# Praise the Lord with the Harp

*A Journal of Faith*
*365 Daily Devotionals*
*with Scripture and Prayer*

# Susann McDonald

Bloomington, IN  Milton Keynes, UK

author-HOUSE®

*AuthorHouse™*
*1663 Liberty Drive, Suite 200*
*Bloomington, IN 47403*
*www.authorhouse.com*
*Phone: 1-800-839-8640*

*AuthorHouse™ UK Ltd.*
*500 Avebury Boulevard*
*Central Milton Keynes, MK9 2BE*
*www.authorhouse.co.uk*
*Phone: 08001974150*

*First published by AuthorHouse 3/13/2007*

*ISBN: 978-1-4259-8067-2 (sc)*

*Library of Congress Control Number: 2006910766*

*Printed in the United States of America*
*Bloomington, Indiana*

*This book is printed on acid-free paper.*

This book is dedicated to all my students, past, present and future, and to my dear friend, Diane Bish, who has always encouraged me in my walk with Christ

# Preface

In April, 2002, I felt led to begin a series of devotions, really as a way to deepen my faith and share God's many blessings in my life as an artist and musician. I am a Professor of Music at Indiana University, chairing one of the largest harp departments in the world. I was using the little devotional book <u>Daily Strength for Daily Needs</u> for my own study time mornings. I decided I would give myself the task of writing a meditation each day based on the scripture for that same day in <u>Daily Strength.</u>

So, this plan worked well and friends and colleagues encouraged me to eventually publish the devotions as a book. Then on November 1, 2003, around 1 AM, my house was swept away by fire, destroying most of my belongings, and the home I had lived in for almost 20 years. My two concert harps were totaled, as was the entire house. Among the lost items were my Bibles and it seemed that two months of these devotions were lost, as well as my little book with the scriptures.

This was a real discouragement spiritually for me. I wondered why God had permitted this fire and I felt perhaps I should forget about finishing the devotions. It was also such a painful time, living in a rental house, making hard decisions whether to rebuild or buy a new house, or just what was best to do. My vast music library of scores and recordings, most of them blackened and scorched, were piled into cardboard boxes. I had so much to deal with that the devotionals were not my main focus.

For almost six months, fire inspections were done to determine the cause of the fire. It was never directly proven, but the consensus was that an electrical problem in the attic heated insulation material which began to smolder, and finally caught fire and raced through the attic across the house to the furnace room. By the time the alarm went off, flames were shooting through the roof, and I was really fortunate to escape out the garage door with my little dog.

However, months after the fire, while sorting through hundreds of books from my library, most of which had to be discarded because they were scorched and covered with soot, I found the devotions for the month of September, which I believed had been burned! Then, my neighbor and prayer group friend, Ethel Smith, found a copy of the little book, Daily Strength. By then it was January. With this great encouragement, I began writing again every morning.

So, dear reader, this book was written in several stages, and over a period of three years. There may be repetitions, but, throughout this time, I have felt so close to God, and protected and blessed by His mighty power, that I have been compelled to finish this witness to His goodness to me during this real trial by fire.

I could not have finished the book without the wonderfully kind help from several friends, Shirley Smith, Ethel Smith, Nancy Miller, and Linda Wood Rollo, and my student Jaymee Haefner. My special thanks to Beverly Larson who did some much needed editing and Betty Thomas and Mr. and Mrs. Peter Doyle for their encouragement. All of them helped me, some by typing my handwritten devotions, and others by their warm support. It is truly thanks to all of them that this book has been completed.

# APRIL

## April 1

*2 Timothy 2.21: He shall be a vessel unto honor, sanctified, and meet for the Master's use, and prepared unto every good work.*

For us to become instruments for God's use, we must first be completely committed, and yielded to God. As He fills us with His wisdom, love, joy and peace, we are cleansed and purified. Although we are but poor earthen vessels, He transforms us into a source of light and we can become instruments that He can use.

Sometimes God finds uses for us in our everyday conversations; at other times, it may be in writing a letter to a friend or loved one. We can never know the impact we may have on others. For example, one of my constant memories of my dear mother, from early childhood until she passed away, was of her leading me and my family in morning prayer and devotional readings. It is no wonder now that I am drawn to write a devotional!

The closer we draw to Him, our source of all light and wisdom, the more we will reflect His light. When we ourselves are selfishly hoarding the joy and peace He gives us, we are not being used by Him. I feel my mother "reflected" His holy light.

God is all knowing and all powerful. He is patiently preparing us. Formed by His loving hand, He equips us for "every good work."

*Dear Father: We want to live useful and honorable lives, conformed to the blessed image of our Lord and Savior, Jesus Christ, in whose name we pray, Amen.*

# April 2

*1 Corinthians 3.16: Know ye not that ye are the temple of God, and that the Spirit of God dwelleth in you?*

What a responsibility we have to live righteous and upright lives when we realize that God's own Spirit resides in us! To have that privilege is such an honor.

I often pray before lessons that I will have an encouraging and helpful spirit toward each student. Each one is so different with such diverse needs. If correction is needed I pray that I may be able to do it in a kindly way.

Sometimes one of my students, not knowing I am present, will use a swear word. Then when she sees me, invariably, she quickly apologizes. Although I have never even talked about not swearing, the students never use such language in my presence.

How much more should we live in ways that are not offensive to our Father God. Of course we should refrain from taking His Holy name in vain. But we should also refrain from all kinds of behavior inappropriate in His presence. Imagine our thoughts and conversation if Jesus walked with us!

*Dear Father: Thank you for your indwelling spirit. Help us to live worthy of thy precious presence each day. In Christ's name, Amen.*

# April 3

*Deuteronomy 18.14: As for thee, the Lord thy God hath not suffered thee so to do.*

This verse says that God has not permitted us to do certain things. In Deuteronomy, Moses is telling the Israelites that God has not allowed them to practice sorcery or spiritualism. He has spared them believing in falsehoods, or forces of evil and witchcraft.

Our faith in God is a stronghold against idols and witchcraft of many kinds. What a waste when people put their faith in astrology or pagan practices, hoping to find enlightenment.

Taking this verse one step further, God has mercifully spared most of us the terrible bondage of drug use or other addictions. I know of several families whose lives have been shattered by children's drug use. It is a tragedy that brings heartbreak to so many. Anything which takes over our minds, and makes us not in control of ourselves, is to be avoided and it is a blessing to have God's protection against such things.

We should also depend only on God. As part of our sanctification, we are to not be dependent on anyone else. As little children, we depend naturally on our parents, but as adults we are to put aside any other dependency and to guard our hearts for the Lord.

*Dear Father: Help us to rely totally on you. Thank you for protecting us from false gods and false dependencies. In Christ's name, Amen.*

# April 4

*Matthew 25.23: Well done, good and faithful servant; thou hast been faithful over a few things, I will make thee ruler over many things; enter then into the joy of the Lord.*

It is truly in the smallest details of life that we see character and faithfulness. Just as in music, where the details and nuances of color, phrasing and balance, all play critical roles, so in our lives, how we manage the details, faithful in even the petty annoyances, serene amidst angry words, and calm while doing those small irksome tasks, these issues show our character. If we can abide in our Lord and do these duties, we will, one day, enter into His joy. We already have that joy and peace even now as we seek to honor Him in all areas of our lives.

What a reward it would be for us to hear the Lord, the Creator of the universe, give such words of praise – "Well done, good and faithful servant."

These words should encourage us to stay the course, even when others discourage us and put us down in petty ways. We can accept belittlement if we commit it to the Lord. Nothing that befalls us escapes His eyes, and everything is of importance to Him.

If we do the smallest task in His name, He knows it and rewards will be ours when we arrive at Judgment Day.

*Dear Father: Thank you for your words of encouragement, and help us to be faithful in every circumstance. In Christ's name, Amen.*

# April 5

*1 Kings 19.18: Yet I have left me seven thousand in Israel, all the knees which have not bowed unto Baal, and every mouth which hath not kissed him.*

God knows and searches every heart, and He is aware of those who belong to him. We may feel that we are saved and are free from sin, but we must always totally rely on Jesus' finished work and place our confidence in His grace alone.

We must, day by day, follow Him. Nothing we do is hidden, and we never know what kind of influence the details of our lives have on others.

In Israel, in the midst of a corrupt and idol-worshipping society, 7000 remained upright and God-fearing. They refused to bow to idols.

We too are called to set our sights higher than the culture we live in. We have such examples of the great souls who came before us: Corrie ten Boom, Amy Carmichael, Mother Theresa, Elizabeth Elliott, Francis and Edith Schaeffer; and some in our own time, like Charles Colson, who has literally turned around prisons through his worldwide Prison Fellowship Christian ministry. Each of them inspire and encourage us.

When God is directing a life wholly yielded to Him, one person can accomplish miracles – through His power and strength.

*Dear Father: We are grateful for the lives of your saints. They inspire and encourage us. Help us to be faithful as they were faithful. In Jesus' name, Amen.*

# April 6

*Psalm 94.19: In the multitude of my thoughts within me, Thy comfort delighted my soul.*

*2 Corinthians 4.8, 9: Perplexed, but not in despair, cast down, but not destroyed.*

I am here in this charming city of Roanoke with vistas of the Shenandoah Valley and the Blue Ridge Mountains. This afternoon one of my most successful and beautiful students will perform a recital here. I came to hear her and at the same time visit my dear friends, Jane Stuart Smith and Betty Carlson. They were neighbors of mine in Huemoz, Switzerland, where L'Abri is located and where I had a chalet for many years. They are authors of many fine Christian books. Other dear friends came for this occasion too, so we are all enjoying a fine reunion.

Friendships are such a wonderful blessing, and can be a great encouragement. However, even the dearest friendships pale beside the love and comfort of our personal relationship with Jesus Christ. He is the friend who will never disappoint us, or abandon us.

When our thoughts are turned to sadness or circumstances perplex us, we can search for answers. We try to understand why we are downcast. Relationships that should be uplifting can become hurtful and painful.

At such times, there is no greater comfort than to turn to our Lord and commit everything to Him, "Jesus, Lover of my Soul." His love never fails us.

*Dear Lord: You are our Savior, Redeemer and our Friend. We are so thankful and we praise your Holy Name, Amen.*

# April 7

*Romans 12.2: That ye may prove what is that good and acceptable and perfect will of God.*

The recital here in Roanoke went beautifully yesterday. Before, that morning, I went to a Primitive Baptist Church service, the first time for me to even hear of that special denomination. The young pastor and his wife have become friends. He gave one of the finest sermons I have ever heard. He preached on solitude, safety and sovereignty.

In the evening, they came over with a group of our friends. We ordered in Chinese food, and after dinner we sang hymns for over an hour. It was such a happy time of fellowship. Surely it is God's will for us to enjoy such times together.

Sometimes though, it is hard to discern God's will when we face anguishing decisions, life-changing choices, we often struggle with fear and anxiety.

One sign, surely, that we are in God's will is the peace and freedom He gives us, when we are on the right track. Without that connection, we must tread very slowly and wait for His still small voice to give us sure guidance.

*Dear Father: Thank you for times of wonderful and uplifting fellowship. Be with all those today struggling to find their way. In Jesus' name, Amen.*

# April 8

*Psalm 23.1: The Lord is my shepherd; I shall not want.*

*Psalm 34.10: They that seek the Lord shall not want for any good thing.*

If we really took these words to heart and lived by them, all fear and anxiety would disappear from our lives. Most of the time we bumble along, trying to work out solutions to our trials, and acting like a rudderless ship. We behave as if we were alone and had no leader or guide.

But God has said – "Ask and you shall receive, seek and you shall find, knock and it shall be opened unto you." He patiently waits, for us to ask Him, to trust Him and He has promised to be our guide – shepherding us through the rocky crags and murky pitfalls of our lives.

Then He says that He will supply everything that we need.

I flew back to Indiana yesterday in time for some teaching. It has turned cold and wintry again here, but the beautiful young pear tree in my front yard is a promise that spring is just around the corner. How I thank and praise God for the wonder and beauty of His creation each spring.

*Dear Father: Thank you for the wonderful surprises you give us. You are our good shepherd. In Jesus' name, Amen.*

# April 9

*Matthew 26.41: Watch and pray, that ye enter not into temptation.*

Jesus said these words to His disciples who had fallen asleep while He was praying in the garden, knowing He was facing a cruel death by crucifixion. They needed to pray for they behaved with weakness and cowardice after Jesus was arrested. They had protested their loyalty, but deserted Jesus out of fear.

We all face many kinds of temptations. We each know the different kinds of weaknesses by which we are prone to be tempted. For one person it may be sexual immorality, while for another it may be smoking or drinking to excess, or gossiping.

God tells us to watch, to be on guard, to avoid situations where we know we could be tempted. We are to "flee evil."

The Lord's Prayer includes the words "lead us not into temptation." We must pray for God's protection every day. He knows we are weak and that we will often fail. But He forgives us when we confess our sins and He lifts us up and helps us to go on. Jesus faced every temptation known to man and yet lived without sin. He has compassion for sinners, and we can go to Him at any time, and He will open His arms to us. In spite of the sin which we all carry at some time or another, His forgiveness is always available to us, as well as His power and strength to face and conquer temptation.

*Dear Father God: Thank you for sending us your son, our Savior Jesus Christ, who carried our sins, and the sins of all mankind. In Jesus' precious name, Amen.*

# April 10

*Colossians 3.23: Whatsoever ye do, do it heartily, as to the Lord, and not unto men.*

*Colossians 3.22: Not with eye-service, as men-pleasers; but in simpleness of heart, fearing God.*

I have always felt special appreciation for people who serve us with manual labor, doing work we cannot do or are not willing to do. I am so grateful to have a new cleaning lady. I have been very impressed by the caring quality of her work. For the first time, I felt someone really taking an interest in such things as a clean kitchen rug, shining tables and floors, and order everywhere. She obviously is doing her work "as unto the Lord."

We have all seen some young people doing their housework or after-school jobs half-heartedly. Some do it very slowly; others arrive late and leave early; and others seem half asleep at their jobs. If they realized that God is their real boss and overseer, might it not change their attitude?

God calls each of us to work as if He were our boss; if we can please Him, we will have performed well. We should take seriously the smallest duty as an act of obedience. Nothing we do, or neglect to do escapes His notice.

*Dear Father: Thank you for those who do their work with their hearts as well as their hands. Help us to do the same. In Christ's name, Amen.*

# April 11

*2 Peter 3.14: Wherefore, beloved...be diligent that ye may be found of Him in peace, without spot and blameless.*

I have looked forward to this day for several months. A harpist colleague and dear friend came for me early this morning,and we flew to Chicago to go to the Lyon-Healy harp factory, to replace my two gold harps that were lost in the fire. My former student, who is now the principal harpist with the Chicago Symphony and another dear friend, met us there and the three of us played for each other and quickly narrowed the choice to two beautiful harps. Both had different qualities, but both seemed capable of great strength, resonance, yet sensitivity, with a wide range of color. What a joyful time! The owners of the company took us to a celebration lunch, photos were taken to commemorate the event, and then we flew home, tired but happy.

I have not purchased a new harp for over 30 years, so it is profoundly moving to me to have these wonderful new instruments.

I praise God for His great goodness and provision. I feel such peace in His love. I know that I am surely not blameless and, while I long to be without sinful "spots," only my Lord, Jesus Christ was without sin. I thank Him and praise Him for His forgiveness and mercy.

*Dear Father: Thank you for the gift of your son, our Lord, Jesus Christ. In Him is our peace as we seek to follow Him and conform to His model. In His name we pray, Amen.*

# April 12

*2 Corinthians 13.11: Be perfect, be of good comfort, be of one mind, live in peace; and the God of love and peace shall be with you.*

*1 John 4.20: He that loveth not his brother whom he has seen, how can he love God whom he has not seen?*

The past week I had to deal with a recalcitrant student, who had not done what I had asked her to do and had upset many of my other students, harassing them to substitute for her in ensemble so she could play an outside job. I had to express my dismay and strong defense of the others in our class and I felt angry about it. But I realized she needed understanding and compassion too, and I was able to just concentrate on teaching her lesson. We both were soon involved in the music and then, as she left, she apologized and thanked me for my patience with her in this situation. I thanked God that He had helped me end a confrontation peacefully.

It is so easy to love those who are loving and kind to us. It is also easy to feel love and compassion for those in far-away lands who are oppressed or persecuted.

But when it comes to our homes and workplaces, where dissension and strife and unkindness can abound, our hearts can close up like clam shells. It is so much harder to love the unlovely, to forgive those who irritate and hurt us and disturb our peace.

We are called, wherever and however it lies in our power, to be peacemakers, to live in peace with all men, no matter how difficult the situation may be.

*Dear Lord: Help us to always search for peaceful solutions in all our dealings with others today. In Christ's name, Amen.*

# April 13

*Romans 8.37: In all these things we are more than conquerors through Him that loved us.*

Today is Palm Sunday. As I prepared breakfast, I turned on the television to hear the latest news from Iraq. What a joy to hear that the seven POWs have been safely found. There had been no word from them for two weeks, and the whole world feared for their safety. The thanksgiving of their families is touching to see. Most of them thanked God and expressed their appreciation for all the prayers offered on their behalf. One mother said she felt her son was alive, but either way, she trusted God.

Yesterday, the builder staked my old lot, so I could see the outline of where the new house will be placed. Sadly, several big old trees will have to be removed. They seem like faithful friends and it is painful to lose them.

It is a time of great highs and some lows too. But, we are more than conquerors in all these things, through Christ's love for us. I look forward to praising Him this special Sunday in church with fellow believers. The dear little children from our large Sunday School classes usually parade through the sanctuary, waving palm fronds. It will be a joyous time of worship. It is always very uplifting to see the many families with their children who are so faithful to our church.

*Dear Father: We thank you and praise you for our Savior Jesus Christ, in whose name we pray, Amen.*

# April 14

*1 Corinthians 3.21-23: All things are yours; whether Paul or Apollos or Cephes, or the world, or life, or death, or things present, or things to come, all are yours; and ye are Christ's; and Christ is God's.*

*2 Corinthians 6.10: As sorrowful, yet always rejoicing; as poor, yet making many rich; as having nothing, and yet possessing all things.*

*1 Corinthians 3.19 which precedes this first verse says, "For the wisdom of the world is foolishness in God's sight."*

God calls us to be humble, as though we are nothing and have nothing, because in Him, we have everything. With Christ's spirit living in us, we want for nothing.

One of my graduate students played a wonderful recital last night. Her demeanor was humble and modest, but she played with great depth, strength and sensitivity.

My pastor spoke movingly in church yesterday of the need for us to be credible Christians in the eyes of the world. We cannot be loving to our neighbor and then be mean-spirited to a student or colleague. We cannot profess that Jesus is the Lord of our lives and cut in front of someone at the supermarket or in traffic. We must be consistent in our walk. We are called to be positive, thankful and helpful, <u>always</u>, not just when we feel like it! We cannot do this in our own strength, but through the power of the Holy Spirit working in us.

*Dear Lord: Grant us today to walk humbly before you and our fellowmen, secure in the knowledge that we belong to you. In your precious name, Amen.*

# April 15

*Romans 8.28: We know that all things work together for good to them that love God, to them who are called according to his purpose.*

*Genesis 50.20: As for you, ye thought evil against me; but God meant it unto good.*

How often in our lives we experience change or circumstances that are exceedingly painful. Some of the time we are to blame by making wrong choices or by our own sinful behavior.

At other times trials and misfortunes seem to arrive "out of the blue." We are blind-sided by bereavement, or the loss of a job or a physical catastrophe.

These verses are among the most comforting in God's word. At any time, and in the worst outward circumstances, we know God can and will turn whatever happens to us into good. We are not at the mercy of a cruel fate, but rather we are in the hands of a loving and compassionate Father.

To those who love God, all the things that happen to us will work together for good. There is no situation that is without hope, for we have the ultimate hope in the resurrection of Jesus Christ and our eventual eternal life with Him. We need never truly despair.

*Dear Father: Thank you for giving us your promise of goodness from all that befalls us. In Christ's name, Amen.*

# April 16

*1 Thessalonians 5.23, 24: The very God of peace sanctify you wholly, and I pray God your whole spirit, and soul, and body be preserved blameless until the coming of our Lord Jesus Christ. Faithful is He that calleth you, who also will do it.*

Spring has come to Bloomington with such beautiful flowering trees and shrubs. Every street glows with redbud, brilliant crabapples, dogwoods and weeping cherry trees. Beneath them there is usually a fine array of tulips and daffodils. I went to my old house lot and picked an armful of flowers, before the bulldozers came again and swept away the shrubs and bushes I had planted so many years ago.

It was painful, but I know that God is faithful, and I trust that He will give me another garden around the new house that will start soon.

This is a time of new beginnings, like having two new gold harps to replace the fire-damaged ones! They are beautiful, but they will need time to be broken in, and I will need time with them to come to know them intimately.

I am so thankful for each blessing. But most of all for His peace. I am so far from being "blameless," but God can cleanse my spirit and soul and body as long as I abide in Him. As He faithfully causes the buried tulip and daffodil bulbs beneath the soil to push through the clay and bloom victoriously each spring, so He can give us victory over sin and make us as new creatures.

*Dear Father: Thank you for your great faithfulness. In Christ's name, Amen.*

# April 17

*Psalm 40.4: Blessed is that man that maketh the Lord his trust.*

*1 Timothy 2.2: That we may lead a quiet and peaceable life.*

We must ask ourselves why we are not living in peace and quiet, if indeed that is the case. While we may always be able to blame someone else, or some hard and troubling circumstance, most of all we are probably to blame ourselves.

If we permit any outside person or situation to disturb our inner peace and tranquility, it is our own fault for allowing it. Sometimes, it may be true, we are blind-sided, caught by surprise and therefore not braced to turn aside from the antagonist, and to remain calm, even while confronting the problem.

Trusting God's perfect will and knowing that He is in control should protect us from becoming upset and disturbed. When we take matters into our own hands, we can quickly become unraveled, and anger and bitterness can erupt. Wisdom is not found that way, nor is reconciliation..

God's will for us is perfect peace. It can, I believe, even be achieved in the midst of a very busy, occupied life. He wants us to work, in peace, and to live, in peace. A quiet heart, resting in God, is the prescription for a peaceful life, even in the hardest circumstances.

*Dear Father: We are so thankful that we can bring any problem and heartache to you, and you have promised to bless us with your perfect peace. What an incomparable gift! In Jesus' name, Amen.*

# April 18

*Deuteronomy 10.12: What doth the Lord thy God require of thee, but to fear the Lord thy God, to walk in all His ways, with all thy heart and with all thy soul?*

A well-known church has this credo – Excellence in all things, and all things to God's glory. He wants our very best, nothing less.

I often tell my students that I don't want them to just be good harpists. I want them to be great harpists. It is exciting when they truly attain that status. The difference between good and great is not so very big. But, it entails complete dedication and attention to detail.

The Bible says, "the fear of the Lord is the beginning of wisdom." Some people don't like the idea of fearing God. They say God is loving and we should not fear Him. But when one reads God's word, it is clear that, although He is loving, He is also all-powerful, all-knowing and all-seeing. The creator of the universe is totally awesome, and I believe we are wise to fear Him.

He also asks us to serve Him and seek Him with all our heart and soul. He wants no tepid, half-hearted worship or service. He wants us to be completely His. God wants us to be great servants, walking carefully in all His ways, loving Him with our whole heart, heeding His commands and trusting Him totally.

*Dear Father: We want to belong to you completely. Take our lives and mold us and shape us into your people. We ask it in Christ's name, our resurrected Savior, Amen.*

# April 19

*Ezra 8.22: The hand of our God is upon all them for good that seek Him.*

*Psalm 31.5: Into Thy hand I commit my spirit.*

Yesterday, I went to school and forgot to take my date book with my teaching schedule. It included two out-of-town students whom I had not even met, and four chamber coachings involving groups of instrumentalists. I was truly dismayed for I did not know who was arriving or when they were due! But, they knew when they were expected, and the day want smoothly, as each showed up in the proper place.

When we muddle along, not sure where we should be, we can trust God to be faithful and to never be late to meet us and to bless us.

When we are committed to God and seeking His constant will in our lives, He will send us blessings beyond measure.

Too often we fret and stew, our imagination occupying our minds. Instead, we should come away to a quiet place. We should put aside our own thoughts and concentrate wholly on the presence of God.

His thoughts are as high above our thoughts as the heaven is above the earth. He will replace our worries and useless imaginings with His peace and wisdom.

*Dear Father: We commit our spirit unto your loving hands today and every day. In Christ's name, Amen.*

# April 20

*Psalm 40:1: I waited patiently for the Lord: and He inclined unto me, and heard my cry.*

*Romans 5:3,4: Tribulation worketh patience: and patience, experience, and experience, hope.*

It is often necessary for us to practice even when we feel very tired or depressed or too sad to have the needed energy. At these times, I sit at my harp anyway, and begin to do slow warm-up exercises and scales and arpeggios.

Once begun, the simple exercises flow into each other, my fingers become supple and take on life and vitality, and almost before I know it consciously, I am playing with full energy and strength! Sitting down at the harp and beginning is always the hardest part. Almost 50 years of daily practice has proven this to me, and experiencing this gives me the confidence and hope that it will always be true.

I think it is the same in life. We must choose to take up the task that lies before us, to make that difficult phone call, to begin that unappealing task, to make a hard decision that one has postponed. Procrastination is only overcome by taking the first step, beginning to do what is the next thing, doing what is the right thing to do.

As we trust God, in His mercy and goodness toward us, He makes each of our efforts, small though they may be, a pathway to real inner peace. Our willpower is strengthened by each step we take, and our souls are filled with hope. In His mysterious providence our humble abilities are empowered. Our hope is not in our own abilities, but in <u>His</u>, and in His mighty power to bless and help us.

*Dear Lord: Thank you for giving us courage, every day, to face up to those duties that are hard for us, and for the hope and patience to complete those tasks you would have us do. In Christ's name, Amen*

# April 21

*Matthew 5:48: Be ye perfect, even as your Father which is in heaven is perfect.*

*Psalm 17:15: As for me, I will behold Thy face in righteousness; I shall be satisfied, when I awake, with Thy likeness.*

We are urged in Matt. 5:48 to be "perfect even as our Father in heaven is perfect."

As musicians, we strive to play perfectly, at first perhaps just to please our teachers, later to please ourselves and reach the highest possible standard of execution of a work. So we also strive to live lives that are pleasing to our Father, our God and Creator.

God is perfection, holy, pure, truthful, infinite, beyond anything that we can imagine from our human perspective. We can never hope to attain to any such perfection by our own strivings. Only by the atoning blood of Jesus Christ who serves as our intercessor can we hope to come into the presence of Holy God, the creator of the universe. Only if Jesus knows us and claims us as His, can we enter heaven.

There is a beautiful song I heard recently, that touched me deeply. The lyrics tell about a young woman a devout Christian, who has died and is standing at the gates of heaven, and Jesus says, "Let her in," she is "one of the family." He paid the price of our sins on the cross of Calvary. It is a moving picture of belonging to the family of God, and one that gives us hope.

In our earthly lives and in our work in music we can please God by obeying Him, loving his character, searching for truth and purpose in our lives, striving for kindness and goodness, and loving those things that are beautiful and pure. We can turn away from what is evil, from laziness, wastefulness, and procrastination. We can seek to embrace mankind and the great blessings God has given us.

We can choose to do those things that are worthwhile and uplifting. As musicians, or professionals in any field, including home-makers, we can give our best efforts to our work and practice, knowing that our human efforts, although far from perfect, are known and approved by Him who watches over us. He loves us and accepts us with all our imperfections.

*Dear Father: Transform our imperfect ways so that our poor efforts may be used to bless others, in Jesus' name, Amen.*

21

# April 22

*1 Peter 1.8:  Whom having not seen, ye love; in whom, though now ye see Him not, yet believing, ye rejoice with joy unspeakable and full of glory.*

Simplicity is the ability to see life and act upon it in an uncomplicated and direct way. I believe it is a real gift. My great French harp teacher, a renowned pedagogue, Henriette Renié, often spoke of her admiration of the simple. She had experienced many students, some of whom asked fruitless questions and interrupted the smooth flow of her wise teaching.  Listening simply to what she wished to share or demonstrate would give better results. While one can sometimes analyze and dissect a musical passage or work with its technical ramifications with good results, I believe most great music-making is a combination of good, hard work, and a simplicity of sentiment, singing from the heart, not just the mind.

Our love of God, who is Love, can be simple too. To strive to spend each day, moment by moment in His presence, simply abiding in Him, delighting in Him, spending time in His word, this is true joy and peace forever.  To bring our every thought to Him and know that he accepts and loves us in return – this is to simplify our lives.  Our fears, cares, depressions will lighten in His presence, until they are fewer, and our time with Him becomes everything.

*Dear Lord: Thank you for the amazing gift of your love and constant presence with us, In Christ's name, Amen.*

22

# April 23

*1 Chronicles 4:23: These were the potters and those that dwelt among plants and hedges: there they dwelt with the king for his work.*

I believe, in God's timing, we can flourish as musicians and artists, in both humble and lofty situations. Particularly in music, which is such an apprenticeship, we generally need many years of experience to prepare us for the rigorous tests of concert work in important venues, or teaching artist students. I know in retrospect, how important were my apprentice years in preparing me for the career that came later.

When I returned to America after my studies in France, ready to start my career, a good friend and fellow artist advised me – "Don't go to New York and do a debut recital there right away  Make a name for yourself elsewhere first so that when you play in New York they will pay more attention to you!" I thought this was good advice, so I played debut recitals in Los Angeles and Chicago, and had concert management there first. It was several years later before I played in New York.

At one point in my career I was without concert management, and was very worried what would become of me. A dear friend, Sister Cecelia Ann Miller,  offered to become my prayer manager, and she literally prayed me into a wonderful management, which booked me on college campuses for many years.

Today, I urge my students to go where there is a need for a harpist, even if it is abroad, or in a more remote area. They can gain experience there and will be appreciated there. They should, of course, always keep their eyes on their ultimate goal, but the most important thing is to do each job to the best of our abilities, never assuming that an engagement is beneath us or too small to be important. Every opportunity to perform should be taken seriously and prepared for fully. I have been amazed how many times a seemingly unimportant engagement has led to a major opportunity because it was done with excellence and made such a strong impression that those involved actively sought to help the performer in any way possible. This is particularly true in being a good and helpful colleague. Having the respect and friendship of your fellow musicians or colleagues is vital and will help you flourish wherever you are.

God does not lose track of us wherever we are, and He will direct our careers in His timing. How reassuring it is to know that He is in charge!

*Dear Father: Help us to be patient and bloom and grow exactly where you have placed us, knowing you have planned for our every move. In Jesus' name, Amen.*

# April 24

*Galatians. 6.2: Bear ye one another's burdens, and so fulfill the law of Christ.*

One of my French professors of music once told me, only half jokingly, "You don't go to the Paris Conservatory to make friends, but to meet rivals!"

Perhaps because of the fierce competition in the music world for positions with orchestras or management, I have always felt it was very important to foster a spirit of cooperation and friendship in my harp classes. Most of all, among talented young virtuosos, nothing is more important than having good and loving relationships with each other.

Learning to share each other's burdens and to help a colleague in distress is one of life's great opportunities. When a harpist needs a substitute to replace him or her in an orchestra rehearsal, due to illness or a serious schedule conflict, I have always felt it was a kind and generous thing for a classmate to put aside her own needs and activities, accepting to go into what is not an easy situation. I believe God always blesses such sacrifices, and I also feel that these people are rewarded by Him in many tangible ways.

What a precious thing too it is for me to witness students, after performing in a major competition, give each other a warm hug in the midst of the natural disappointments of not winning a prize. I feel these students will be winners in life.

There is always someone whom we can help. During the years when young musicians often are struggling to support themselves, if they can reach out, play for a hospital or retirement home, and share their talents with people who need encouragement, they will be encouraged themselves. God is always present to help us carry our burdens. He is often only waiting for us to ask him for help. We receive not because we ask not!

*Dear Lord: Give us eyes to see the needs of others around us, and compassionate hearts to reach out to them in love. In Christ's name, Amen.*

# April 25

*Psalm 131.2: But I have stilled and quieted my soul,; like a weaned child with its mother, like a weaned child is my soul within me.*

Earlier in this Psalm David writes, my heart is not proud, my eyes are not haughty. Later in the Bible Jesus said "Unless we become like little children we cannot enter the kingdom of heaven."

I have remarked often how many of the world's greatest artists have a precious child-like quality about them. They seem to have the ability to enjoy the simple, small pleasures in life, like a child, and their faces reflect this joy.

In writing earlier about simplicity I omitted this quality which I think is such an important one. It comes from an appreciation, I think, of each one of God's gifts to us. The ability to take joy from - a beautiful small wildflower, a sparkling mountain lake, the passing smile of a stranger, the cavorting of a puppy, the expression on baby's face, the exhilaration of playing a passage exactly the way you always wanted, the excitement of discovering a new piece that you love, the fun of risking a very fast tempo in favorite piece. Or, we can just enjoy a bowl of hot popcorn, an evening free to see a video that you have wanted to see, an unexpected day off due to a cancellation.

Each of us has favorite things and events that give us special joy. But sometimes we take ourselves too seriously, and this can rob life of spontaneous fun. I remember falling in love with the Impromptu by the French composer, Albert Roussel. I loved it so much that I learned and memorized it all in one day and played it at a party that same night. It was a childlike joy in that music that propelled me to do that.

I think as we remain free of distrust and artifice, striving to keep a childlike acceptance of the simple large and small gifts given to us by our loving Father, we develop a quiet and mature faith. Maybe the older we become, the more childlike and simple we can dare to become?

*Lord, Thank you for the gift of laughter and all the many joys and simple pleasures you provide for us, In Jesus' name, Amen*

# April 26

*Romans 8.25: If we hope for that we see not, then do we with patience wait for it.*

*2 Peter 3.8: One day is with the Lord as a thousand years and a thousand years as one day.*

I think one of the most important attributes in life is a spirit of hope. Each of us needs to live with a sense of optimism for the immediate and long-range future.

Those of us who place our faith in Christ and His promise of salvation have a hope that is unchanging, even when life's circumstances in the short term seem hopeless. When serious illness strikes, or we lose a loved one, or we lose our job, or our security, or our financial situation is turned upside-down, only trust in God and His assurance that He will never leave us nor forsake us is of any real comfort.

For the musician, hope should be a constant companion. The job market in music is so very tight, that it is hard to imagine that one day the hard disciplined hours will pay off with a good living doing what one loves. Research has proven that students who have studied music consistently make the best lawyers, doctors and other specialists. The discipline they have learned will apply to every area of their lives, in a music career or not.

God is always ready to guide and direct us with His wisdom and hope. We are His creation and he wants us to achieve our highest ideals. Not all of us are destined to become concert artists, but all of us are His children, secure in His everlasting love.

He is the reason for all our hope.

*Dear Father: Thank you for your faithfulness in renewing our spirit of hope, every day. In Jesus' name, Amen.*

# April 27

*Zechariah. 8.16: Speak ye every man the truth to his neighbor.*

*2 Corinthians 1.12: For our rejoicing is this, the testimony of our conscience, that in simplicity and godly sincerity...we have had our conversation in the world.*

I see a teacher's role as a mixture of encouragement and exhortation. For sure, we must teach our students what is right from wrong in their notes and rhythm. That is a relatively easy job, for we are dealing with absolutes, notes and rhythm are either right or wrong. But the subtle differences of tempo, hand positions, articulation, expressiveness, sentiment, intensity and energy or lack of it, (to name but a few) are harder to teach. I have always felt that for me to take the harp and play the passage is worth hundreds of words of explanation. Imitation is one of the best tools in teaching music. The details above mentioned form the very fabric and essence of music-making, and are part of the fascination of teaching.

But how easy it is for a teacher to diminish a student's real love of what they are doing. I believe we must teach our students with Godly sincerity, speaking the truth as we know it with kindness and patience. I always have hope in my heart for the future development of each student.

There have been many occasions when I have felt that perhaps I should discourage a student from pursuing a future as a harpist. Perhaps they seemed unusually slow to learn or seemed to have fewer natural musical gifts. However, in looking back after over 50 years of teaching, I have seen many of these same students achieve real success and happiness as musicians. I am glad that God stayed my hand, and permitted me to give them the encouragement, so vital to achieving their dreams, rather than dampening their spirits by words of discouragement.

Encouragement is not false flattery. Everyone has some natural abilities and attributes which we can praise, and our appreciation of their very real gifts can serve to inspire them to achieve greatness.

*Dear Lord: Thank you for the encouraging words, from you, that we read in the Bible, and which lift us up in hope. In Jesus' name, Amen.*

# April 28

*Psalm 121:5: The Lord is thy keeper: the Lord is thy shade upon thy right hand.*

*Psalm 119:165: Great peace have they which love thy law: and nothing shall make them stumble.*

Many professions carry great amounts of stress and nervous tension. I recently talked with a highly successful criminal trial lawyer. He and I compared the stress of his work with that of a performing artist. He said part of the stress he experienced was never knowing exactly how a trial would turn out. He also carried the strain of knowing in some cases a life depended upon his work.

While a live concert is not a matter of life and death (although sometimes it almost feels that way!), it can involve a lot of tension. There are so many variables. No matter how well–prepared an artist is to perform the music, there is uncertainty about many details which can affect the performance. A string can break, a pedal slip, the lighting can confuse visually, the acoustics may be troubling, and of course there is always the possibility of a memory slip.

One certainty in life, if one has placed one's trust and faith in God through His son, Jesus Christ, is the knowledge that He is always with us, upholding us with His right hand. His love and presence bring us peace of mind and the strength to see us through concerts and other stressful times in our lives. This peace is always so meaningful to me before a concert. You may be sure in those last few moments before going on stage I always do two things, I wash my hands in warm water to soften my calluses, (the tips of a harpist's fingers are calloused to protect them from blistering due to the friction of the strings) and I pray for God's protection and help. When I know I have done my part in working and preparing the concert to the best of my ability, I then leave it in God's hands. I trust that He will be with me. This gives me enormous peace.

And by His mercy and grace, if we consecrate our humble efforts to Him, an ordinary performance may become a great one, enabling us to touch people's hearts. God can make our efforts holy work.

*Dear Lord: Thank you for your peace which we need so badly in our stressful lives, In Jesus' name, Amen*

# April 29

*Luke 15:18: I will arise and go to my father.*

The story of the prodigal son is well–known. After spending and losing his father's inheritance foolishly the son decides to return to his father and ask to be one of his servants. But the father rejoices at his return and welcomes him home with a fatted calf. This story is a wonderful example of God's patience with our human weaknesses and frailties. He totally forgives our mistakes, past, present and future.

One of the hardest things in performing is the ability to keep one's concentration after having a memory slip or playing wrong notes. We need to forgive ourselves instantly, and not become fixated on the mishap.

We must keep going, focusing on the continuing music. It is very hard to do. I teach my students a system of safe places or bases in the score, repair points, which they must learn almost independently of the music. I ask them to practice beginning at each of these places – cold— that is, not hearing the notes before these spots. Hopefully this system enables them to keep their equilibrium after a memory blank, and continue to perform smoothly. Often, when this is well–done, the audience is not even aware that a memory lapse has occurred.

In our lives, I believe God is our repair point, always faithful to forget and forgive our mistakes and His mercy allows us to go forward with our lives, striving to do His will, secure in His never failing love for us.

*Dear Father – Thank you for the gift of your forgiveness, which allows us to put our mistakes behind us and move forward with hope. In Christ's name, Amen*

# April 30

*Exodus 14:15: Speak unto the children of Israel, that they go forward.*

*Luke 9:62: No man, having put his hand to the plough, and looking back, is fit for the kingdom of God.*

What a comfort it is to practice every day!  It is a constant source of reliability amid life's many uncertainties and anxieties.  During times of trials or discouragements, it is always strengthening inwardly for me to sit at the harp and patiently practice.  It always gives me a sense of being in the right place doing the right thing!  And other problems seem to recede in importance.

Luke 9 is telling us not to stew over our past failures and mistakes, in life or in music, and to forge ahead, upward and onward.  We constantly have to make choices in life.  Some are not wise.  However, we should not second guess our decisions, regretting them or constantly worrying that they may not be right.  We need to keep our eyes lifted up, as the wonderful hymn goes, keeping our eyes on Jesus. We need to go forward, trusting His guidance, knowing He has forgiven our past and that He is in charge of our future.  My dear friend, French poet Francoise des Varennes wrote, "To live is to walk, ones forehead facing heavenward." That is to live courageously.

*Dear Lord – We ask for courage today, to live as you would have us live, with kindness and love in our hearts to all whom we will meet.  In Christ's name, Amen*

# MAY

## May 1

*Psalms 34.1: I will bless the Lord at all times! His praise shall be continually in my mouth*

*Psalms 9.1: I will praise thee O Lord with my whole heart. I will show forth all thy marvelous works.*

*Psalms 43.4: I will praise you with the harp, O God, my God.*

I hope it is pleasing to God when we come into His presence simply to thank Him or to praise Him. We all too often bring our pain, suffering, worry and distress to Him. He does assure us that He wants us to bring everything to Him in prayer. But I can't help but wonder if it is sometimes a relief for Him when we simply come to thank Him with a heart full of gratitude! It may be much like a parent feels when instead of whining about their homework, their child comes up and gives them a hug!

It sets the tone for the whole day when we wake with thanksgiving on our lips. When we spend time with God in the morning upon arising, He seems able to expand our time so that we are able to do everything we need to do on our busiest day with time spent alone with God first. So we should never feel too busy to have quiet, alone time with Him, and to make it our first priority. It may mean getting up half an hour earlier. The old saying is true, if we are too busy to pray we are <u>too</u> busy.

In the student-teacher relationship I see some parallels. How easy it is for the teacher when a student soaks up their suggestions for repertoire, fingering, contest preparation, and so forth, rather than the student pushing for their own agenda, often at variance with the teacher's best goals for the student. There is of course a need for a beneficial give and take between them. I had such a wonderful role model with Mlle. Renié, whose wisdom was so great. I just soaked up everything she chose to share with me with gratitude and simplicity. She gave me so much of herself and I trusted her judgment totally.

I want to be like that with God, to accept all that comes from His hand with thanksgiving and unquestioned obedience.

*Dear Lord – Help us to simply take what you give us each day, which is always more than enough, and to be thankful. In Jesus' name, Amen.*

# May 2

*1 Peter 3.4: The unfading beauty of a gentle and quiet spirit, which is of great worth in God's sight.*

*Colossians 1.22: To present you holy, blameless and without accusation in His sight.*

Our culture does not seem to value those qualities such as quietness, self-effacement, modesty and gentleness. Even in the field of classical music, where one might expect conservative dress and customs to be the standard, we increasingly see shorter and shorter skirts, and more and more bare skin in artist's attire.

How can a Christian musician live and survive in this milieu, choosing to dress and live in a less provocative way? Our society seems to put so much too much emphasis on outer, physical beauty, which can be so fleeting. By cultivating our inner, spiritual life, we find favor with God. By our behavior, and by our apparel, we can make a stand for more modesty, and the right kind of man, who is looking for a godly wife, will appreciate it!

Unfortunately, so many young people start living together during their college years, trying marriage out, without the blessing of God on their union. They postpone marriage, and statistics show that even when these couples finally do decide to marry (and so many don't) the percentage that ends in divorce is very high.

On a brighter note, the movement for chastity and sexual abstinence outside of marriage is growing in size, notably among high school age young people. This is definitely a ray of hope for the future.

*Dear Lord God – Show us how you would have us live, we want to be holy before you, our holy God, and our culture would influence us in other directions. In Jesus' name, Amen.*

# May 3

*Nahum 1.7: The Lord is good, a stronghold in the day of trouble; and He knows them that trust in Him*

We all have days that seem to go wrong from the very beginning and keep going increasingly wrong as the day progresses. Problems can pile up and threaten to destroy our peace and inner tranquility. We can receive criticism that hurts, a family member can be rushed to the emergency room, or we can lose a very important audition.

What a comfort it is to know that we can turn these problems over to God. He is our fortress, our safe base. To use a harp expression, He is our "Repair Point." The trust we place in Him never disappoints. He wants us to cast our cares upon Him, because He cares for us. He knows us like no one else can ever know us, our every thought and feeling.

We may have close friends or colleagues with whom we depend and share much of life, but even they can and will let us down on occasion.

God will never let us down. He is there for us always, no matter what we are going through in our lives. He will never leave us.

God does not promise that we won't have problems, tribulations, trials, grief and loss in our lives. Not until heaven will be free of those. But God is good. He has promised to be with us, in every situation we face, if we trust in Him and in His son Jesus Christ.

*Dear Father – You never disappoint us and we thank you for your precious presence, day by day, through our ups and downs. In Christ's name, Amen.*

# May 4

*Hebrews 11.33, 34: Who through faith subdued kingdoms, wrought righteousness, obtained promises, stopped the mouths of lions, out of weakness were made strong.*

The writer of Hebrews encourages his readers by citing examples from the Old Testament of what those saintly heroes had done and achieved by their great faith. Many of them were martyred for their faith; others saw great miracles of faith performed such as the parting of the Red Sea and the falling of the walls of Jericho. A little later after this passage, in Hebrews 12.1 he urges us "since we are surrounded by such a great cloud of witnesses, let us throw off everything that hinders…. And let us run with perseverance the race marked out for us."

I think perseverance is one of the greatest attributes for a musician. Keeping on keeping on is critical in a musical career. Often there are harpists who began harp studies later in high school or even college who despair of ever having the facility of those who began as children at a much younger age. I tell them, wait and see, when you accumulate the necessary years of playing you will have the technical facility and strength! There are usually lean and challenging years at the beginning of a career. But to those who stay the course, great rewards ensue! It is often amazing to know of many famous artists who were never heard of until they were in the forties!

We too need to have perseverance in our prayers, persisting until God has answered us, even though sometimes His answer is to wait! The essential is that we have faith and trust in His wisdom and His wonderful promises.

*Dear Father – Thank you for hearing our prayers. Please give us patience and persistence and perseverance, as you guide and direct our daily lives. In Jesus' name, Amen.*

# May 5

*Jeremiah 12.5: If you have raced with men on foot, and they have worn you out, how can you compete with horses? If you stumble in safe country, how will you manage in the thickets by the Jordan?*

If we cannot endure a little pain or discomfort, how could we endure a cross? I think these words of Jeremiah are a reminder that no matter how hard our lives can sometimes feel, there are so many others whose lives are so much harder. When we consider others suffering, we ought not to grow weary in facing and rising above our momentary and often petty discomforts.

Of course in the physical domain, American harpists and other musicians are mostly very spoiled with the ready availability of wonderful instruments, plentiful strings and every possible piece of music or recording one could desire. I remember when I first saw whole harp concertos which had been painstakingly hand-copied by diligent and dedicated students who could not have played the work without hand-copying it. It was not possible for them to buy the music scores. I was so humbled and impressed by this. I also felt so sad when I saw a harp without all the strings, with a rubber band strung in place of missing strings, because there was no hope of their being able to purchase strings.

On a spiritual level, how we need to learn to overlook small hurts and affronts and injustices. How else can we prepare to face a flood of suffering which we may have to encounter, and for which we will need to have great strength of character, endurance and courage. We need to let petty quarrels and annoyances flow by us. When we have friends who are girding up to battle cancer or grieving the loss of a child, how can we complain about a missed appointment or a friend's lack of understanding?

We need to develop spiritual maturity, and strong backbones, and depend on God for courage as we need it.

*Dear Father – Please give us courage to face whatever comes to us this day. Help us to be peacemakers, and do all we can to diminish other's suffering. Help us to be part of the solution to problems which confront us, rather than adding to those problems. In Jesus' name, Amen.*

# May 6

*Romans 12.10: Be kindly affectioned one to another with brotherly love.*

*Proverbs 31.26: In her tongue is the law of kindness.*

One does not have to look long or far to find examples of rudeness or a lack of simple civility in our society. From road rage to impatience with clerks or airline workers, everywhere we go we are confronted with this plague of unkindness to our fellow man. It is most unfortunate when it occurs in our own homes. How quickly an irritable remark or a dour expression can make a sunny day cloud over.

I think we have a godly duty to be pleasant, not in a Pollyanna kind of way, but in observing the small amenities - of politeness, gentleness and kindness with whomever we meet, and most of all in our own homes. There, where we must interact with the same family members day after day, year after year, that is where is most needed the kindness and caring that we often seem to save for outer friends or even perfect strangers.

In the mundane, ordinary days of our lives, we need to be extra careful not to take for granted our parents, siblings, husbands, wives, or roommates. They need most of all our thoughtfulness and consideration. It is our first duty. How simple things like saying thank you or a quick hug can change and lift the atmosphere in the home.

I often pray for my students before I go to teach. I am mindful of the responsibility I have to each of them – to be patient with the last student the same as with the first. To temper my advice and suggestions with encouragement and praise for the things they are doing well. Only in this atmosphere of mutual respect can lessons be truly fruitful. The student too has a responsibility to be open and courteous.

In every situation we face, kindness is the key to a life of peace and joy.

*Dear Father – Help me to treat everyone I meet today with the kindness and affection that you have placed in my heart. Help me to have your law of kindness on my tongue. In Jesus' name, Amen.*

# May 7, 2003

*Psalms 147: 3, 4, 7: He heals the broken-hearted and binds up their wounds. He determines the number of stars and calls them by name. Sing to the Lord with thanksgiving: make music to our God on the harp.*

This is one of my favorite psalms, partially of course because it mentions praising God with the harp, but also because of what it says about God's omnipotence. It is amazing to know that the same God who created the universe and named every star which he placed in the heavenly realm, cares for me and knows my name.

When the inevitable times of loss and suffering occur, it is a great comfort to know that He knows our brokenness, and that He compassionately cares for each of us.

I love to read of the results of latest scientific research about the origins of the universe. So many learned physicists believe the evidence is overwhelming for the creation to have been by intelligent design, not a big bang! And archeologists as well continue to support the historical accuracy of the Bible. Increasingly, the saying among many Christians – "The Bible says it and I believe it and that's the end of it" is supported by hard evidence in the scientific community. In this vast universe, God has planned the smallest details.

*Dear Father – Today I give thanks and praise you for your wonderful creation. And I am especially thankful that I know your love and your mercy personally. In Jesus' name, Amen.*

# May 8

*Psalms 118.24: This is the day that the Lord has made; we will rejoice and be glad in it.*

*Matthew 20.6: Why are you standing here idle all day?*

I remember reading words by Charles Spurgeon to the effect that until he had thanked God, on his knees every morning, he was not ready to face a new day! If our first thoughts and words were always of thanksgiving and praise to our great God, would that not set the tone and manner of our conduct for the rest of the day?

After those prayers, we should be able to set aside small cares and petty anxieties, and perform the duties and responsibilities that we all must shoulder with a peaceful heart. Is this not the key to a life of joy and serenity, lived close to the Lord?

I often feel restless and ill at ease until I have practiced every morning, even if only for one hour. It has been a constant in my life, this daily practicing. It is hard for me to truly focus on other things until my practicing is done. After that, I can make the necessary phone calls or tend to correspondence, do household or university tasks. There is also a real sense of peace in tending to these small, but important chores, and creating a sense of order out of the often chaotic business of living.

However, if we feel resentment over these daily tasks they can become a real obstacle to peace and a close walk with our Lord. The least significant jobs, (emptying the dishwasher!!) if done with a happy frame of mind and peaceful heart will bring us closer to God. I think where the trouble lies, at least in my life, is when I try to squeeze too many jobs into too short a time and of course that leads to frustration.

*Dear Lord – Help me to do just as much as you want me to do today, direct my steps and my stops, In Jesus' name, Amen.*

# May 9

*Job 1.21: The Lord gave and the Lord has taken away! Blessed be the name of the Lord!*

Often we see events in our lives or the lives of others that seem unjust or very unfair. Only God knows the reason why some of these hard things happen to good, innocent people.

The tragic losses of 9/11 brought to mind again the whole problem of evil. Satan can and does use the forces of nature, illness and wicked people to achieve his aims. The struggle between God and Satan will continue until the end of time as we know it. But in the end God will triumph and Satan will be cast out.

As a teacher I have often seen gifted students struck down with a devastating hand or arm problem which incapacitates them completely, often at the worst time in their careers. We wonder how can our loving God give us great gifts and then take them away?

Or we know of a wonderful, loving mother, in the prime of life with little children to raise, taken away by breast cancer, leaving behind a broken-hearted family.

God causes it to rain on the just and the unjust.

We cannot answer these hard questions completely, but we can search for answers in the Bible. Most suffering makes us more fully dependent on God. We realize all that we are and have is His, our homes and families, our career success, our material and physical well-being, everything is in His hands.

We have a choice, to trust God entirely and cooperate with His plans, or rebel and struggle against Him pointlessly. We can choose to obey Him and have faith that only in eternity will we see and understand why some of these things happened. We will see, I believe, God's love, mercy and justice. For now, we can just choose to praise Him.

*Father —We cannot understand the plans you have for us, but we trust you, that in everything, you are wanting the best for us, far more than we can imagine for ourselves. Thank you, in Jesus name, Amen.*

# May 10

*Psalms 34.22: The Lord redeems the soul of His servants, and none of them that trust in Him shall be desolate.*

*Job 13.15: Though He slay me, yet will I trust Him.*

We never know when our circumstances may change, bright with hope one day, then completely demolished the next.

I actually know many people who seem to never have had to experience great sorrow. Lives that have gone along on an even keel, children, marriage, job – all have gone well without any major problems of any kind. It is very rare though I believe.

I think however, that without experiencing suffering and sorrow, it is harder for them to draw nearer to God than for those for whom pain and despair are frequent companions.

For without experiencing great loss or heart-break, we can feel that we are pretty self-sufficient, that we can cope just fine, thank you, in our own strength and abilities. We can live good lives, even very considerately doing good deeds and works, without any reliance on the One who is greater than all He created.

I certainly do not wish people to have to experience sorrow in their lives in order to know God and to commit their lives to Him, but I know for myself I need the completeness of joy and peace – in good times and hard times – of trusting God for everything.

*Dear Lord – Help us to come to you, like a child, in simple trust, no matter what happens. Thank you that you love us. In Jesus' name, Amen.*

# May 11

*Job 2.10: Shall we receive good at the hands of God, and we not receive evil?*

*Psalms 119.65: Thou hast dealt well with Thy servant, O Lord, according to Thy word.*

I believe that whether or not we are content with our lives depends a great deal on whether we accept that all that comes our way is Divine Providence, God's will for our lives. If we could see the choices in our lives as God sees them, we would surely know that He chooses the best for us.

My dear teacher and mentor, Mlle. Renié, was never offered the most prestigious teaching position in France, at the Paris Conservatory, although she deserved it. It had to have been a great disappointment in her life. But rather than living in resentment, she lived a radiant life, performing, teaching and composing some of the most important works for solo harp. Her incomparable Harp Method is a monumental work. She also dedicated her resources and fame to helping less fortunate artists and musicians by creating a fund to pay for their retirement. Her faith in God defined her life. And perhaps she achieved a greater fame without the position of prestige that she deserved.

Joni Eareckson Tada's life was changed abruptly after a terrible diving accident that left her paralyzed from the neck down when she was just a young woman. Instead of living a life of self-pity, she has inspired millions throughout the world with her uplifting and positive faith. She has also written many best-selling books that have given hope to many others, and created a program to help supply wheelchairs to those unable to afford them. She is a living example of courage and faith in spite of tremendous hardships.

God wants the best for each of us and wants to use us. His ways in dealing with us are often beyond our human understanding at the time we experience them. Years later we may be able to better understand why certain things happened and how He led us in certain paths rather than others. The main thing is that we know that He is in control and that all He ordains will turn out for our ultimate good.

*Dear Father – Help us to trust you during stormy times as well as fair weather. In Jesus' name, Amen.*

# May 12

*Revelations 2.10: Do not be afraid of what you are about to suffer. Be faithful, even to the point of death and I will give you the crown of life.*

It is normal for us mortals to fear suffering. A trip to the dentist for a root canal, undergoing major surgery or chemotherapy, or watching a loved one suffer, these are just a few things which we quite normally fear. No one wants to suffer.

The Bible says over and over, "Fear not," "Be not afraid" and we are exhorted to stand firm and be faithful. Is. 41.10 says "Fear not, for I am with you."

I have known a few people who have experienced near death experiences, almost dying during surgery for example and being brought back. They say after that, they do not fear death anymore.

Mental anguish is one of the hardest kinds of suffering to bear. To perform, for me, has always been hard. I usually feel a kind of dread and oppression as a concert date draws nearer. I feel a heavy weight on my shoulders. I experience a kind of drawing inward, rationing my emotions, needing to be very still. Fortunately, all these feelings disappear when I begin to play, and of course there is a tremendous exhilaration afterwards.

Is this not a kind of picture of what we can look forward to, after the sufferings we face in our earthly lives, the incredible victory and joy of the crown of life? This is the reward we can expect, if we have put our faith and trust in Jesus Christ as our Lord and Savior.

*Dear Father – We know that there are times in our lives when we will suffer, but You have promised to be with us in them. Thank you for that assurance. In Christ's name, Amen.*

# May 13

*John 12.15: I pray not that you should take them out of the world, but that you should protect them from evil.*

God has never promised that we would not suffer in this life, but He has promised to be with us when we "pass through the water."

He has given us free will, and this is a great responsibility. How often, in this freedom, we make foolish choices and wrong decisions. Satan is a very real presence in the world and he is always waiting and trying to tempt us or cause us to stumble.

Although we can and do suffer the consequences of our mistakes, as we seek God's forgiveness and confess our sins to Him, we can be assured that He will sustain us and protect us from evil. We have only to call out to Him. If we commit our ways to Him, I believe He truly protects us from future mistakes and many of our human weaknesses.

When we are considering whether a choice is right for us, if it is God's will for us, it is helpful to ask ourselves these questions:

1 Is this course of action consistent with God's word?
2 Will this action hurt someone else?
3 Do we have peace of mind about it?

We should pray, without ceasing, for God's wisdom, and then let the matter rest, secure in the future and in the knowledge of His presence with us.

*Father : Thank you for your constant protection. In Jesus' name, Amen.*

# May 14

*Micah 6.8: And what does the Lord require of thee, but to do justly, and to love mercy, and to walk humbly with thy God.*

*Colossians 3.12: Put on therefore. . .kindness, humbleness of mind, meekness, long-suffering.*

Surely such words as humbleness, kindness, meekness and gentleness are not what our society usually is teaching us today. No, the lay world emphasizes self-awareness, self-confidence, self-expression and an attitude which asks "what is in it for me?"

How different these two world views! Even the lack of manners that we experience in daily life can be traced to the "me first" attitude. And I think in general, our culture disdains someone who is self-effacing and modest.

There is great peace in having a humble opinion of oneself, not proud, expecting very little in the way of recognition, and content with one's situation. There is joy in valuing others' needs as more important than one's own. Because God loves us, we are able to love others and to forgive them their human frailties, because we are keenly aware of our own. We want to be merciful in judging others, because of His great mercy to us, and forgiveness of our frailties. This is specially needed in our day to day dealings with those closest to us. To overlook petty irritations and annoyances is to walk closely with our Lord.

The image of walking humbly with God is so beautiful. His presence and strength are all we need and will always be more than enough. When we have His approval, we should need no other!

*Dear Father – Thank you for walking beside me wherever I may go today! Amen*

# May 15

*Exodus 33.14: My presence shall be with you, and I will give you rest.*

*Psalms 16.11: You will show me the path of life: in your presence is fullness of joy: at your right hand there are pleasures forever more.*

Billy Graham's wife, Ruth, wrote in *Decision* magazine recently about her life. She said the most important thing in her life was her personal relationship with Jesus Christ. She talked also of the joy her family has brought her, and then she mentioned aging. She said while there are special joys in growing old, aging can bring physical ailments. However, she has a very positive outlook on life and accepts each part of life with its ups and downs. Ruth Bell Graham is known by all as a joyful person and she has surely been a blessing to her husband, family and everyone she encounters.

How God showers His children with blessings! There are many who may think the Christians life must be dull and boring. How wrong that is! It is a joyful path, sometimes in bright sunshine amidst fields of flowers, sometimes through dark storms of doubt and despair. But when we walk beside Christ, held by His right hand, we can live victoriously in both the bright and the dark times in our lives.

If we focus on Christ, we need not fear aging, but can, like Ruth Graham, accept each stage as an opportunity to grow closer to Him. Then, in death, we will finally stand fully in His presence, and He will welcome us home as a beloved child.

*Father – Thank you for each period in our lives. Help us to appreciate each stage. You bless us and bring us joy and rest. In Chirst's name, Amen.*

# May 16

*Ephesians 6.10: Finally, my brethren, be strong in the Lord and in the power of His might.*

*Matthew 6.24: No man can serve two masters.*

Have you ever tried to do two things at once? Have you ever tried to do one task while still fretting over something else, a recent disagreement? Or something which you forgot to do and which needs to be done?

I have sometimes tried to practice and to concentrate on the music when there are some letters or school reports that are waiting to be done. It is truly impossible to have two things on your mind at once and do either of them very well!

It is surely the same in the spiritual realm. We cannot be double-minded. We will always be most devoted to what we love the most. Matthew said further in verse 24 "You cannot serve both God and money." Money can also be represented by our work (as important as that may be) or a relationship or an addiction. Where your treasure is, there will your heart be. In other words, we will put first in our lives what we love the most.

We need to value most all those things that are eternal, not the values of the world which are here today and gone tomorrow.

Our first priority should always be our personal, daily walk with Jesus Christ. If He remains our hope and our strength, all the other areas of our life will fall into their proper place. Time spent studying the Bible and reading inspirational messages by fine Christian writers is time well spent. We will gain wisdom and power to cope with all of life's circumstances.

*Father – Help us to worship you single-mindedly, you are our treasure! In Jesus' name, Amen.*

# May 17

*1 Thessalonians 5.11: Therefore encourage one another and build each other up, just as in fact you are doing.*

*Matthew 19.19: Love your neighbor as yourself.*

It is often much easier to show kindness and patience to strangers or colleagues than to those whose lives are enmeshed with ours, those with whom we share life on a daily basis.

The small irritations that we encounter in our home lives become more and more abrasive over years. Familiarity breeding contempt is the opposite of loving and encouraging each other. We need to bear each others weaknesses and faults with patience and kindness. Alas, it is not always easy to do that.

We are familiar with the kind of man who is an outstanding philanthropist, but who is mean to his servants, and a poor father to his children, and often abusive to his wife.

While that may seem an extreme case, we all need to constantly be on guard at home and at work. We must never take our closest friends, colleagues and family members for granted. We need to treat them all with the utmost consideration and care and appreciation, always mindful of how much they really mean to us and how greatly we need them and love them.

We also need to remember how we need their love and patience with our many weaknesses and foibles. Charity truly begins at home!

*Dear Father – Help me to show my appreciation and love to those closest to me today. In Jesus' name, Amen.*

# May 18

*1 John 3.14:   We know that we have passed from death to life, because we love our brothers.*

*1 John 4.8:   Whoever does not love does not know God, for God is love.*

What does it truly mean to love your brother?  Jesus said in John 15.12: "Love each other as I have loved you."

I think that it begins with a love of God, a holy, divine love. It is a command.  If we cannot believe in a power greater than ourselves, we make ourselves much greater than we are.

In these days of rampant secular humanism, so many people put themselves in the center of their world.  They base their actions on what they like or what makes them feel good.  They don't believe in any moral absolute, and certainly don't believe in a higher power.

But if one's allegiance is to Jesus Christ, we want to follow him, to serve Him, and to obey Him.  Our love and obedience, although far from perfect, lead us to unselfishness and a love of everyone.  Because all of His creatures are loved by Him, we love them too.

Throughout the history of Christianity, hospitals, prison ministries, and social programs and services have been an overflow of Christian love to our brothers in need.  We need to be a generation which continues this outreach to those in need.  Mother Teresa with her ministry to "the lowest of the low" epitomizes this brotherly love.

Charles Colson's revolutionary work in prison ministry throughout the world and to the children of prisoners is an incredible example of God's love and the power of the Holy Spirit, moving in the life of Colson, once a prisoner himself during the Watergate scandal.  What a testimony to the life-changing love only God can effect!

*Dear Father - Help me to show forth your love to my brothers today.  In Jesus' name, Amen.*

# May 19

*Psalms 37.7: Rest in the Lord, and wait patiently for Him.*

*Psalms 62.8: Trust in Him at all times.*

When a friend or student comes to me with a problem, I want to jump in and help them with suggestions and solutions. I want to be genuinely helpful and share their burden.

However, perhaps a better way is to listen to their problems, to be silent and let them express their needs. To pray with them is the best answer, for we need to have God's wisdom. He alone can provide the solutions to everyone's needs.

But how hard it is to be silent! I long to offer practical solutions and human ideas of what may be needed. But God's ways are not our ways. Most deep problems are based on needs of the heart and soul of a person. Only God can touch those needs and provide the comfort, wisdom and reassurance that they crave.

To hear his Holy Spirit speak to us, we need to halt the busyness and clamor of our lives, to bow before Him and be silent. It is helpful,too, to simply hold the Bible, and to read some favorite passage of scripture. By meditating on these precious verses we allow God to speak to us through them.

He has promised to answer us when we ask in complete faith and trust.

*Father – Help me to be silent and get out of the way, so that you can speak and be heard. In Christ's name, Amen.*

# May 20

*Romans 8.6: To be spiritually minded is life and peace.*

As I read Romans 8 it is clear that Paul is writing very specifically about the Spirit of God. If the Spirit of God lives in you, that is life and peace.

We live in a sinful and broken world. Even after we have surrendered our life to the Lordship of Christ, sin will continue to knock at our door. Satan will try to ensnare us. We can have the Holy Spirit abiding in us, and that gives us the power and strength to resist sin and temptation. But, we will still often fail. However, when we confess our failures to God, and ask forgiveness, we can nevertheless, keep moving forward in victorious and confident living.

The important thing is not to focus on our mistakes, but to keep moving in the right direction, surrendering our lives day by day and moment by moment to the control of the Holy Spirit. Only when we are one with Christ will we human beings be completely free from the influence of sin.

Paul writes in Romans 8.16-17 "that we are God's children, heirs of God and co-heirs with Christ – if we share in His sufferings – we may also share in His glory."

Then in Rom. 8.28 those wonderful words of hope and comfort "and we know that in all things God works for the good of those who love Him, who have been called according to His purpose." These words give life and peace to all who believe in Jesus Christ.

*Dear Father – I surrender my life to the guidance of your Holy Spirit. Please keep me from stumbling today. In Jesus' name, Amen.*

# May 21

*Deuteronomy 33.12: The beloved of the Lord shall dwell in safety by Him: and the Lord shall cover him all the day long.*

What does it mean to "dwell safely" by the Lord? I have an image of a baby bird safely covered by the wings of a parent in its nest. I also remember walking proudly beside my father, feeling buoyed and protected by his presence.

We cannot always be physically safe and protected. Many times we have to venture out on our own and confront potentially dangerous situations, dark streets or storms in the skies during a flight. In these days of suicide bombings, almost anyplace has the potential for great danger.

I remember flying to South America as a young artist for concerts in Peru. The plane hit serious turbulence and it was very frightening, even though I was a seasoned flyer by then. After that frightening experience I decided that I would not fly anymore and only travel by car or train! Well, that lasted about one year, and then I realized if I was to be a concert harpist, I simply would have to get over my fear of flying. I committed the fears to the Lord, and have flown ever since, trusting Him for my safety, at home and in the air.

Spiritually, when we trust the Lord, we do dwell in peace and walk safely, for we are walking beside one who loves us. He is with us in every situation we face in our life on earth, and we can look forward to the day when we will truly be united with Him in eternal life.

*Dear Father – Help me to realize your presence beside me throughout this day. In Jesus' name, Amen.*

# May 22

*Psalms 91.1: He who dwells in the shelter of the Most High will abide under the shadow of the Almighty.*

I find such comfort in the words of this great Psalm 91. It is so important to me to daily confirm God's promise of protection and safety.

I really believe it is the most important part of every day, beginning by thanking God for his blessings and seeking his shelter and protection for the new day.

We truly never know what each new day will bring. Sometimes I am rushed in the morning before school and I do not get to spend time in prayer. Later during the day, I can suddenly be presented with a serious problem, or a strained relationship or a frustrating misunderstanding. How I need His under-girding at such times, to be braced for whatever happens. And then I regret so much not having had the quiet, alone time in prayer with God.

Time spent in His presence is the best way I know to prepare for the many pressures we experience in life. Psalm 91.2 says "I will say of the Lord, He is my refuge and my fortress, my God, in whom I trust." These words are truly a source of great courage and strength for whatever we have to face in this life.

*Dear Father – Thank you for your shelter and provision for this new day. In Jesus' name, Amen.*

# May 23

*Hebrews 13.5: Keep your lives free from the love of money and be content with what you have.*

*Philippians 4.11: I have learned to be content whatever the circumstances.*

*1 Timothy 6.6: But Godliness with contentment is great gain.*

These are some of my favorite Bible verses. I deeply believe that the secret of a happy life is being content with our God-given circumstances.

Constantly regretting the past and decisions made long ago, pining for a former job or home or relationship are sure paths to unhappiness in the present and a prescription for lifelong misery.

I think the same thing applies to one's longing for a bigger home, a more exciting spouse or hitting the jackpot in the future. How different it is to face each day with a thankful heart and to remain firmly focused in the present.

It doesn't mean that we can't have big dreams and make needed changes in our life as God directs us. But I believe being rooted in the present is pivotal to our being content. I know, for myself, I want to value each moment of every day and appreciate everything I am given by God.

I want to live a holy life, that is, a life praising and glorifying God. I want to please him by my actions and my attitudes. Of course I know that I will often fail, but this is the path and the direction I choose to follow. I believe if we ask God to give us this gift of contentment, He will bless us with it.

*Dear Father – Thank you for your blessings today, help me to be content with each circumstance I experience today. In Jesus' name, Amen.*

# May 24

*Hebrews 12.11: No discipline seems pleasant at the moment, but grievous: Nevertheless, afterward it produces the peaceable fruit of righteousness for those trained by it.*

Discipline is a word which is rather out of fashion these days. Yet, how sad it is to see a child misbehaving without any correction . It is not his fault that his parents have not trained him and yes, disciplined him. Such discipline, administered with love yet firmness, is what gives the kind of life-long results and habits that are so needed in each person's life, and indeed, in our whole society.

In musical training, of course discipline is a vital necessity. There is no substitute for daily practicing, years of scales and exercises. There is no way to cram for that!

As a world famous pianist once said, "If I miss practice for one day, I know it, if I miss practice for two days, fellow musicians know it, and if I miss practice for 3 days, the entire audience knows it!"

So it is crucial to have discipline. God has created each of us with consciences to prod us and to correct us. He has instilled in each of us the ability to choose right from wrong. There are consequences to wrong choices, but if we learn from them and hence are trained by them – we may experience the fruit of a new and better way of living, full of peace and righteousness.

*Dear Father – Please discipline me as you feel I need it and help me to grow in wisdom under your loving and firm hand. In Jesus' name, Amen.*

# May 25

*Matthew 26.39: O my Father, if it be possible let this cup pass from me: nevertheless, not as I will but as you will.*

My teacher wrote this same prayer before one of her concerts. It was sometimes so difficult to face the real anguish of solo harp performance. No matter how prepared she was and supremely gifted as an artist, many things could go wrong.

I too have always prayed before recitals, knowing I would soon go on stage, I prayed that God would give me steady fingers, a clear mind, a solid memory, and that my music would glorify Him. I often felt very weak before concerts, and I needed to trust God totally to enable me to have the courage to go out and play!

I have always felt, above any other considerations, that I wanted to be in God's will for my life. That does not mean that I have not made many mistakes and suffered some hard consequences, but I believe the main thing is to commit one's life to Christ, to follow Him and to believe in Him. He alone can take our failures and shortcomings and turn them to good.

"He who began a good work in you will be faithful to complete it."

"For all things work together for good to them who love the Lord and are called according to His purpose."

*Dear Father - May your will be done in my life today, and thank you for turning my weakness into your strength. In Jesus' name, Amen.*

# May 26

*Exodus 16.8: The Lord hears your murmurings, which you murmur against Him.*

Complaining, if we allow it, can become our habitual re-action to everything, large and small, that we don't like or we wish were different. We who are Christians can be the worst offenders and complainers. We complain about the church music, too fast or loud, the sermon is too short or too long, the parking lot is too crowded, the list can go on and on!

I had dinner with friends this week. The husband said he had told his wife "that if she couldn't say something nice about him, to say nothing at all." He went on to say that "it's sure been quiet around here lately!"

How hard it is for us to try to even go one whole day without complaining about something!

Even if we succeed in not verbalizing our feelings, it is humbling to know that the Lord knows our hearts and minds. He knows exactly how we feel.

When I think of the Christians in Sudan and other areas of the world who are persecuted for their faith and who are not even able to worship openly in a church, I realize that we should only be thankful that we can attend church at all. We can work to improve or correct genuine grievances, when change is possible and desirable, but the rest of the time, let's just give thanks!

*Dear Father – Thank you that we can worship you in such peace and freedom. Be a comfort and great Savior for those who are dying because of their faith in you. In Jesus' name, Amen.*

# May 27, 2002

*Luke 16:10: He that is faithful in that which is least is faithful also in much.*

*Psalms 31:23: The Lord preserves the faithful.*

How much of life is spent doing mundane, daily chores like loading and unloading the dishwasher, sorting the laundry, picking up dishes, wiping the kitchen counters, hanging up clothes, sweeping the garage and preparing meals. The list is endless!

Our attitude toward these small jobs is everything. If we do them cheerfully, I think they can be a real blessing in the fabric of our lives. They need not be stressful. They can bring a peaceful contentedness to our lives. I get real pleasure from seeing a clean kitchen floor or a neatly folded pile of towels.

Of course, excessive tidiness can become a burden, to ourselves and to those around us. But I think every chore, if done as unto the Lord, can be a source of blessing.

Of course, we all derive great pleasure in preparing a meal for friends and seeing their happy faces as the food disappears. Less obvious is the possible delight in cleaning out a messy dresser, file cabinet, or closet.

I think getting ones outer life in order brings a great sense of peace and helps restore balance in our inner lives and even our spiritual life. I often wonder if people who live in general disorder may have the same disorder in their inner lives as well.

*Dear Father – Help us to do everything that you place before us, cheerfully and with good spirit, In Jesus' name, Amen.*

# May 28, 2002

*Colossians 1:11: Being strengthened with all power according to the glorious might so that you may have great endurance and patience, with joyfulness.*

When we are weakened by worries and care and feel unable to go on, this verse is such a powerful reminder that we have strength beyond our mortal selves! It is so wonderful to realize we can lean on God's strength and power when ours seems to just be gone. We can lean on Him for patience when ours has withered up. He gives us, not a little more patience, but great patience. We can trust Him to give us endurance to stay our course, not a little endurance, but great endurance. And, He promises that we will even have joy in the midst of those times when we feel so weak!

I think often of circumstances when one or another of my students was so discouraged they were ready to seek other employment outside of music. And then, at the final audition, they have won a major orchestra position and were instantly established with a great career. I believe it is when we have reached the limit of what we can do by ourselves that God's power is the greatest. When we must totally rely on Him, miracles happen, and then, He can bless us beyond our wildest dreams.

*Father – Thank you for your incredible strength and grace when we reach the end of all we can do on our own. In Jesus' name, Amen.*

# May 29, 2002

*Hebrews 6:12: Be not lazy, but imitate those who through faith and patience inherit the promises.*

The book of Hebrews tells of how God worked in the lives of the Old Testament believers, and the faith in Jesus Christ of the New Testament. The writer exhorted the early Christians to stick to the new covenant in Christ, and not to fall back on the legalism and rituals found in the Old Testament.

It is a real inspiration, when we go through various trials, to have the example of those who have gone before us and come out victorious. Famous bicyclist, Lance Armstrong, who overcame cancer to win the Tour de France, not once but 7 times, is such a model. It must be comforting and helpful to someone suffering with cancer to be able to look at his victories in spite of it.

My strong role model was my teacher, Henriette Renié, who spent one hour every morning in prayer and devotion. Her constancy and her deep faith were an inspiration to me, a young eighteen-year-old American in Paris. Her example deepened my own faith. Also, I was encouraged by the fact that after her time of worship and prayer, she practiced an hour every morning, doing this still when she was 80 years old! Her character and discipline impressed me deeply.

In a similar way, as believers, we are impressed and influenced "by a great cloud of witnesses," those Christians who have gone before us. They are cheering us on in our life adventure. Their faith in Jesus Christ is a poignant and constant encouragement to us.

Heb. 11:1 says "Now faith is being sure of what we hope for and certain of what we do not see."

*Dear Lord, We thank you for the incredible gift of faith. In Jesus' name, Amen*

# May 30, 2002

*Judges 5:18: The people of Zebulun risked their very lives; so did Naphtali on the heights of the field.*

In these days of patriotic fervor following the attack on the World Trade Center, our country has asked for help from the rest of the world in our battle to defeat terrorism. The help from our closest allies, Britain and Canada, has been very encouraging. And, other countries as well have sent troops and supplies. All of these allied troops are risking their lives for this cause in support of us.

In Judges, this was somewhat the case. Some of the tribes of Israel stayed home, rather than get involved in the battle of other tribes.

War is always hard, but sometimes necessary. We owe so much to our brave military men and women who are risking "their very lives" again today in order for us to live in freedom and security. We need sometimes to fight for justice against real and great evil.

In touring the Normandy D-day battlefields, it is humbling to see the cliffs, covered with barbed wire and German pillbox bunkers, which our brave men scaled, heedless of the horrific danger they faced. So many of them died in order for the others climbing the hill below them to survive. We owe them such a debt of gratitude. They and their families paid the ultimate price for our cherished freedom.

*Father, Help us never to take for granted the precious freedom we enjoy. Be with our military men and women and their families. In Jesus' name, Amen.*

# May 31, 2002

*Psalms 5:11: Let all those that put their trust in Thee rejoice: let them also that love Thy name be joyful in Thee.*

*Psalms 23:2: He maketh me to lie down in green pastures.*

There are special times in God's creation that fill my heart with such joy. Springtime in Bloomington is one. I don't understand how anyone cannot appreciate the beauty of God's creation as evidenced by flowering trees and flowers, grass, sky and clouds. After the dark days of winter, they specially seem to show us His love.

When I see a field of daffodils, a line of rose and red peony bushes, a forest filled with brilliant white dogwood trees, turn a corner and see a row of gorgeous red flowering crab trees or glistening white pear trees, look at each petal of an iris, so delicately and intricately painted by the Master's hand, I cannot help but be filled with awe and wonder. I love to walk on a carpet of freshly mown grass, velvet in texture, and inhale the fragrance that is so very special in spring.

In Switzerland, where I have taught summer classes for many years, I feel especially close to the Lord. "I will lift up my eyes unto the hills, from whence cometh my help." How often I have walked and gazed at the beauty of the snow-covered mountains and prayed to God for deliverance and help during trying times.

I am so thankful for the beauty of God's created world, and I do feel close to God in my garden and in all of nature. How blessed we are to have eyes to see all He has designed to give us joy!

*Thank you, Lord, for the beauty of nature. Help us to take time to really look at a flower today and appreciate each detail you have created so lovingly for us. In Jesus' name, Amen.*

# JUNE

## June 1

*Psalms 27:4: One thing I ask of the Lord, this is what I seek: that I may dwell in the house of the Lord all the days of my life, to gaze upon the beauty of the Lord and to seek Him in His temple.*

Having lived in the same house for almost 20 years, I understand what it means to truly dwell there, until the fire took that dwelling place away! What can it mean to "dwell in the house of the Lord?" I am sure it does not refer to spending great amounts of time in a physical church. Rather, I think we are called to live close to God in our hearts, to consecrate and dedicate each of our days to Him and to spend time with Him in prayer, seeking to know and to do His will.

We will experience the "beauty of the Lord" when we reflect on His character. His love, strength, omnipotence, courage, wisdom, gentleness inspire us to seek these qualities in our own lives. "To seek Him in His temple" I believe means for us to seek to live lives that are holy.

The psalmist says "this one thing I will seek." If we put as our first priority in life our devotion to God, our faith in Jesus Christ, I believe all the other aspects of our life will fall into place. He will empower us to do the work He has graciously provided for us. He will also provide for our physical and spiritual wellbeing. In reality, we who love Him, are already dwelling with Him. That is what I want for myself and those I love.

*Father, please allow me to draw ever closer to you, that I might experience more of You each day. In Jesus' name, Amen.*

# June 2

*2 Corinthians 3:18: We all, with open faces that reflect the glory of the Lord, are being changed into His likeness, from glory to glory, as by the spirit of the Lord.*

I feel as if I have many "harpist grand-children!" Many former students bring one of their own young students to work with me in a summer class. I often marvel at how their hand positions absolutely mirror the hand positions of their teachers, whose hands I came to know so well in years of lessons. This fact has always touched me somehow, proof of the faithfulness students exhibit in trying to imitate their teachers. My students rarely look like me, since most of them came to work with me in later years, for graduate study, after their hand positions were established.

As we, in a similar way seek to imitate our Lord, and to conform ourselves to Him, His holy spirit can change and transform us into His likeness. Of course, we cannot do it on our own, any more than a student can achieve a good hand position without a model. But, as we behold the glorious face of Jesus, His power can flow into us and can make us into the children He plans for us to be. And, the end result is that as His people we will glorify Him in our lives.

*Lord, Please mold me and shape me so that I may conform to your will, In Jesus' name, Amen*

# June 3

*Psalms 64:10: Let the righteous rejoice in the Lord and trust in Him; let all the upright in heart praise Him!*

*Proverbs 16:20: Blessed is he who trusts in the Lord.*

If we truly trust God, we will not fear tomorrow. We will not spend our days worrying about our future, short term or long term. We must commit everything to Him and then do our work and remain vigilant, depending on Him for help and guidance. When we memorize our music, we must do our part in that often hard intellectual work, but then, we should trust God to see us through the actual performance.

This trust is especially important in decision making. There are always pros and cons to each choice we must make. But, if we truly commit the decision to God, we should have a pretty clear sense of which choice would have God's blessing on it, the greatest good, the least self interest. Then we should move forward and act with confidence and courage, not looking back or fretting that we have chosen wrong.

God is in control and He can overrule even our wrong choices. So, our hearts can rejoice and we can be at peace. We can praise God with all our heart.

*Father, thank you for guiding us and helping us to make wise, godly decisions. In Jesus' name, Amen.*

# June 4

*I Corinthians 15:58: Therefore, my dear brothers, be stead-fast, immovable, always abounding in the work of the Lord because you know your labor in the Lord is not in vain.*

I believe that God will always enable us and empower us to do what is right. If we sincerely seek to do what is good and noble, He will give us the necessary strength and ability.

He knows our hearts; He knows our every thought. We must ask Him simply and directly, with firmness. We must be immovable in our faith in Him.

Some of us are called to enter the ministry, some to be missionaries, some to be teachers, some to be doctors, some to be artists and some to be engineers or architects. Some people struggle for many years before finding their niche or the work that is suited to them. But, if we commit our work, whatever it may be, even work which seems menial or without meaning, to the Lord, He has promised we will not work in vain. He will be in our work and He will bless it.

*Dear Father, I commit all my work to you today—my practice, my teaching, my phone calls, my thoughts. Please help me and enable me to do what is right in all I do. In Jesus' name, Amen*

# June 5

*I Samuel 3:9: Speak, Lord; for Thy servant heareth.*

My favorite time of day, in the morning, is to read scripture and afterwards spend time praying. This time is wonderfully calming and stabilizing to me before I begin the day's work.

How can we hear God speak to us in the midst of the noise, clamor and rush in our world? We will surely not hear His voice in our cell phones, e-mails and fax machines. We will not see His face in our scanners, videos or computer screens.

We must seek Him in silence and solitude. What an effort it takes to shut out the world—to close the newspaper, to turn off the television and to truly be alone with Him.

But, what peace and joy await us when we do this. Then, and only then, we can hear His still, small voice—a mere whisper in our ears. Only then can He speak to us, and give us all wisdom and guidance.

*Dear Father, please speak to me today. I need to hear you; I need you. In Jesus' name, Amen.*

# June 6

*Revelations 3.12: Him who overcomes I will make a pillar in the temple of my God.*

*Ephesians 2.22: And in him you too are being built together to become a dwelling in which God lives by his Spirit.*

As God molds us and transforms us into His likeness, we become a pillar in His temple, a living and evolving part of the church universal. And, because His Holy Spirit dwells within us, we are being constantly changed into someone more acceptable to God.

I have always loved the verse from Rom.12.2: "Be not conformed to the world, but be transformed by the renewing of your mind. Then you will be able to test and approve what is God's good, pleasing and perfect will." I feel these words give us great hope and encouragement. We do not need to be locked into harmful thought patterns or past behaviors. If we study the Bible and fill our hearts and minds with God's words, we can truly become new people, from the inside out!

Paul writes also in Rom. 8.6: The mind of sinful man is death, but the mind controlled by the Spirit is life and peace. Later in Rom. 8, Paul continues to write, that nothing can separate us from the love of God which is in Christ Jesus our Lord.

This is how we are transformed, by His great love. We then can be deemed worthy to be a living pillar in His temple.

*Dear Father: May your Holy Spirit guide me and shape me into the person you would have me become. In Jesus' name, Amen.*

# June 7

*1 Thessalonians 5.5: You are all sons of the light and sons of the day. We do not belong to the night or to darkness.*

*Psalms 97.11: Light is shed upon the righteous and joy on the upright in heart.*

I love sunshine and sometimes I really have to struggle to keep my spirits up during dark, gray days. We have a lot of them in southern Indiana. Light and sunshine seem to symbolize joy and happiness to me.

As Christians we need to be able to hold our thoughts and attitudes and actions up to the light of God's wisdom and judgment. We need to be conscious and aware, vigilant to keep areas of darkness and sin out of our lives.

If we live free of guilt and conscious wrong-doing, God will fill our hearts with his light and joy. Not that we won't make mistakes, which of course we all do. But if we bring those mistakes to God, ask His forgiveness and repent of our actions, He will forgive us and grant us a peaceful heart.

We can walk in obedience and be cloaked in the sunshine of His great love and protection on even the darkest days.

*Father – Thank you for Jesus Christ who came to be the light of the world. In His name, Amen.*

# June 8

*Zechariah 4.10: Who despises the day of small things?*

A good friend who is a great violin teacher and who has taught many young prodigies once spoke to one of my summer classes. I loved what she told them. She said "the difference between a good performance and a great one is often not very big. The difference lies in the details, like a clearer bass line here, the melody more singing there, or more time on the final notes." What an encouragement and inspiration! Small details are so very important in music.

Andrew Jackson's mother gave him this advice when he was young, she said "never forget a kindness." He never forgot her wisdom and continued to show appreciation during his days as president.

In Matthew 25.23 Jesus said "Well done good and faithful servant, you have been faithful over a few things, I will make you ruler over many things. Enter into the joy of your Lord."

In Luke 16.10 Jesus said again "Whom can be trusted with very little can also be trusted with much."

How we handle the small daily duties shows much about how we will deal with a large crisis or opportunity. How we treat those who are seemingly unimportant in our lives shows also an important side of our character. We should treat everyone the same, the lowly in station and the powerful. Our kindness and attitude of evenly appreciating everyone, can make a real difference.

*Father – Help me to pay attention and be faithful in the small details of life, everyday! In Christ's name, Amen.*

# June 9

*Proverbs 15.32: He that is slow to anger is better than the mighty; and he that rules his spirit than he who takes a city.*

Self-control is such an important character trait, and yet it can be so hard to learn. Some people seem to just naturally be self-controlled. I tend to be too impulsive and spontaneous, and this can lead me into trouble. In my zeal to make things right or to help a situation I can get carried away, and before I know it I am losing my head and am "out of control!"

I think that is why this verse is so important, to be slow to anger, that is to cool off and to wait to express an opinion. Less said is always better than too much. Listening is of much greater value, and defuses anger. The ability to simply say "I am sorry" is such a sign of maturity and self-control. To not need to be right all the time is also such a good and easy way to live.

*Father – Please help me to be thoughtful and to guard my words today, that I may not cause hurt to anyone. In Jesus' name, Amen*

# June 10

*Isaiah 50:10: Who among you fears the Lord and obeys the work of his servant? Let him who walks in the dark, who has no light, trust in the name of the Lord and rely on his God.*

*Psalms 18:28: The Lord my God will enlighten my darkness.*

Some of my darkest hours have been spent worrying about things which never happened. Times when I doubted that I could perform due to various finger problems, or times when I had to make hard decisions, truly which would change my life.

Hebrews 11:1 tells us, "Faith is the substance of things hoped for, the evidence of things not seen." When we are in the darkness of uncertainty, feeling alone or abandoned, that is when we most need faith. We need this most of all—to trust God and to believe that He will work all things for our good. It is hard to believe that when we are in the midst of heartache and despair, when life and our circumstances seem hopeless, God will give us hope and a future. In Jer. 29:11 we hear, "If we could see ahead the plan God has for us, that would not be faith. God will enlighten us in His timing."

Sometimes we need to cry our sorrow and let the pain come out. But, then, we should try to do some simple chore and get on with our life, secure that He who watches over us will bind up our wounds and lead us gently through the present darkness.

*Thank you, Father, for walking with us in the dark and giving us your Holy Spirit to enlighten us. In Jesus' name, Amen.*

# June 11

*Psalms 138:3: In the day I cried you answered me, and strengthened me with strength in my soul.*

I Peter 5:7 says we are "to cast out all our anxiety on Him because He cares for you." I have recently had to face some hard news. Instead of a carefree summer with friends, I have just heard that I will have to travel alone and work alone most of the summer. This change in plans has hit me hard and I am feeling very sad about it. I have actually shed many tears about it and prayed for courage to face this lonely, hard time ahead. I believe God has answered my prayers and is giving me the strength I need to go on. He encouraged me over a period of a few days. My sad feelings are still very real, but I feel He is giving me the strength I need day by day. As I continue to bring my pain to Him, He is faithful to relieve it. How wonderful to know that we have a heavenly Father who cares for us.

*Father, great is Thy faithfulness! Thank you for caring for me today. In Jesus' name. Amen.*

# June 12

*Joshua 1:9: Have I not commanded thee? Be strong and of good courage; be not afraid, neither be dismayed: for the Lord thy God is with thee wherever thou goest.*

Although I have traveled extensively all my life, I am a real "homebody." It is like pulling teeth for me to leave home. So, when I must travel, I truly need to be strong and have courage.

As security precautions have tightened, travel by air has become less comfortable. I think we all share a sense of heightened tension and anxiety when we travel these days.

However, how wonderful is God's promise to be with us, wherever we go! If we are high in the air over the Atlantic or on a ship in the Pacific, He is with us. We can count on it.

When I am teaching in Switzerland, daily I "lift my eyes unto the hills from whence cometh my help. My help cometh from the Lord, the maker of heaven and earth." Psalm 121 1:2

*Dear Father, Thank you that you are with us, wherever we go. In Jesus' name, Amen.*

# June 13

*1 John 1:7: If we walk in the light, as He is in the light, we have fellowship one with another.*

*Hebrews 6:10: God is not unjust to forget your work, and the love you have shown Him as you have ministered to His people and do minister.*

I attended a women's Bible study at my church last year. It met at 9:30 every Tuesday morning. It was a very special time. There is a sweetness in being with sisters in Christ, fellow believers who are so open about their faith in Christ. Truly, I could feel a beautiful aura coming from fellowship with these godly women.

But we are called to minister to those who are in need and who do not know Christ. It is not easy to reach out to strangers, but He empowers us to share our love of Him with them, with kindness and gentleness. Not in a self-righteous way, but humbly telling them what He has done for us. Not that we are finished products by any means, for each of us remain a "work in progress."

If we try to help others to know Christ in our own strength, we will often fail. But, He knows our efforts and He will bless whatever we endeavor in His name.

*Dear Lord, Please help me to be strong to tell others about you today. In Jesus' name. Amen*

# June 14

*Isaiah 14:3: The Lord shall give you rest from your sorrow and fear and hard bondage wherein you were made to serve.*

I have always admired Charles Colson for his wonderful Prison Ministry. He brings hope and encouragement to prisoners who are often living in total despair and hopelessness. And it seems huge percentages of these prisoners, when finally released back into society, because of their faith, are able to stay out of prison and live new and productive lives.

True peace, that is deep peace of the soul, can only be found in the Lord. He above can satisfy our longing for rest and peace; He alone can offer forgiveness of past sins. He alone can offer comfort and hope when we grieve; He alone can calm our fears, real and imagined.

Then, we can find that rest, which is so elusive in our busy and often, tormented lives. As we seek His will and submit to His chastening, He will cleanse us and renew us.

But, we must have complete faith and trust in Him. "Faith is our pathway to Heaven," said Charles Stanley. Without faith, communication is blocked. The Lord hears our prayers before we utter them and answers every request asked in faith. He will grant us peace and rest when we ask Him.

*Dear Father, Thank you for the gift of your peace and rest today as we submit ourselves to you. In Jesus' name, Amen.*

# June 15

*Psalms 46:1-2: God is our refuge and strength, a very present help in trouble. Therefore we will not fear, though the earth be moved; though the mountain be carried into the midst of the sea.*

Trouble can come so suddenly into our lives. Like a sudden change in the weather or a severe storm. One moment we are calmly going about the daily routine of our lives, and the next moment we can be shattered by devastating news or an unexpected blow to our future plans—indeed our whole future.

Surely our hearts and mind cannot ever fathom the pain when a close friend or neighbor loses a child. It seems the papers are so often full of such tragic news. When a child is killed, the gaping wound in a family's heart is unbearable.

No human words can console at such a time of grief. But, God is our refuge and strength, a very present help in our times of trouble. He can heal our wounds. He can see us through the times when our circumstances seem hopeless.

*Thank you, Father, for bearing our burdens. Jesus was a man of sorrow and acquainted with grief. Please place your healing hand on those suffering loss today. In Jesus' name. Amen.*

# June 16

*Ephesians 3:20-21: Now unto Him that is able to do exceeding abundantly above all that we ask or think, according to the power that works in us, to Him be glory in the church by Christ Jesus throughout all ages. World without end. Amen*

I cannot help but remember my wonderful father on this and every Father's Day. He was such a dear, good man. He really was a family man who, along with my mother, made a wonderful home for me and my brother. He was an attorney for a large insurance company. He loved to take us on family vacations, and we were the center of his life.

I think God's promise above is amazing, that He wants to do for us more than we can even imagine. We often pray for help or a solution to a particular problem but, if we stop and realize that God is able to do for us way beyond what we can even imagine, we might ask so much more of Him.

I could compare it to a young harpist who dreams of owning a small lap harp or Irish folk harp, whose parents surprise her by buying her a big, gold concert harp! If our human parents can give us such gifts, what greater gifts does our heavenly Father have in store for us, His children who love Him and worship Him?

What peace it brings to know that He wants our best in all circumstances, and that His best for us is beyond the best we can even imagine!

*Our heavenly Father, On this Father's Day, we honor and praise you. We thank you for loving us. In Jesus' name. Amen.*

# June 17

*Matthew 6:28: Consider the lilies of the field, how they grow.*

I love flowers of all kinds. Each season is different. My favorite time is probably spring, when I watch every day the hundreds of bulbs I have planted in the yard bravely start pushing through the soil. Daffodils and tulips are among my favorites, and peonies and violets. I am not at all an expert gardener, but I love to work in my garden. I am also a dedicated walker and love to watch the various flowers and gardens as I roam my quiet neighborhood in the mornings. I feel in touch somehow with God's world as I observe the changes each season brings.

I am also so aware that "only God can make a flower" as the dear children's song says. My best gardening efforts are useless without the sun and rain He sends. Only the Master Gardener could ever have designed the beauty and immense variety of colorful flowers, painted in unimaginable delicacy and intricacy.

As I walk in the Swiss Alps in the summer, I marvel at each tiny wildflower. Often the most beautiful ones grow in the most rugged and wind-swept, rocky areas. One of the most colorful is the golden globe, delicate, like a tiny anemone. What lessons we can learn from flowers—to be content where God has placed us, to trust Him alone for our welfare, and to not be anxious about outer garments or circumstances!

*Father, Thank you for the gift of flowers. How they brighten our world. Help us to brighten the lives of those around us as your love shines through us. In Jesus' name, Amen.*

# June 18

*Matthew 6:30: Wherefore, if God so clothe the grass of the field, which today is alive  and tomorrow is cast into the oven, shall He not much more clothe you, O ye of little faith?*

*Psalms 52:8: I trust in the mercy of God for ever and ever.*

How silly it would seem to us to imagine a daisy worrying or a rose fretting whether their colors and fragrance might not turn out right? Who can picture a daffodil anxious whether it will pierce the hard crust of winter and be able to brighten the world with its cheerful, yellow petals?

If we could only have the simplicity to trust God to "grow us up," molding our character and circumstances as He wills, just as he causes the flowers and fields to blossom and flourish. How much better we would be! Yet, don't we continually look back and regret many of our actions and look forward with fear and trepidation about our future?

We need big faith—large enough to enable us to completely yield our lives to God. His mercy is forever and ever.

*Dear Father, Thank you for your patience and mercy toward us. Help us today to simply abide in you and entrust all we do to your loving care. In Jesus' name, Amen.*

# June 19

*Psalms 121:7 The Lord shall preserve you from all evil. He shall preserve your soul.*

Psalm 121 is one of the most beautiful and comforting passages in the Bible. It describes how God is in control of every circumstance of our lives, with love and compassion. He watches over us wherever we are and whatever we do. The maker of heaven and earth never slumbers. When I think of the word preserve, I think of the times I have been alone in Europe or Asia or South America and how God has protected me on each trip and at each concert.

He is omnipotent, omniscient and omnipresent, in plain words, He is all-powerful, all knowing and present everywhere. We can know that He cares for each one of us, personally and intimately wherever we are, at home or in a distant country.

Jesus said, "In this world you will have tribulation, but be not dismayed, I have overcome the world." While God may allow great trials and challenges in our life, if our goal is eternal life through faith in Jesus Christ, we should remain focused on Him and the future He promises us with Him. Therefore, we need not fear whatever happens to us in this world. It is our souls that are being preserved by Him for heaven.

*Dear Father, Thank you for being in control of our destinies. Help us to keep our focus on Jesus. In His name I we pray, Amen*

# June 20

*Psalms 57:1: Be merciful unto me, O God, be merciful unto me for my soul trusts in Thee! Yea, in the shadow of Thy wings will I make my refuge until these calamities be over past.*

Elizabeth Elliot has been such an example of courage. After her missionary husband was killed by the Aucan Indians in South America, she went to live with the very tribe responsible for killing him. There she witnessed to them and today that tribe has renounced violence and many have become Christians. Through Elizabeth Elliott's newsletter and radio broadcasts, she has inspired many to follow Christ and to live lives of hope and encouragement. I was thrilled to have her and her brother stay several years ago in my guest-house.

What an example of faith and courage Todd Beaver's widow has been also. She has consistently praised God for how He has used her husband's death in the tragic 9/11 plane hijacking for good. The lives of countless people have been uplifted through her faith.

We need God's mercy every day, but particularly when we are faced with a true tragedy. How precious then to be able to turn to Him with our pain and grief; and to trust Him to see us through the veil of tears. God is truly our refuge in time of trouble. His mercies are everlasting

*Dear Father, Thank you for your mercy to me this day, and for showing me the way to go when I cannot see it. In Jesus' name, Amen.*

# June 21

*Psalms 81:7: In your distress you called and I rescued you.*

*1 Chronicles 22:13: Be strong and of courage; dread not, nor be dismayed.*

Resignation to God's will for our lives can seem easy much of the time. I feel most of the time that I am where God has placed me, and that I am doing the work He has equipped me to do. So, I feel great peace in my heart.

But, how hard it has to be to accept those blows that come into every life sometime like when the doctor says you are seriously ill or your child is hurt or your spouse is suffering. The pain and distress are so enormous, and we need God-given courage to bear such circumstances.

Times such as these make resignation and acceptance of God's will extremely difficult . But, we can remain strong in the face of such hard problems if we trust God. We may feel alone but He has promised never to leave us. He is faithful even when we feel our world collapsing.

*Dear Father, I thank you for every normal, peaceful day. Comfort and sustain those today whose lives are filled with pain. In Jesus' name, Amen.*

# June 22

*1 Corinthians 10:13-14: There hath no temptation taken you, but as is common to man; but God is faithful who will not suffer you to be tempted above what you are able, but will with the temptation also make a way to escape that you may be able to bear it.*

Temptations come in all sizes and shapes. Everyone has areas and weak points where they may be tempted. I believe when you know what tempts you, the best defense is to avoid it! If dieting, avoid the store where you might be tempted to buy a milkshake or hamburger.

We are most prone to temptations of all kinds when we are discouraged or lonely or tired. Esau sold his birthright because he was simply too hungry! My pastor suggested that we remember the word HALT to help us avoid possible temptations. He said when we are hungry, angry, lonely or tired we are more susceptible to succumbing to weaknesses. Remembering HALT can prevent us from saying or doing things we shouldn't do, when really we should probably just try to get some rest or eat a healthy snack.

God will graciously and faithfully make the way for us to escape temptation if we call upon Him. He knows how weak we are and will protect us.

*Dear Father, Keep me from temptation, today. Thank you, Father, Amen*

# June 23

*Psalms 42:11: Why are thou cast down, O my soul? And, why are thou disquieted within me? Hope thou in God for I shall yet praise Him who is the health of my countenance and my God.*

As I flew last night across the country to Vancouver and looked down at snow-covered mountains and the tiny twinkling of cities, I felt God's awesome power over all of creation and His abiding love for each of His creatures. I was going to teach a harp class, then enjoy a wonderful cruise to Alaska. Unfortunately, I was also worried about a number of professional problems, when I wanted to just relax and enjoy the trip.

It is not always easy to praise God and have a thankful heart when we are worried or frustrated by hard decisions or difficult circumstances. But, I know that is exactly what we should do to experience His hope, confidence and power. He wants us healthy and whole, and He never wants us to live lives of despair and anxiety.

His will for us is peace and contentment, not in just good circumstances, but in all circumstances. The very act of thanking and praising God lifts our spirits and I believe those attitudes and expressions of faith "plug" us into God's great power. We position ourselves for His blessings and peace of mind. One thing that always helps me is to remember up-lifting words from Bible verses or hymns.

*Dear Father, Thank you for your words that give us peace and hope. In Jesus' name, Amen.*

# June 24

*Matthew 11:26: Even so, Father, for so it seemed good in thy sight.*

Paul Fleming wrote, "What God hath ordered must be right, then find in it thine own delight." Who are we to find fault with God's will. Yet, how often we do just that! We are upset whenever our human plans seem thwarted by unexpected events, over which we have no control; events which, if we search our hearts, we must admit that God allowed to happen. Yet, we foolishly complain about many such things.

As I write today, I am about to board a beautiful cruise ship to Alaska for the next ten days. I am sure there will be many surprises, not always easy or comfortable, during this trip. But, I have prepared myself and I have prayed that I will be thankful for all that happens during this cruise. I am very grateful to have this wonderful opportunity to see the beauty of Alaska. And, it will also be an opportunity to share my love of Jesus Christ with many people. I pray that God will bless this trip and help me to accept all as coming from His hand.

*Father, Thank you for the wonderful opportunities you give us. Help us to accept your good and perfect will for us each day. In Jesus' name, Amen.*

# June 25

*Psalms 31:15: My times are in Thy hand.*

*Jeremiah 11:29: Every purpose of the Lord shall be performed.*

There are so many things that happen in our lives that we cannot understand. But, it gives great peace to know that God has ordained all of it. He will continue to choose and to direct our path. Our small part is to simply obey Him and to accept our conditions.

When I think of hands, I of course think of hands playing the harp, how my students' hands faithfully perform their music. Each hand is different, but all are used to make beautiful sounds on the harp. God will see to it that each of us perform his purposes.

Sometimes we think we can run away from a certain work or duty. But, in reality, if God has appointed us to do it, we will be enabled to do it. Other times we think we should pursue a course that will be beneficial to us but, without His hand guiding us, we could easily lose our way. The only way is to wait patiently for His purposes. Only in placing our lives in His control can we be sure that His will is being done. What we can do is accept our present situation as coming from His hand, and do the good and kind thing to each person in our sphere of influence.

*Dear Father, Help me to simply abide in you today; humbly and gratefully accepting all that you have intended for me today. In Christ's name, Amen.*

# June 26

*Mark 11:25, 26: And when you stand praying, forgive, if you have ought against any: that your Father also which is in heaven may forgive you your trespasses. But if you do not forgive, neither will your Father which is in heaven forgive your trespasses.*

When I have trouble releasing hurt feelings or painful misunderstandings, it often helps me to imagine how I would feel if God withheld his forgiveness from me for my many shortcomings, mistakes and sins! The Bible says "if we confess our sins He is faithful and just to forgive our sins." This forgiveness that He promises us should be our model.

As followers of Christ, we must forgive all who have offended us, no matter what they may have done to hurt us. And in addition we are supposed to love them. I don't think we can easily do this in our own abilities. Only by the grace of God working through the Holy Spirit in our lives can we accomplish the miracle of forgiveness. Sometimes the hardest words we will ever utter, are "I'm sorry."

But, what blessed relief it is to be able to truly forgive! It is the only cure, along with love, that can ease the pain of hurt or damaged relationships. The love of God can banish the misery of an unforgiving heart and bring light to each situation. His love can restore relationships and bring us blessed peace.

*Dear Father, Help me to forgive others as you have so graciously forgiven me! In Jesus' name. Amen.*

# June 27

*Luke 17:21: The kingdom of God is within you.*

As I write this morning we are cruising under grey skies, approaching Sitka, Alaska. Yesterday morning was the same, very grey and foggy. I went to see a movie in the ship's theater in the afternoon since it was too cold to be out on deck.

Imagine my thrill when I emerged from the dark theater into radiant sunshine, and was surrounded by absolutely gorgeous scenery. The snow covered mountains glistened in the sunlight and the coast was lined with beautiful evergreens. What a transformation!

This is how it can be when our lives are transformed by the love of God, when we accept Christ with our heart and live in submission to Him, His light banishes the dark areas of sin in our lives and our selfish wills. He will rule in our hearts if we make Him the Lord of our lives.

It is very humbling to think that through His grace and power the Holy Spirit actually dwells in us. What a responsibility to have that precious fellowship. If we live in loving trust and obedience, His spirit will reign in us.

*Dear Father, Thank you for coming into my heart. Help me to be worthy. In Jesus' name, Amen.*

# June 28

*Psalms 116:6   The Lord preserves the simple.*

There is the story of a church congregation who decided to reward a member whom they felt was the most
humble and self-effacing in their church by giving a medal
in recognition of his humility.  They finally chose the man
and gave him the medal. But they had to rescind the medal
a few weeks later, because he kept wearing it!  Gone was
his humility!

Perhaps being simple is similar. Once we become aware
of it, we have lost our simplicity. The candor and lack of
guile or self-interest inherent in simplicity requires a kind
of lack of self-awareness.  I think often musicians and artists are rewarded by great fame and financial success, and
these can lead them to become arrogant and even lose their
gifts in the process.

True simplicity is very accepting of circumstances out
of our control. It is unselfish and comfortable with a resignation which says—"this is God's will for me right now,
therefore I am at peace and content."

Such an attitude can bring a sense of perfect freedom.
It eliminates striving and a spirit of competitiveness.

*Dear Lord, Thank you for preserving me, help me to rest,
simply, in your loving care. In Jesus' name, Amen.*

# June 29

*I Kings 20:11: Let not him that girds his harness boast himself as he that puts it off.*

*Ephesians 6:11: Put on the whole armor of God.*

We are called to be warriors, part of the victorious army of God. We are to be dutiful, willing to do the hard chore. We should leave the world better for our having been here.

But even though our hearts have been loyal, how often have we failed to really make a difference in someone's life by openly recounting what Christ means to us. When a friend or companion is hurting is such a good time to talk about Christ and how He can share their burdens and ease their pain.

I have often wanted to share the gospel and have shrunk from doing it out of fear of offending someone or of being rejected. I have wished to be that quiet, open person that students and others might confide in. Instead I have often filled silences with meaningless conversation when they might have left an opening to witness to Jesus Christ.

If we put on the whole armor of God, He will equip us for the battle. We will find the right words and we will be empowered. The world is hungry for meaning to life and Christ alone can fill that void.

*Dear Father, Please give me courage and honor and equip me this day to be a humble foot-soldier for you. In Jesus' name, Amen.*

# June 30

*Isaiah 32:17: And the work of righteousness shall be peace; and the effect of righteousness, quietness and assurance forever.*

*1 John 2.5: But whoso keepeth his word, in him verily is the love of God perfected : hereby know we that we are in him.*

When we do the right thing, peace of mind is the result. The opposite is true too. If we leave undone a duty, or even just an opportunity to do something nice for someone, we are filled with a restlessness and disquiet. How much better is the first way.

God created us be His hands in this world, carrying out faithfully His will.

It is not easy many times, to reach out to those who may have hurt us with a healing touch or a kind word. I know what it means to receive a loving smile of forgiveness from a friend or colleague when I have said something foolish. How wonderful it is to be able to work together again in restored harmony.

If we do these things in Jesus' name, and for His sake, He will give us the needed courage, and reward us with His inner peace and quiet confidence.

*Dear Father, Forgive us for being slow or reluctant to do those good and right things you present us. In thy strength, help me to show your love to others today. In Jesus' name, Amen.*

# JULY

## July 1

*Exodus 16:7: In the morning, then ye shall see the glory of the Lord.*

*Romans 12: 11–1: Serving the Lord; rejoicing in hope.*

I am on a beautiful cruise through Alaska and each morning we have truly seen the glory of God's creation. Yesterday in Glacier Bay, there were huge glaciers, cracking loudly as large chucks broke off and crashed into the water. Its scope was truly awesome, and inspirational. The vastness of this great wilderness is humbling.

As we visit Ketchikon this morning under grey and rainy skies, I realize how fortunate we have been to have had such fine, sunshine-filled days for most of our cruise.

A few of us played for the ship's church services yesterday. I have had a concert harp in my stateroom, loaned by a dear student. While only a small proportion of the ship's population attended services, it was a special time of praising God and rejoicing together in the beauty we have shared.

Truly each day brings us new possibilities, to serve the Lord, to praise Him and to enjoy the wonders of His creation.

*Dear Lord, We thank you for each new day with the possibility of a fresh start, forgiveness for our failures, and joy in knowing you. In Jesus' name, Amen.*

# July 2

*Acts 24:16: Herein do I exercise myself, to have always a conscience void of offence toward God, and toward men.*

*Psalms 32:8: I will instruct thee and teach thee in the way which thou shall go: I will guide with mine eye.*

Today we are cruising between Alaska and San Francisco. The ocean seems so vast; I think of God's view of our ship. We are less than a grain of sand in the universe.

As we sail through these often rough seas, I have thought a lot about how God has promised to guide us and direct us, if we listen to His voice, even across these endless miles of churning ocean waves. If we spend quiet time in prayer, asking and listening, hopefully, we will grow in our understanding of His Word and His will for us.

A trip like this is a wonderful opportunity for me to spend quality time in His presence.

Then, the Holy Spirit can work in us. As we seek God's will and search to do what is right in His sight, our hearts and minds—our consciences, will be at peace. I know I will often make mistakes, but I have the assurance of God's forgiveness. He is my Guide and will lead me gently back on His path.

*Dear Lord, Thank you for caring about each of one of us. Please keep me on your pathway today. In Jesus' name, Amen.*

# July 3

*Psalms 130:8: He shall redeem Israel from all his iniquities.*

Psalm 130 assures us of God's mercy and forgiveness. It also says: "I wait for the Lord, my soul waits, and in His word I hope."

A friend and I noticed two sisters who were in the adjoining suite to ours on the ship. They came to the church service Sunday, and we struck up an acquaintance. We later spent time with them. One of them was going to take this cruise with her husband to celebrate an anniversary. He died suddenly a few weeks before the cruise. She was going to cancel the trip, but her sister offered to go along with her. Although they both were still grieving, they told us that they could not have gotten through this hard time without their deep faith in Christ and His enduring love.

"Out of the depths Israel called unto God, and cried out for mercy and forgiveness. And He was faithful to forgive their iniquities." He is faithful the same today, to hear our cries and give us His hope. I am grateful for the moving testimony of these new friends.

*Dear Father, Please comfort those who mourn, and thank you that you bring hope to all ho call upon you. In Jesus' name, Amen.*

# July 4

*Ecclesiastes 2:10: Look at the generation of old, and see; did ever any trust in the Lord, and was confounded? Or did any abide in His fear, and was forsaken? Or whom did He ever despise, that called upon Him?*

*Psalms 25:6: Remember O Lord, thy tender mercies, and thy loving kindness; for they have been ever of old.*

We docked early this morning in San Francisco. It was beautiful to see the lights of the city appear out of the vast darkness of the ocean.

Tonight we will see the night lit up with fireworks to commemorate the Fourth of July.

In a similar way, Jesus, the Light of the World, came into the world to seek and to save sinners. He has been so faithful to protect me on this long journey. I have felt very fortunate to have been invited on the wonderful cruise ship.

Even when the future seems unclear and filled with fears and uncertainties, if we remember His love and kindness to us in the past, we can have courage to face the future. We are secure in His faithfulness to all who call upon His name. He has said "I will never forsake you." I have felt so close to God in the beauty I experienced in Alaska.

*Dear Father, On this important American holiday, I commemorate your faithfulness to me. Help me to always trust you in every situation I face. In Jesus' name, Amen.*

# July 5

*Isaiah 27:8: He stayeth the rough wind in the day of the east wind.*

*Isaiah 42:3: A bruised reed shall He not break.*

God never gives us trials that are more than we can bear. If we were to have all our trials piled together from our whole lives, they would be overwhelming. But God measures each one, and gives us the strength we need—for that one trial, that day.

I think when I am performing music, how hard it would be if I tried to carry in my mind the whole program at once! It would be confusing and overwhelming.

But if I concentrate on one piece at a time, and each phrase of that piece, note by note, I can manage to be in control and am able to play the entire program with confidence and ease. I believe in mental practice and always play entire programs in my head before each performance, reviewing mentally, every note and every pedal.

So in life, if we accept hour by hour each burden God places on us, we will find He always provides the endurance and ability we need. And He also will teach us the lessons He wants to learn from each trial.

*Dear Father, Thank you for never giving me more than I can bear. Please give me your strength and wisdom for all you would have me learn today. In Jesus' name, Amen.*

# July 6

*Isaiah 42:6: I the Lord have called thee in righteousness, and will hold thine hand, and will keep thee.*

*Psalm 25:20: O keep my soul and deliver me: for I put my trust in Thee.*

As I travel home from San Francisco I realize again how God has blessed me during this time. I did some teaching again while in the Bay area and saw dear friends and former students. The world, so vast, can seem small when we are reunited with loved ones who live far away from us.

Billy Graham wrote "The world does not give peace, for it doesn't have any peace to give. It fights for peace, it negotiates for peace, but there is no ultimate peace in the world." But Jesus gives peace to all those who put their trust in Him. His peace is available to everyone who will receive it.

God has called us to live good, up-right lives, to be His hands in our world. He promised to keep us and give us His wisdom and truth. He is our faithful Guide, and protects us wherever we may be..

*Dear Father, As I prepare to fly home after this wonderful trip to Alaska, filled with so much beauty, I thank you for each moment and pray for the trip home. In Jesus' name, Amen.*

# July 7

*Psalm 27:1: The Lord is my light and my salvation; whom shall I fear? The Lord is the strength of my life; of whom shall I be afraid?*

Fear is such a paralyzing emotion. When I was a young girl, I would hear strange sounds when I was alone in the house and fear that someone had broken in.

I have always loved to read mysteries and spy novels. When I was studying in France I used to read Agatha Christie books in French partly because it helped me develop my French vocabulary. However, as I matured I began to realize that some of these books, which included some violence and killing, were leaving me with a sense of fearfulness. I had made some poor choices in my reading material. As I stopped reading frightening books,

I found myself freed from most of the fears I used to experience.

When I read spiritually up-lifting books, and the Bible, I found that I slept peacefully without being troubled by fearful images. This has taught me that it is important to fill my mind with uplifting reading material. It also is true about films which can be entertaining without needing to have violence or bad language.

Of course, the best reading is always the Bible, and reading it fills our minds with God's wisdom and love.

*Dear Father, Please guard my mind today and help me make wise choices about what I put into it! In Jesus' name, Amen.*

# July 8

*Ephesians 4:32: Be ye kind one to another.*

A good life is built of many small moments of kindness. I often think that one of the best and noblest acts we can do is simply to have a ready smile.

On the flight home from San Francisco after the cruise, there was a flight attendant who had such a radiant smile. While passengers, some tired and grumpy, were boarding, she greeted each with a warm smile and helped them get comfortable. Throughout the flight I noticed she continued to smile at each passenger as though they were a dear friend.

Sometimes on my morning walks as I pass strangers I try to remember simply to give them a warm smile. I know when someone passes me with such a smile, it lifts my entire day. In cold or rainy weather I usually walk in the mall. I love to see the young mothers walking with their babies in strollers. They usually call out friendly greetings to each other and to total strangers.

Serendipity is doing something kind for another, without expecting anything in return. Much of the world's loneliness could be cured by a simple smile.

*Dear Father: Please help me to show your loving kindness to everyone I encounter today. In Jesus' name, Amen.*

# July 9

*1 John 4:7: Love is of God: and everyone that loveth is born of God, and knoweth God.*

*Col. 3:13: Forbearing one another, and forgiving one another, if any man bear a grudge against any; even as Christ forgive you, so also do you.*

It is so important that we look for the best in one another. We all have faults and shortcomings which can blind us to others' good points and attributes. Having a forgiving, loving spirit is a great gift from God. We can, by His grace, overlook each others' faults and focus on their best traits. Everyone has redeeming traits if we honestly look for them. And we all try to hide our shortcomings!

I believe as a teacher it is so important to emphasize what a student does well, and of course also to hold up to them a higher standard of performance in the areas where they may be weak.

By doing this we mirror that which God surely does with us! He calls us to live holy and pure lives. He asks us to follow Him, to make Him the center of our world. And He is always there to lovingly forgive us when we stumble. We must always be ready to forgive others when they too may stumble.

*Dear Father, Help me to see the good in everyone I meet today. In Jesus' name, Amen.*

# July 10

*Psalm 138:8: The Lord will perfect that which concerns me. Thy mercy, O Lord, evolves forever, forsake not the work of thine own hands.*

How often I fret and stew about the future, or decisions I have to make. Should I accept a performance when my schedule at school is very busy and I will have such limited time to practice? Should I tell a student that she is not measuring up to our department's standards, knowing how that would be discouraging for her. And often, it seems that just when I do decide to say something, the student comes around on her own and improves.

I wish I would remember this verse at such times, and simply trust God to guide and direct me in His timing.

We waste so much time and energy on matters that are not in our control. Is this or that trip right for us? Should we accept this or that responsibility? When we commit everything to God we can trust Him to guide us and we can know we are doing His will. When we cannot see clearly what lies ahead, God will give us all the light we need for the daily path. He gives us guidance and wisdom as we need them. He wants the best for us; more than we even can imagine ourselves. He will perfect that which concerns us. What a great promise!

*Dear Lord, Thank you for the guidance and wisdom you give us every day. In Jesus' name, Amen.*

# July 11

*Job 34: 29: But if He remains silent, who can condemn Him?*

*Acts 20: 24: None of these things move me.*

Paul, in looking ahead to possible imprisonment and death, wrote in Acts 20, "none of these things move me." He meant that his life itself was not important to him, only his faithfulness to testify to the gospel of Jesus Christ. He was urging the early Christians to also not be swayed by those opposed to their faith, to stand firm.

Job is writing about our inability to understand God's will. When God remains silent in the face of a person's suffering, we cannot understand it. I know I truly suffered after losing my home to the fire. I did not understand how that could be God's will, and I felt abandoned and lost.

However God has promised no evil will go unpunished and no good act will go unrewarded. When God remains silent we are forced to find solutions and answers in ourselves that He desires us to know. He rules over all. Sometimes God may test the loyalty of those who follow Him, but He remains in complete control.

*Dear Father: Forgive us for questioning your will. When we do not understand, help us to be faithful. In Jesus' name, Amen.*

# July 12

*Deuteronomy 31:6: Be strong, and of good courage, fear not nor be afraid...for the Lord thy God, He it is that goes with you. He will not fail you, nor forsake you.*

One of the hardest things for me to do is to have to pack for a trip and leave home. I am such a homebody. It does not seem to make much difference if a trip is for pleasure or work. I hate to leave home! Partly, I know it is the reluctance I experience in leaving my little poodle. Even though I know he is happy and content with the friends who keep him, I miss him terribly every day.

So today, as I prepare to leave home and my dear pet for three weeks for a harp conference in Salt Lake City, I need this verse greatly. While I look forward to seeing friends and colleagues, it still feels very hard to leave. God will give me the strength and courage I will need to face the weeks ahead. He has promised to be with me.

I know He will enable me to go with His peace and do those tasks He has set before me.

*Dear Father: I am so grateful to know that you will go with me, wherever I must travel. Thank you Lord for your courage. In Jesus' name, Amen.*

# July 13

*Isaiah 58:11: The Lord will guide you always, He will satisfy your soul in drought.*

Even when we are not sure what path to follow, if we know the Lord is guiding us, all we need to do is walk beside him. Our one true Guide throughout our lives will see us through every decision and challenge.

Phil. 4:6 says, "to be anxious about nothing; but in everything with prayer and petitions with thanksgiving make your requests to God, and the peace of God which transcends all understanding will guard your hearts and minds in Christ Jesus."

Once in Europe attending a conference, I was so very lonely, and I felt I could not stay. Then friends surrounded me and I truly believe God sent them to comfort me and allow me to stay the course!

I picture a hot, arid desert and a deep thirst, where God brings cooling water to my lips and burning throat. He knows our every need. When He speaks we must listen; when He tells us to go, we must go; and when He tells us to stay, we must stay.

For Him to be our guide, we must listen closely for his words and we must obey – even when we do not understand at all why or where.

*Dear Father: Thank you for guiding me, every day. Help me to listen even more closely to your small still voice and obey. In Jesus' name, Amen.*

# July 14

*Romans 12:2 Be not conformed to this world: but be ye transformed by the renewing of your mind.*

I am easily influenced some times, by the opinions of friends or colleagues. If I am complimented about an outfit I am wearing, I tend to wear it too often! We are all bombarded with opinions about politics, religion, music, and everyone seems to have strong feelings about many things.

Memorizing Bible verses, studying worthwhile devotional material and reading inspirational books by Billy Graham or Charles Stanley or Elizabeth Elliot, I find these are ways of transforming my mind and renewing my spirit. What we read becomes a part of us, and will be an influence on us and those about us.

Phil. 4:8 is another verse I love that expresses a way to transform our minds. "Finally, brother, whatever is true, whatever is noble, whatever is right, whatever is pure, whatever is lovely, whatever is admirable – if anything is excellent or praiseworthy – think about such things."

My beloved teacher, Henriette Renié, had as her credo:

To Serve Beauty in Art
Truth in my life
Goodness in others

She exemplified these attributes in her life and work as a great artist and teacher.

*Dear Father: Help us to be renewed every day by the truth of your holy word. Help us to resist conforming to a society that does not honor you.*

# July 15

*Psalm 24:9: Lift up your heads, O ye gates: even lift them up ye everlasting doors: and the King of Glory shall come in.*

*2 Corinthians 6:16: Ye are the temple of the living God.*

As I face having to leave my beloved home for almost a month of mostly hard work in Europe, I am relying on Him to help me leave with good will and an uncomplaining spirit. I am thankful He has equipped me for all the work ahead, and that He has given me this work to do. But, how sweet it will feel to come home again!

What a source of comfort it is to know that God goes with me and before me in these long travels. Surely He will help us to live in ways that are obedient and pleasing to Him.

God does not leave us alone. He has sent us the Holy Spirit. It is He who will protect us and give us the necessary courage to do whatever work is before us.

*Dear Father, Please abide in my heart each day and help me to be courageous. In Jesus' name, Amen.*

# July 16

*Psalm 31:19: O how great is Thy goodness, which Thou hast laid up for them that fear Thee; which Thou has wrought for them that trust in Thee.*

*Psalm 13:6: I will sing unto the Lord, because He hath dealt bountifully with me.*

It hit me like a weight on my heart when I woke early this morning. Today I have to leave home for almost one month. The last few days have been such a flurry of activity, workmen remodeling a bathroom, a friend's injury to her head, and constant last minute e-mails – and of course packing and re-packing.

I was thankful to finally sink into my seat on the plane only to have the pilot announce engine trouble. We sat captive for three hours and then finally left Indianapolis. It was a hard way to start the trip, knowing I had missed my flight to Paris and the subsequent connection to Geneva. I realized how many times we really have little control over what happens to us while traveling.

But, I am thankful to the Lord. He is so good and I trust Him to work it all out. There will be other flights and in His time I will reach my destination.

*Dear Father: Thank you for your goodness and your faithfulness. I need you more than ever as I travel alone. You are my travel companion. Thank you Lord. In Jesus' name, Amen.*

# July 17

*Romans 8:18: For I reckon that the sufferings of this present time are not worthy to be compared with the glory which shall be revealed in us.*

*Hebrews 7:25: Therefore he is able to save completely those who come to God through him, because he always lives to intercede for them.*

I read about a Christian mother whose two babies had both died of a rare disease. She suffered greatly, and yet felt a special closeness to Jesus through and in her suffering. She said God does allow suffering, but all suffering has meaning.

My teacher wrote a beautiful work, *Piece Symphonique,* which I have played and recorded many times. For the theme she chose the words, "Faith does not diminish our pain, but transfigures it."

This verse also points to the fact that our suffering in this present life refines our faith and draws us closer to Christ who suffered for our sins. God's merciful plan of salvation meant Jesus had to pay the ultimate cost of our salvation by dying on a cross.

If salvation were available to all who are good and kind and go to church, He would not have had to suffer and die. He is our pathway to heaven and eternal life. He will always be there to intercede for us.

*Dear Father – You allow us to suffer, but never without meaning. Thank you for your great love to us, your son, our Savior, Jesus Christ. In Jesus' name, Amen.*

# July 18

*John 13:34: A new commandment I give unto you, that you love one another; as I have loved you, that you also love one another.*

*1 Thessalonians 3:12: And the Lord make you to increase and abound in love, one toward another, and toward all men.*

I am grateful to have safely arrived and settled into my hotel here in Geneva. I arrived a day early in order to be more rested before the Congress begins. Over 700 harpists will gather here from around the world this weekend.

I hope and want to be a source of love and encouragement to them, many of whom are old friends or former students. I am so pleased that there will be numerous church services on Sunday, with harpists playing at the different churches, alone or with choirs.

Many, if not all of the performers, may be nervous and lonely, far from their homes. I hope I may have time to welcome them in a personal way. What an opportunity to possibly be used to show them the love and light of Jesus Christ.

*Dear Lord, Please make me an instrument of your love and peace and joy during this week. In Jesus' name, Amen.*

# July 19

*Psalm 145:9: The Lord is good to all: and His tender mercies are over all His work.*

*Psalm 50:10: For every beast of the forest is Mine, and the cattle on a thousand hills.*

I have always loved the cows in Switzerland. They have cowbells around their necks so their owners can find them and identify each one. These bells are beautiful and can be heard throughout the hills and valleys for many miles.

It has been a vivid picture to me of God's care and concern for each creature He has created, and His tenderness toward all of them, from the smallest sparrow to these great bovines. He has put all the animal kingdom under the care of man. And we must protect them and love them as part of His great creation.

What a rich dimension He has added to our lives with our pet dogs and cats. These dear animals are precious and trust us completely. They depend upon us totally and it is our responsibility to give them the right care.

*Dear Father, Thank you for your animal kingdom which you have placed in our care. Give us tender hearts to do for them what they cannot do for themselves with love. In Jesus' name, Amen.*

# July 20

*Isaiah 49:4: Then I said, I have labored in vain, I have spent my strength for naught and in vain.*

I once asked a Christian leader who is a friend of mine what I could do to live a more effective life for Christ. I was thinking I should perhaps try to volunteer in several capacities.

He answered me thoughtfully, "Spend more time alone with Him in prayer. Our busyness is not what He desires but us, ourselves. He will show us what tasks He would have us do."

Many times we think that good deeds and busyness in volunteering can mean we are closer to God. In reality, activities, especially those done without inner peace, can be a detriment to our spiritual lives.

We must never forget that "He is the vine, we are the branches." We can only be nourished and grow through our intimate contact with God.

*Dear Father, Help me not to labor in vain. I commit my work to thee today and ask for your presence, moment by moment in all I do. In Jesus' name, Amen.*

# July 21

*2 Corinthians 4:16: For which cause we faint not; but, though our outward man perish, yet the inward man is renewed day by day.*

As I go to opening ceremonies today of the World Harp Congress, I go with love in my heart for all those hundreds of harpists who traveled here, and I pray for God's peace to preside over the gathering. I hope that each of them will be renewed and enriched by this gathering of colleagues from around the world.

When faced trials and problems, those who entrust their lives to Jesus Christ are not in despair. 2 Corinthians 4 speaks of the hope we have, that our afflictions, whatever they may be, are working for us an "eternal weight of glory." That, as we keep our eyes on the cross of Christ, we do not focus on the temporal life but on the eternal. In Chapter 5:7 Paul writes "For we walk by faith, not by sight."

So in our work and in our daily lives, we will have peace and hope if we do everything as unto the Lord. That is my prayer for these many harpists gathered here this week.

*Dear Father, Please renew me in faith and hope each day. In Jesus' name, Amen.*

# July 22

*Psalms 107:43: Who so is wise, and will observe these things, even they shall understand the loving kindness of the Lord.*

This psalm speaks of the beauties and wonders of God's creation. It also shows how God can bring down princes and raise the lowly . . .how He controls the oceans, the forests.

"The beginning of wisdom is the fear of the Lord."

I think, often, that most people do fear the Lord, except, perhaps for atheists. That wisdom, realizing He can and does to us what He will, should not discourage us or make us fearful, but should be encouraging and uplifting to us by understanding that <u>God is love</u>. He loves us, and wants us to be like Him. He sent His son to die for us so that sin is dealt with and can be forgiven. God is holy and He wants us to be holy. He is reaching out to us and longs for us to come to Him.

*Dear Father, Thank you for loving us. When our lives turn grey and frightening, help us to remember your loving kindness and to rest and wait and trust you. In Jesus' name, Amen.*

# July 23

*Luke 10:27: Thou shalt love the Lord thy God with all thy heart, and with all thy soul, and with all thy strength and with all thy mind.*

We sometimes think service is what God seeks from us, and that if some service is good, more is even better.

However good and useful our acts of love and sacrifice for others can be, Jesus says in Luke that if we observe the verse above, "we shall live."

He wants, first of all, our hearts. Then He claims our souls, physical and mental strength and our minds. All we are should be offered to Him on a <u>daily</u> basis: a heart filled with love for Him and thanksgiving; a soul filled with devotion and awe at His holiness; our physical bodies a temple for the Holy Spirit, pure and unsullied; and finally our minds, searching the scriptures for His truth, open to His guiding, obedient and pliable. These are the very real gifts we have to offer God. What a privilege it is to know He accepts them as our loving Father.

*Dear Father, I want to put my whole being at your disposal today. Please help me serve you in love to others and a passion for sharing the Gospel with them.*

# July 24

*1 Thessalonians 2:12: Walk worthy of God who hath called you unto His kingdom and glory.*

*Genesis 28:16: Surely the Lord is in this place; and I knew it not.*

I can sometimes look at the lives of friends and colleagues and long for the marriages or families that they have. Some mornings as I walk in my area, I wonder why God has not placed me in such a situation which seems so desirable. But, then I think of all the blessings He has given me, and I believe His plan is perfect.

The Lord has placed each of us in the circumstances and with the people He chooses for us. How important for us to then live in peace and acceptance of our present situation.

We should not long for other places or different associates. We should love sincerely our daily companions and colleagues, and we should pray for them and encourage them in every way we can.

Living in the present, we will not miss the wonderful opportunities God gives us every day. He gives us plentiful opportunities to obey Him, to lift up others, and to experience the joy which comes from knowing Jesus Christ and having a personal relationship with Him.

"No mind has conceived what God has prepared for those who love Him." 1 Corinthians 2:9.

*Dear Lord, Thank you for your loving kindness. Help us to walk in a way that is worthy of you. In Jesus' name, Amen.*

# July 25

*Job 23:10: He knoweth the way I take.*

*Proverbs 22:24: Man's goings are of the Lord; how can a man then understand his own way?*

God's ways are so far above our understanding as human beings. I often compare our ways to a flock of sheep. On August 1 the National Swiss Day there is always a parade of animals in Villars near my summer chalet.

Cows, goats and sheep all go up a crowded street with their herders. The sheep and goats often butt against each other or rush headlong as a group in this direction or that. The shepherds keep them safe.

How like us, striving for this or that, on our own. Only God knows the way we should go, and how we should go. Our task is to obey and to trust Him to show us the way. He is in complete charge of the circumstances of our life. Our role is to accept His will, and not struggle to have our way. He knows best, and will guide us safely to the shelter of His abiding love.

*Dear Father, Please guide and direct me today in all I do, and in my relations with others. In Jesus' name, Amen.*

# July 26

*Psalms 125:1-2: They that trust in the Lord shall be as Mt. Zion, which cannot be removed, but abideth forever. As the mountains are round about Jerusalem, so the Lord is round about his people from henceforth even for ever.*

While here in Switzerland one cannot help but be moved by the beauty of the mountains. The psalmist compares our faith in God to a mountain. This is a vivid picture of our need to be strong and courageous, unmovable in our faith.

I have a professional acquaintance who through a series of mishaps and health problems turned against God, blaming Him for those difficult, life-changing trials. Faith turned to bitterness. My heart aches for her pain and the turning from the only one who could take away her distress. She is missing out on God's comfort.

God's love is there for all who claim it and turn to Him. His promises, to be with us in every situation and in every place, are meant to encourage and to bolster us during life's most difficult times. We must hold on to our faith, firm as a rock, strong and solid as the Swiss mountains near Geneva.

*Dear Father, I will lift up my eyes unto the hills from whence cometh my help. My help comes from you Lord. I thank you and praise you. In Jesus' name, Amen.*

# July 27

*Matthew 13:23: But he that received seed into the good ground is he who hears the word, and understands it; which also bears fruit and brings forth, some a hundredfold, some sixty, some thirty.*

I love to garden and to plant new flowers, particularly perennials which faithfully come back year after year. If we entrust our lives to God, He will accomplish in us exactly what He wills for us to be and to do, year after year.

It does not matter our weaknesses, or our mistakes of the past. We will bear fruit as long as we are His, our lives will be fruitful, in exactly the way He ordains.

Jeremiah 29: 11 is one of my favorite verses – "For I know the plans I have for you.....plans to help you and not to harm you, plans to give you hope and a future."

We should invite God into our every situation. He will guide us so that we are what He wants us to be, and we do those things which He wants us to do.

And of course it goes without saying He protects us and steers us clear of those situations He would have us avoid.

*Dear Father, Thank you for your protection and guidance. May I do what you will today. In Jesus' name, Amen.*

# July 28

*1 Thessalonians 4:13: But I would not have you to be ignorant, brethren, concerning them which are asleep, that ye sorrow not, even as others which have no hope.*

When we lose someone we love deeply, a parent, friend or child, we who believe that Jesus Christ conquered Death itself, are not left without hope. One day, we believe, we will be reunited with our loved ones. Dying is so final for those who do not have the hope of eternal life. How different it is to view death as a passage into a far better place.

When we are absent in the body (our physical presence, that is,) we are present with the Lord. Our departed ones, when they leave us, go to heaven and will be with God.

I have always loved the comparison to saying goodbye to loved ones to waving to a boat as it leaves harbor, hard to see it go – but across the water on the other side there are those waiting to welcome the boat home.

That is our faith and hope. The Lord himself will welcome us home.

*Dear Father, Thank you for Jesus, without whom we would have no hope of eternal life. In Jesus' name, Amen.*

# July 29

*1 Corinthians 7:29: But this I say, brethren, the time is short.*

As I drove up to my chalet yesterday, I marveled at the beauty of the mountains revealed at each turn in the steep road. The road from Geneva begins with freeways, but soon starts winding upward. Although there are hairpin curves to negotiate, I sneak looks right and left! I always feel closer to God when I look at these awesome snow-capped peaks. There is such an inspirational feeling looking at these mountains, and I am grateful for the privilege of time spent there.

I think we would all do things differently if we knew our days on earth were to be very short. We would not put off saying words to heal old wounds. We would lay down old burdens of guilt over the past and worries for whatever our futures hold.

I think we would all seek to draw closer to our Lord and Creator if we knew our days were numbered, as they all truly are. We would want to spend time alone with Him. When time is short, we would no longer hustle and bustle through life, being endlessly in a hurry to do and to achieve. I ask myself, "Why don't I live every day like that now?"

*Dear Father, Thank you for the gift of time with you. In Jesus' name, Amen.*

# July 30

*Psalms 25:7: Remember not the sins of my youth, nor my transgressions: according to Thy mercy remember Thou me for Thy goodness' sake, O Lord.*

It is easy to keep replaying our mistakes and sins of the past. It can become a comfortable, frequent habit, like a tongue probing a sore tooth! Instead of remembering good and happy performances of the past, I can easily find myself replaying a concert of long ago, where I missed one note in a passage! As I write this I realize how foolish it is to dwell on one wrong note among thousands of right ones!

That is not God's way nor His will for our lives. He wants us to come to Him, asking forgiveness as soon as we err, and then to release that painful burden completely and totally.

God wants us to live free and triumphant lives, unfettered by the past. He is our rock and this allows us to plant our feet firmly in the present, trusting His forgiveness. We will be able to be more helpful to others and more aware of other's problems if we don't cling to our old ones.

*Dear Father, Forgive us all our sins, past and present, and help us today to live freely in your love. In Jesus' name, Amen.*

# July 31

*Isaiah 44: 22: I have blotted out, as a thick cloud, thy transgressions, and as a cloud, thy sins. Return unto Me; for I have redeemed thee.*

*Micah 7:19: He will turn again, He will have compassion upon us; He will subdue our iniquities; and Thou will cast their sins into the depths of the sea.*

We have trouble, sometimes, truly taking in and accepting the depth of God's mercy toward us. Because His forgiveness is so much more compassionate than our ability to forgive, we mustn't fall into the trap of projecting our feeble efforts onto God's infinite power to forgive. Sometimes students will not respond to teaching, or one will say something thoughtless that can be hurtful. I work with so many wonderful students, yet still it can be painful to feel unappreciated or to have one's teaching ignored. Over years of teaching however, I have learned to make special efforts to help this kind of student, and it seems to always be healing. I find myself loving them and wanting more for them, and my own hurts are forgotten as we do exciting work together.

But God's forgiveness is so total and complete. Our sins are blotted out, or buried in the depths of the sea. He truly remembers them no more. He does not replay them, or remember this or that sin or hurt we have committed.

We should be in awe of His great compassion toward us. Our response can only be to worship our great God and thank Him everyday for His love.

*Dear Father, Thank you for taking away the terrible burden of our sins. Help us to walk worthy of this incredible gift. In Jesus' name, Amen.*

# AUGUST

## August 1

*Ecclesiastes 7:9: Be not hasty in thy spirit to be angry: for anger rests in the bosom of fools.*

*Ephesians 4:26: Let not the sun go down upon your wrath.*

It never fails that if I go to bed without taking care of business or any personal concerns, I will have a troubled night's sleep! I know better, that I should always try to handle such cares before going to bed, but that is not always easy or practical to do. If there has been strife, I should make the hard call and apologize.

These verses do not tell us that we should never be angry, but rather how to handle anger. We are not to be impatient with others, or quick to feel anger. And we are not to hold onto anger overnight, and allow it to fester and turn to bitterness.

We should never dwell on hurts or possible offences against us, but let, as much as possible, these feelings be brushed off as not important. We should try to focus on what is good and positive and hopeful instead.

God will reward all of our efforts to be peace-makers, for this is His will. He wants us to live lives of service to others, of gentleness and humility, not overly concerned with ourselves. The sooner we forget past offenses, the more at peace we will be.

*Dear Father, Help us to be slow to anger, and quick to forgive. In Jesus' name, Amen.*

# August 2

*Isaiah 12:2: Behold, God is my salvation; I will trust, and not be afraid: for the Lord Jehovah is my strength and my song; He also is become my salvation.*

*Mark 4:40: Why are you so fearful? How is it that you have no faith?*

Before every concert I always pray, asking God for His protection and that He will be with me, guiding my fingers and feet and mind in the recital. At that point I feel I have done all the work I can to prepare wisely, and then I put my whole trust in Him.

Our faith can disappear and instead of trusting God, we give in to despair and worry. We must remember Jesus is with us, "in the boat," during our performances, in our depressions, during our lessons, among the students, in the meetings, in our conversations. We only need to ask Him and He is there, healing and saving.

We are so often like the disciples in Mark 4. Even though Jesus Christ, the Son of God was in the boat with them, when the furious storm came up, they were still terrified. When we face hard and stormy times we often forget that Jesus is with us in them, and we too, cry out in fear. Our faith must stay strong in every situation.

*Dear Father, Help me to trust you more, and to fear everything less. In Jesus' name, Amen.*

# August 3

*Psalms 12:6: Thou hast made Him exceeding glad with Thy countenance.*

Can there be any greater joy than the joy we feel when we know God has blessed us and looked with favor upon us?

God's presence is like the bright sunshine after days of greyness and rain. I experienced such a day today. August 1, Swiss National Day, was overcast and wet. The parade of cows and goats and Swiss Army Band went on anyway. It is one of my favorite events each summer while I am teaching classes in Switzerland. I always go with my students, and after the parade we walk through the crowded streets, sampling the Swiss specialties cooked outdoors. The cheese fondue, sausages, crepes and rosti, a hash-brown type of potato dish, are all so delicious.

But it was too bad that the mountains were hidden by the fog and heavy grey clouds. Then I awakened yesterday to a brilliant blue sky with every mountain bathed in bright sunlight. The beauty was breath-taking and inspiring.

This is how our delight in God's love should be. He lifts our drooping spirits by the light of His countenance and His great faithfulness, new every day.

*Dear Father, Thank you for the joy we can know by abiding in your unfathomable love. In Jesus' name, Amen.*

# August 4

*Psalms 107:9: He satisfies the longing soul, and the hungry soul He fills with good.*

*Ephesians 3:19: That you might be filled with all the fullness of God.*

I am in the middle of teaching an intensive 10-day summer class here in Switzerland. The students are of all ages and nationalities and varied backgrounds. But they are all, even the youngest, avid lovers of the harp. Many are the only harpists in their cities! So it can be a revelation for them to be with other talented harpists and become friends.

As I listen to each one play, I have two desires. I want to first encourage them, and then to help improve their playing in any way I can. It is fascinating work because each student is unique and needs a different kind of help. I love this aspect of my work. It is specially rewarding to see a student grow in understanding the music and the techniques involved in performing. I am always thrilled to hear the results in the final class recital when they can often play absolutely brilliantly.

How much more deeply however does God look upon our needs. He longs to satisfy them and to "fill us" with all that is good. Blessed by His love, we truly have all that we need.

*Dear Lord, You are the Master Teacher. Show me everything you would have me learn today of your goodness and fullness. Thank you, Father. In Jesus' name, Amen.*

# August 5

*2 Corinthians 9:15: Thanks be to God for His unspeakable gift.*

My teacher, Mademoiselle Renié had a wonderful sense of balance and equilibrium in her life. Her spiritual life had first priority, then her family, and then her work and students. I loved being with her, basking in her strong personality and vibrant teaching. And her deep faith in God was a constant inspiration to me, as her student, during the brief years we had together and since then in my life as an artist.

In Geneva, at the World Harp Congress, we paid tribute to Mlle. Renié. As one of her last students, I was one of the speakers. As I came to describe the last moments I spent with her, I broke down and wept and was unable to continue for a few moments.

Until that very moment, I did not even realize her immense impact on my life and the depths of my gratitude to her, and love I have for her.

And today – as I go back to teach the large international class of harpists, I thank God for this incredible gift of a godly teacher – who is always with me.

*Dear Father, You give us exactly what we need before we know we need it. Thank you for your unspeakable gift – today and everyday. In Jesus' name, Amen.*

# August 6

*Psalms 103:2: Bless the Lord, O my soul, and forget not all his benefits.*

I awoke here in this tiny Swiss village to another grey, rainy day. The mountains have disappeared, covered by a thick layer of clouds and fog. On these rainy days I laughingly tell my students that God has sent the rain so they will stay inside and practice more!

On days like this how important for me to remember all the "benefits" God has provided, like wonderful daily French bread, a warm, dry house, the kindness of a little neighbor girl, the precious wildflowers that are found in every pasture, the gift of music, work I love, the Bible and His forgiveness. All these benefits are mine and so many more. Health, sight, hearing, a mind and a heart turned to God.

All these benefits exist whether it rains or pours. And of course when His sunlight reveals the glory and the majesty of these snow-covered mountains, we are overwhelmed by such an additional "benefit."

*Dear Father, I do praise you and bless you for all your great benefits to me today. In Jesus' name, Amen.*

# August 7

*Mark 9:23: If Thou canst believe, all things are possible to him that believes.*

*Matthew 17:20: Nothing shall be impossible unto you.*

I have always known that in a concert performance, if there is *one* measure where one is not completely sure of the notes or pedals, that is the spot that will trip one up, every time. It is so important to review those spots until one can play them perfectly, mentally, so that one's memory is absolutely solid.

I think it is the same with our faith – if there is one little area of doubt or questioning whether God can and will truly help us, that doubt acts like a short-circuit to His miracles in our lives. We must not pray with any doubt or hesitation. We can trust Him totally.

Both of these accounts in Matthew and Mark tell of Jesus' healing the boy whose father brought him to Jesus to heal his seizures. Jesus drove out the evil spirit and the boy was completely healed. Later Jesus said that the disciples were not able to do this because they "had so little faith." (Matthew 18:20.)

We are told many times that we can ask God for anything, but we must ask in complete faith, no wavering or hesitation. Our faith and belief must be total.

*Dear Father, Thank you for the gift of faith. Be with those who are struggling to believe and help them to believe. In Jesus' name, Amen.*

# August 8

*Galatians 5:1: Stand fast therefore in the liberty where-with Christ has made us free, and be not entangled with the yoke of bondage.*

*2 Corinthians 4:13: I believed, and therefore have I spoken.*

It is so easy and pleasant to be with fellow Christians and talk about our faith in this or that situation. We all nod and agree and enjoy such fellowship. It is comfortable and yet deepens our faith and understanding of Biblical principles lived out in our lives.

But how different it is to be the only believer in a group of cynics and people with no religious faith! Gone is the easy exchange, and on our own we must trust the Holy Spirit to enable us to speak the truth boldly, knowing we may and probably will be ridiculed.

One evening I was having dinner with a group of friends and colleagues. After desert, I spoke briefly about my faith and what it meant to me. A friend spoke up kindly saying, "Well, good, if you feel it helps you." I felt that probably my words did not make an impression, but one never knows. Our faith should give us courage to speak, in any situation.

*Dear Father, Because I believe, please give me the right words today to share my faith. In Jesus' name, Amen.*

# August 9

*Luke 8:27: The things which are impossible with man are possible with God.*

*Psalms 94:17: Unless the Lord had been my help, my soul had almost dwelt in silence.*

We all have experienced moments of heartbreak, when we feel too sad and weak to go on. I have recently experienced such a time, and I simply could not see how I could carry on. After the fire, it was like the bottom had fallen out of my life. I was left with an almost insurmountable void, and in addition my work seemed beyond my capacity to do.

But, I always trusted God, and never lost faith, and He provided for me in a miraculous way throughout that time. He does truly do those things which we human beings cannot do. And I believe that His power to do these wonders is released when humanly we have reached the end of our capabilities and we must totally depend upon Him. That seems to be exactly when God performs miracles.

I love the praise song, "What a Mighty God we serve!" It expresses to me how great God is, and that His strength is always available to us, moment by moment, day by day.

*Dear Father, Thank you for doing the impossible for me. In Jesus' name, Amen.*

# August 10

*John 18:11: The cup which my Father has given me, shall I not drink it?*

*Ecclesiastes 2:4: Whatsoever is brought upon thee, take cheerfully.*

Yesterday, I finished my last class and had the entire group to a party at my chalet. After driving the last group of students and guests up the mountain road I wearily turned to head home and collapse. Just then an acquaintance spotted me and asked if I would drive her to her hotel, which was in the opposite direction! I of course agreed to do that. I knew it was the only right thing to do, but at the time it felt so hard. I wish I could have done it with a better spirit!

Jesus spoke these words in John 18 as he was about to be arrested, telling his disciples not to defend him. What an example to us. He was ready to face arrest and crucifixion as part of God's plan of salvation.

Another earlier time, Jesus had received the terrible news of John the Baptist's death and was grieving. A crowd sought him out for healing, and even in his own time of distress he went out to them in compassion. By contrast, I often struggle to just be courteous, when I am feeling tired and exhausted. How I need His grace.

*Dear Father, Help us to take whatever you hand to us with grace and compassion. And thank you Lord for your help and provision during this past month of hard work. In Jesus' name, Amen.*

# August 11

*Deuteronomy 15:10: The Lord thy God shall bless them in all Thy works, and in all that thou puttest thy hand unto.*

I prayed for several months for God to bless this summer class here in Switzerland. It seemed that there might be fewer students than usual this year. Then, in a flurry of last-minute registrations, the numbers rose to 22, very large for this kind of class which is intensive, with 10 days of performing and coaching. I absolutely felt it was the Lord's blessing.

Although I knew a few of the students, most were strangers to me. I rarely advertise these classes, it just seems the right students come. But, as we worked together, the sweetest bonding occurred, between the students and between me and them. By the end of the class we were all very close and I believe life-long friendships were born.

Only God could have created and produced this beautiful situation and nurtured these relationships.

*Dear Father, Thank you, Lord, for your blessing, guiding, and directing my work.*

# August 12

*Luke 10:25: Master, what shall I do to inherit eternal life?*

*Ecclesiastes 9:10: Whatsoever thy Lord findeth to do, do it with thy might.*

As a teacher of students from all different countries and different backgrounds and schools of harp playing, I try to work with each of them beginning where they are at in the present moment. I do not try to greatly change their position or technique, but I do try to encourage them, each one, to improve in some way. But with every one of them, I try to instill musical intensity, that they play the harp with all of their heart! I think this is the most important aspect that I seek to instill through my teaching.

Is this not true for all of us, in whatever work we are doing? It is necessary that we pour ourselves into it, doing our very best, with our whole heart and soul. If God has given us a certain work to do, we must not hold back, but commit to do it to the best of our ability.

If we do our work half-heartedly, it will never bring us satisfaction or peace. Whether doing mundane chores and duties of our everyday life, or writing a symphony, God wants our best, and He will bless us as we lose ourselves in doing His will.

*Dear Lord, Thank you for giving me work that I love and for providing me with the energy and strength to do it. In Jesus' name, Amen*

# August 13

*Luke 21.19: In your patience possess ye your souls.*

Home at last after a long month of hard work and real loneliness in Switzerland! I am awestruck by God's provision and protection of me during this time.

I felt his hand throughout the tumult of the 8th World Harp Congress in Geneva. I knew His provision by bringing such a dear and wonderful group of students to my master class in Villars. I felt His presence every day and at night as I drove home on the dangerous mountain roads, covered in fog and mist. He was with me in those lonely and dark nights in the mostly deserted small village. He brought Christian friends to support and pray for me.

He gave me an amazing trip home, even up-grading me to business class so that I could get some sleep and even allowed just enough time for me to make my connecting flight, 22 hours later. I can only thank Him and praise Him today for His constant provision.

*Dear Father: I am so thankful to you, beyond any words for your grace and mercy to me this summer. Thank you, Lord. In Jesus' name, Amen.*

**Author's new house after the fire
destroyed former house, 2003**

**Music room stage in new house with IU students performing**

**Unpacking  the two new harps**

**Bulldozer demolishing house after the fire November 1, 2003**

**Author with pets, Tutti and Baby, teacup poodles**

**Diane Bish, Jean and Maurice Biggs with dogs**

**An IU harp department graduation party at McDonald home**

**Magazine cover after winning Premier Prix
(First Prize) from Paris Conservatory, 1955**

With famed organist and friend, Diane Bish,
after recital in Spivey Hall, Atlanta

Naoko Yoshino, a former student, now renowned
concert harpist, and her mother, Atsuko Yoshino,
with the late George and Catherine McDonald.

**With parents in California**

**The IU harp class with guest harpist
from England, Skaila Kanga**

The Swiss chalet "Les Noisetiers" in Huemoz.

International prize-winning students, Maria
Luisa Rayan, Dan Yu, and Kaori Otake

The author with young student Naoko Yoshino

The author with harpist Linda Wood Rollo and her husband, Dr. David Rollo, Chairman of the Board, USA International Harp Competition. Opening reception at McDonald home, 2004

With colleague Elzbieta Szmyt, Clarence and Nance Miller, Eleanor Fell, and John Karaagac, Board members and friends of the USA International Harp Competition

**Members of the jury for the Lily Laskine International Harp Competition, Deauville, France**

**The author during her teaching years at The Juilliard School, 1980**

**The author's brother and sister-in-law,
George and Janet McDonald**

**On balcony of Swiss chalet, "Les Noisetiers"**

Author after a concert

**Author with harpist friends, Eleanor Fell,
Sarah Bullen (principal harpist with Chicago
Symphony, and former student) Elzbieta Szmyt,
colleague and husband John Karaagac.**

148

**View from Swiss chalet**

**Author at her Brown County country home, 1985**

**Prayer circle friends, MaryNelle Schaap, Ethel Smith, Mary
Kominowski, Shirley Smith, and Diane Bish, dining out**

**Jackie Brummet and Darlene Frye,
prayer partners for many years**

**Friends and students watching the Swiss
National parade, August 1st.**

**Cows in the Swiss National Day parade**

**Swiss alphorn players**

**Golfing in California with Linda and David
Rollo and brother, George McDonald**

**Close friend and colleague, Ela Szmyt**

**Baby found in a quiet moment**

**Author ready for golf in Florida, 2005**

**Lunch in Bloomington with Diane
Bish, Ela and John Karaagac**

**At Pine Mountain, Georgia with dear friends, Diane Bish, Jane Stuart Smith, Sissy Eason and Jane Carlson.**

# August 14

*Psalms 121.1: I will lift up mine eyes unto the hills, from whence cometh my help.*

*II Corinthians 12.9: My grace is sufficient for thee.*

I am so thankful to be home. I missed my little dog, Baby, so much. He is just over one year old, a white teacup poodle, so cute and playful and affectionate. Two of my friends are suffering as their old dogs are ill and failing. I pray that they will be given special grace to endure such a painful loss. I feel God gives us the companionship of dear animals that comfort us and enrich our lives.

Now that I am back in Indiana, the mountains of Switzerland seem like a distant dream. But whether I am here or there, I know my help comes from the Lord. He is my constant source of strength and wisdom.

This week I will need to begin school preparations – working on my teaching schedule, getting a parking permit (otherwise known as a "hunting license" because of the almost impossible job of finding a free parking space) and answering almost 100 e-mails. I will need God's grace for all these chores.

*Dear Father: Thank you for your grace, it is indeed all I need, but how I need it. In Jesus' name, Amen.*

# August 15

*II Timothy 1.7: God has not given us the spirit of fear, but of power and of love and of a sound mind.*

I have always felt that being a musician or an artist does not carry special privileges, such as tolerating neurotic or selfish behavior. To the contrary, it seems that great gifts should require great responsibility. The Bible says to whom much is given, much will be required.

This verse in Timothy is such a wonderful encouragement, as it reminds us that when we face difficult problems, loneliness or bereavement, God has given us sound minds and love and power. These real gifts see us through whatever we may be facing.

He does not want us to live with fear. While I savor these precious days of vacation at home, I think ahead about returning to France so soon, facing another jet lag and long hours of hard work judging harpists playing for important prizes. Then knowing I will return late to the opening of school and plunge into lessons the day after I return causes me some concern and worry. So, God's promise above is very meaningful to me.

*Dear Father: Thank you for your great gifts to us. Please fill me with your peace about the future and help me to just live each day, secure in your love. In Jesus' name, Amen.*

# August 16

*Galatians 6.7: Whatsoever a man soweth, that shall he reap.*

A musician's life is really about our commitment and faithfulness to practice every day. We cannot expect our fingers and tendons to perform well if we go one or two days without practice, then attempt to cram our work on the third day! Our fingers would quickly become sore if we worked so irregularly. We can also risk getting tendonitis.

Faithful practice is so necessary, and it pays rich dividends in terms of technical facility and an ease in performance.

The habits we practice in our outer lives are so important too. If we are peacemakers and up-lifters, our lives will be filled with peace and joy. If we are "gloomy Gerties," seeing the downside all the time, our lives will be depressing and filled with worry.

If we anchor ourselves to Jesus Christ, making Him the focus of our lives and our role model, then by His grace and mercy our habits may enable us to become increasingly like Him.

*Dear Lord: Help me to sow habits that will bring joy and peace to others. In Jesus' name, Amen.*

# August 17

*Psalms 86.16: O turn unto me and have mercy upon me: give Thy strength unto Thy servant and save the son of Thine handmaid.*

I have been so happy to just be home. The familiar routine is such a comfort – feeding Baby, doing devotions in a favorite chair, and going for my daily walk around the neighborhood. I realize again just how very precious such normal days are.

I think God gives us these respites in our busy lives to recharge our batteries and prepare for the tumultuous times ahead. In just two weeks, classes begin again. I know I will be swept up in the students' needs. Each will need help in choosing the repertoire they will study. Many will ask for advice about entering contests or applying for certain auditions. And so many will have financial needs and I will try to get scholarship help for them in a situation where there is never enough money to go around. I will need to read and study many new scores to effectively teach. And there will be recitals, orchestra concerts, master classes, and committee meetings and departmental meetings.

I am thankful to God who will give me the strength and courage to face a new year.

*Dear Father: Thank you for giving me work that I love. I pray for your constant presence. In Jesus' name, Amen.*

# August 18

*I John 3.21: Beloved, if our heart condemn us not, then have we confidence toward God.*

As a teacher, I can and do work hard to secure scholarships and financial aid for many of my students who need it desperately. I can also write strong letters of recommendation to help them get accepted into competitions or auditions. These are things I can do. I cannot join the Peace Corps or work in the missions overseas, but I can give financially to help others who serve there. God blesses us, so that we can be a blessing to others.

Our hearts and our conscience will bother us if we allow ourselves to stray from good and truthful actions. The opposite is also true, our hearts and minds will be at peace if we live lives of love toward those in need. If we have pity and compassion toward the hungry and hurting in the world, God will work through us and we will be His hands.

If we obey his commands and do what pleases him, we may ask and receive from him whatever we ask. If we believe in Jesus Christ, that he is the Son of God and we have love for one another, he will live in us, and his Holy Spirit will guide and direct us.

We need to spend time alone with Him daily, to get away from our cares and worries and to have confidence that he hears us and answers every sincere prayer. He will direct our giving and use our gifts.

*Dear Father: I have complete confidence that you have blessed me to be able to bless others. Thank you Lord. In Jesus' name, Amen.*

# August 19

*Psalms 27.11: Teach me Thy way, O Lord, and lead me in a plain path.*

This weekend I read an article about two teachers, a husband-and-wife team, who had been lauded for their effectiveness as music professors. I was keenly interested for I always hope to be a more effective teacher. One point they made was so good. They said each student is a "Number One" with them. I agreed, feeling that we must seek to develop each student's special and innate gifts. We need to find the right positions and technical solutions that will free them to play comfortably. We need to select repertoire and etudes that will develop their musicality and expressiveness. Each student should receive our undivided attention and our care.

Isn't this how God teaches us? He patiently guides us, choosing special experiences to train us in His ways. He also protects and spares us from those things he deems unwise for us. If we are good students, we will listen carefully to His teaching. We will be anxious to read and study his Word – the Holy Bible – and consult Him in prayer before every decision, trusting Him with our whole life.

*Dear Father: Thank you for your precious teaching and guidance. In Jesus' name, Amen.*

# August 20

*Psalms 27.14: Wait on the Lord: be of good courage, and He shall strengthen thine heart: wait, I say, on the Lord.*

*Isaiah 40.29: He gives power to the faint; and to them that have no might He increases strength.*

How hard it sometimes is for us to be patient! We live in a time when we expect instant gratification. We do not want to sit in traffic jams, even when we might benefit from that quiet time to think or to pray. We are dependent on our computers working and when they crash or our printers are out of ink, we are terribly frustrated!

I see this impatience sometimes in some of my students. They want to play repertoire that is too difficult for their technical abilities, rather than waiting for their fingers to strengthen and develop. Wanting to encourage them, I try to select repertoire that they will enjoy, but that is appropriate for their present ability. I pray for wisdom in making wise choices for my students.

I know that if we ask God to make us more patient He will do it, and He will give us strength and courage in every area of our lives. He knows what we need before we are even aware of our need.

*Dear Father: Give me your patience to face the needs of this day with courage and strength. In Jesus' name, Amen.*

# August 21

*Romans 15.1: We then that are strong ought to bear the infirmities of the weak, and not to please ourselves.*

Isaiah 10.4: The Lord God has given me the tongue of the learned, that I should know how to speak a word in season to him that is weary.

God has given each of us special gifts. How easily we can forget that each gift from God is to be used in His service. We are not to please ourselves but to be used to help others and to serve others who are hurting. Every month when I sit down to pay my bills, I thank God that he has given me the resources to pay them. And in addition He has given me enough to help numerous people in need through World Vision and In Touch Ministries.

There is always someone near us in need of a kind word or a compassionate note or just a warm smile. How sad that we too often live to ourselves, doing what brings us pleasure instead of looking out for others. When we think of the lonely, sick and hurting people in our lives, what a responsibility we have to reach out of our comfort-zone and try to help them, to ease their loneliness and to let them know someone cares. We too will one day be weak, weary and infirm.

*Dear Lord: I pray that you will give me a heart full of compassion. Show me where and how I can be used today to lift up someone who is in need. In Jesus' name, Amen.*

# August 22

*Romans 12.1: I beseech you therefore, brethren, by the mercies of God, that ye present your bodies a living sacrifice, holy, acceptable unto God, which is your reasonable service.*

As I get older, I am aware of so many parts of my body that I used to take for granted! Now, often when I get up in the morning, I am so stiff I can hardly walk! And when I go to the harp, it takes me longer to warm up and get my fingers working comfortably. I must accept the new aches and pains as part of the aging process. It is very humbling.

In our own strength and abilities, we are not able to approach a standard of holiness, acceptable to our Holy God. But He who created us, by His mercy and love toward us, can bring about such a change.

Paul adds that "presenting our bodies as a living sacrifice"is a reasonable service for us to do. Perhaps some blatant and obvious sacrifices such as gluttony or sexual immorality seem reasonable to make. But what about getting up out of an easy-chair and helping a friend? Or leaving the comfort of a warm house to run an errand for someone in need during bad weather? Or making that hard but necessary phone call? Or just patiently listening to someone's problem when you long to be alone and just read or relax?

By God's grace we are enabled to live lives of small but meaningful sacrifices, as we strive to be ever more like our Lord and Savior, Jesus Christ.

*Dear Father: Please mold me and make me acceptable as I strive to live a holy, obedient life. In Jesus' name, Amen.*

# August 23

*Jeremiah 45.5: Seekest thou great things for thyself? Seek them not.*

A friend of mine who has undergone several surgeries to fix a painful condition just called to report that the most recent surgery was still not successful. He keeps praying and still trusts God to work out His plan. That is great faith.

I leave again for France tomorrow. I will be a judge at an international competition in Deauville. I have committed the trip and the competition to God. I pray for His hand to be upon the contestants and the jury and for His justice to oversee the entire event.

It has been said, "Excellence in all things, and in all things to God's glory." I believe this verse encourages achievement that honors God. But we are not to seek glory and honor for ourselves but to use them to bring praise to God.

God wants the best for us, better than we could dream or imagine for ourselves. If we commit all we do, every effort we make, every endeavor we undertake, to Him, we will be astounded at what He will bring to pass.

*Dear Father: Thank you for the great opportunities you give us to honor you. In Jesus' name, Amen.*

# August 24

*Luke 8.14: And that which fell among thorns are they, which, when they have heard, go forth, and are choked with cares, and riches and pleasures of this life, and bring no fruit to perfection.*

How like a garden our lives can be! When I returned after five weeks in Switzerland, no one had tended my fenced garden. Two other areas were neat and tidy because they had been weeded and mulched. But in the fenced area, weeds were choking the roses and black-eyed Susans, and it was a sorry sight. The weeds had overwhelmed the flowers.

Sin in our lives will effectively smother the Holy Spirit's voice, which urges us always to live holy lives. How easy it can be to be seduced by world pleasures or success, so we become too busy and self-concerned. Or we allow our work to become all-consuming, so that those nearest to us are neglected. Being overly concerned with worries is another form of sin, because it blocks us from positive and helpful living. We need to put aside anything which prevents us from hearing God's voice and doing His will.

*Dear Father: Help me to turn from anything that would keep me from closer communion with you. In Jesus' name, Amen.*

# August 25

*Hebrews 12.25: See that he refuse not Him that speaketh.*

Sometimes I will give a student very specific advice about taking a certain tempo in a passage of music or playing with stronger dynamics or slowing at the end of a phrase. Then later, I hear that the student has listened to other advice about these passages and is no longer following my suggestions. It is natural for me to feel undercut and a bit hurt.

I wonder how much more strongly God must feel when He has spoken to us clearly, in the Bible, or through the promptings of the Holy Spirit, and then we go off in an opposite track. It must seem bewildering to Him, as it was to me with my student.

We need to be careful to whom we listen and to what voice we heed and obey. The world will always try to get our attention. Satan is always ready to try to confuse us with messages like, "just one time will not hurt…" or "they won't even miss you…" or "it is really not important that you call."

Today I leave for France. I am sure while serving on the jury I will hear many opinions about the music, the performers and the interpretations. I pray for wisdom to keep my own counsel and judge wisely.

*Dear Father: Help me to only listen to Your voice and protect me from all others. In Jesus' name, Amen.*

# August 26

*Zachariah 2.13: Be silent, O all flesh, before the Lord.*

The long trip back to Europe after such a short time at home went well. Although my plane was late leaving Atlanta, a young French harpist colleague had waited faithfully for me in Paris, despite my two-hour delay. She drove me straight to Deauville, where the jury had assembled for the opening ceremony of this international harp contest.

After the contestants drew numbers for their performance order the next day, the jury had a chance to renew our old friendships. Then I had the bliss of getting to bed early for a long night's sleep. I awoke this morning, gratefully feeling already on French time! I always dread having a jet lag on these trips. Specially, when needing to listen attentively to harp music for long hours, one needs to be well rested!

I am happy to have quite a lot of time to be alone with God on these trips. Although the work keeps me busy, there are times when I can return to my room and rest, pray and have the peace of quiet communion with my Lord.

To be alone with Him is to be refreshed as from an eternal fountain. There is no exercise as important as seeking alone time with Him.

*Dear Lord: I am so thankful that in the silence I can hear your words of guidance and encouragement and love very clearly. They will sustain me during this week so far from home. In Jesus name, Amen.*

# August 27

*Philippians 1.6: Being confident of this very thing, that He who began a good work in you will perform it.*

*Matthew 10.22: He that endures to the end shall be saved.*

There is a praise song often sung in church these days based on Philippians 1.6, "He who began a good work in you, will be faithful to complete it." Being back in France reminds me of my days here as a student. I was very shy and lacked confidence. I had not yet grown fluent in French in those first years studying in Paris.

It is a great contrast for me to return here, welcomed and respected as an artist, so different from my simple days as a student. I can only marvel at how God has blessed me as a harpist.

In moments of weakness or discouragement, it is a great comfort to lean on the promise of these verses. Our great God does not lead us only so far and then cast us off. When we are weakest, His strength is greatest. He will complete in us the work He would have us do.

The Holy Spirit works powerfully in us, if we bathe our every decision in faith-based prayer. And the fruits of the spirit are love, joy, peace, patience, kindness, goodness, faithfulness, gentleness and self-control. (Galatians 5.22)

The deeper our faith, the more buoyed up we shall be as we pass through turbulent waters. He will finish in us the work He has given us to do.

*Dear Father: Help me to endure to the end, so that in all I do you will be honored and glorified. In Jesus' name, Amen*

# August 28

*Psalms 9.10: They that know Thy name will put their trust in Thee: for Thou, Lord, hast not forsaken them that seek Thee.*

*Psalms 85.12: Yea, the Lord shall give that which is good.*

Yesterday we finished hearing thirty harpists in the first stage of this international contest. The jury passed eleven to the second stage. In the evening, the mayor gave a reception for participants and jury. Of course, those who did not pass crowded around us, asking for our comments and explanations. Many were in tears.

We tried to console them and encourage them. Life is not a contest, and contests often do not show the person's depth and real musicianship. It is often a show of "iron nerves" and "fast fingers." I pray for justice to be done in this contest, and that God will give us insight and wisdom in choosing the final laureates. It can often happen that the most deserving contestant does not win. Judges have different tastes and preferences and a contest can be very unwieldy. One can never be sure of the outcome.

I am grateful that God does not judge us superficially, by our actions or our outer shell, but that He knows our hearts and our souls. We can absolutely trust Him to give us what is good for us.

*Dear Father: I put my trust in you for the right outcome of this day and I will seek you with all my heart. In Jesus' name, Amen.*

# August 29

*Genesis 4.9: Am I my brother's keeper?*

One of the wonderful perks of being on the jury of an international harp competition in France is having a chance to enjoy the great food. The seafood is so fresh and delicious on the Normandy coast. The mussels, and tiny shell fish and shrimp are the best anywhere. We are wined and dined between the three stages of the contest.

Even with the heavy schedule of the competition, the schedule here seems much easier than at home, where so often I attempt to do more than I should in a given time. I become so committed to household chores, practicing, errands and e-mail, that interruptions are difficult to accommodate graciously!

But, that is exactly what God would have us do. We should never be so intent on doing our own business that we brush aside someone in need. This is surely easier said than done. We are to put aside our personal priorities and plans, and help anyone in need. Often it is simply to listen to someone who needs to talk, on the phone or in person. It means building suppleness into our schedules so we are freer to change course to help another.

*Dear Father: Help me to not be so attached to achieving that I am unavailable to help those in need. In Jesus' name, Amen.*

# August 30

*Ephesians 4.1, 2: Walk worthy of the vocation wherewith ye are called, with all lowliness and meekness, with long-suffering, forbearing one another in love.*

God has truly blessed my career as a harpist and teacher, beyond any of my hopes and dreams. Not a day goes by that I don't realize with deep gratitude what He has done in my life, allowing me wonderful students, a prestigious university position and a certain amount of fame in the world harp community.

But the vocation Paul refers to in Ephesians 4 is that of belonging to the Lord. He has called us and made himself know to us. Therefore we cannot live to ourselves but for Him. He asks us to live lives of simplicity and humility, putting the well being of others before our own. He calls us to be patient with others in love.

This is the blessed life He calls us to live. As we walk in meekness and humbleness closer and closer to our Savior and Master, we will increasingly live in total peace and harmony. As he reigns in our hearts, we will experience a deep joy, which no "career" can give us.

*Dear Father: I am so thankful to know you. Please mold me today into your true and humble servant. In Jesus' name, Amen.*

# August 31

*Romans 15.5: Now the God of patience and consolation grant you to be likeminded one toward another according to Christ Jesus.*

*Psalms 121.8: The Lord shall preserve thy going out and thy coming in.*

*Psalms 121.7: The Lord shall preserve thee from all evil.*

One of the joys for me in my life as a harpist is having many warm friendships with harpists around the world. This time in France with this particular jury has been very special. We all have so much in common and have shared so many similar professional experiences that we feel like a family! We have had many happy and light-hearted times together this week.

However, as this international contest comes to the final two days, the jury is faced with hard decisions. The results can be heart-breaking for some of the young people. I pray for us to judge with wisdom and insight.

How I pray for and need God's protection every day and in every situation. One moment we can be at perfect peace and the next can bring unexpected woe. We need to be so anchored in Christ that we can surmount difficulties and problems without sinking into them and being pulled down by them

We are also to bear our burdens bravely, and not to complain to others about them. We must try to be cheerful even when we are hurting. We must be ever ready to console others and not be overly concerned with our consolation.

*Dear Lord: I commit each day to you, and thank you for your patience and protection. In Jesus' name, Amen.*

# SEPTEMBER

## September 1

*I Peter 4.19: Let them that suffer according to the will of God commit the keeping of their souls to Him in well-doing, as unto a faithful Creator.*

*James 5.11: The Lord is very pitiful and of tender mercy.*

Today is the final stage of this contest in this charming Normandy coast city of France in Deauville. Three finalists will play the Reinecke Harp Concerto with orchestra and all three will receive substantial cash rewards. But, the First Prize winner will be catapulted into fame and an already constructed career of recordings and concert engagements, not to mention much worldwide publicity.

One of my students is a finalist, and so I am filled with prayers for her. I am praying not that she will necessarily win, but that God's will be done in her life and in the lives of the other harpists. It will be life-changing for all of them, winning or not. The tension and stress on the harpists and the jury is great. The rules of the contest of course prohibit judges voting for their own students, so I will abstain from the final vote. I hope that the voting will be just and fair. No one can ever predict the outcome.

I will start the long journey home tomorrow, and God willing, I will be back in my own bed tomorrow night. These days spent in Deauville will be added to my memories of special times the Lord has given me—-times of friendship with dear colleagues and the great pleasure of being with French friends from my days as a student in Paris. I have felt God's great faithfulness while here, in a very special and meaningful way.

*Dear Father: Thank you for your love and compassion which never fails, no matter where we may be. In Jesus' name, Amen.*

# September 2

*Matthew 5.9: Blessed are the peacemakers for they shall be called the children of God.*

How we are blessed when we are given the Godly wisdom to utter the soft, kind words which can defuse a tumultuous or angry situation! Words can be so healing or so destructive.

Yesterday, after the results of the contest were announced, and my student had the joy of being named the winner, several disgruntled French friends came to me and railed at me because their favorite harpist had not won the first prize. I tried to explain to them that it was the jury's decision, but I mostly just let them vent their feelings. I told them I was sorry that they felt that way, and at the end, they apologized to me for having been hurtful.

I was struck again by the verse, "a soft answer turneth away wrath." It was important to me not to defend myself or the jury and to match anger with their anger, and I was grateful I was able to do that. I wanted to leave Deauville, knowing that everyone was at peace about the contest, but that was not possible.

But, one of the surest ways to obtain peace in this life is to try to be someone who seeks to insert kindness and patience into the lives of those around us who are hurting. I know I cannot do that in my own strength, but Christ can do it working in me.

*Dear Father: Thank you for your faithfulness during the contest and this time in France. I pray that you will bring me safely home tonight. In Jesus' name, Amen.*

# September 3

*Psalms 145:15: The eyes of all wait upon Thee: and Thou givest them their meat in due season.*

*Psalms 56:6: What time I am afraid, I will trust in Thee.*

What joy it is to be safely back home after travels abroad! I had such a good trip home—both flights on time, no crowded lines in Atlanta for immigration and customs. And, best of all, to be met by my little dog, Baby, in Indianapolis, thanks to a friend who brought him.

A lady who spoke no English on my flight from Paris quickly crossed herself when we had safely landed. I realized she had been very frightened flying. I thank God over and over for this good trip and His protection and mercy.

Today I return to my university teaching after my year of sabbatical. It will be a shock to again be teaching long hours every day. But, I do trust that the Lord will meet my needs and give me the strength and courage to do the work with which He has blessed me. As I commit this year, day by day into His keeping, I feel great peace. I am truly back home where I belong.

*Dearest Lord—I thank you for giving me work that I love. I look to Thee to bring all my students what they need. In Jesus' name, Amen.*

# September 4

*Psalms 1:2, 3: His delight is in the law of the Lord. And he shall be like a tree planted by the rivers of water that bringeth forth his fruits in his season; his leaf also shall not wither: and whatsoever he doeth shall prosper.*

One of the good things for me about having jetlag is that I wake up very early in the morning. Of course, over a week or so, that keeps changing later and later until I am back to my usual wake-up time.

But, these early fall days are so beautiful in Indiana. The humidity is mostly gone and the air is fresh. The tomatoes which I planted in May are bearing fruit now. The grapes are also so sweet. There is a hint of fall in the air but the leaves have not yet started turning.

It felt quite normal to be back teaching my lessons yesterday afternoon. I am so thankful to be home, and I felt so welcomed by my dear students.

God so blesses us with the changing seasons—each season with its special joys and beauty. Fall is surely a time to savor, a time of new beginnings and of fresh hope.

*Dear Father—Thank you for your incredible, beautiful universe. In Jesus' name, Amen.*

# September 5

*Isaiah 38:14: O Lord, I am oppressed: undertake for me.*

What a blessed relief, when we face problems or obstacles that fill us with doubt and fear, to quickly commit them to our Lord. Today was the first masterclass with all my students and I felt tired and weak to face such a large class.

I prayed for His strength to fill me with all I needed. And, when the room filled up with my large class, some twenty-four students, He filled me with tremendous love and energy for them. I truly felt lifted up. Their smiling, welcoming faces completely energized me. When I left school, I almost floated home, praising God for this special time.

I know that His strength is made perfect in our weakness. I have personally experienced it so many, many times. When we falter, He takes over for us.

Too often our trouble is that we don't ask and we try to carry burdens for ourselves. His love and compassion are always there for us—only a prayer away. To God be the glory!

*Dear Father—Your love for us is so wide, so deep and so constant. Thank you, Lord, for knowing what we need before we can even tell you about it. In Jesus' name, Amen.*

# September 6

*Luke 9:23: If any man will come after me, let him deny himself, and take up his cross daily and follow me.*

I pray that God will give me a heart for others and that He will enable me to grow in selflessness. As I look into the young, smiling, hope-filled faces of my students, I realize He has blessed me beyond measure. I hope that He will grant me the wisdom to help each of them. They all have different needs and different gifts. To whom much has been given, much is required.

To take up one's cross daily is not easy to do. Perhaps even harder is the second part—to deny oneself. Sometimes we are willing and able to do things to help other people. But, very often we do not have to give up our own needs or priorities to act in kindness.

More than anything, I want to follow my Savior.

I am sure Jesus, in speaking of the cross, meant the sacrificial giving up our own needs. We are to put them aside. Jesus died on the cross for our salvation. We are to die to selfishness, self-centeredness and pride. Only as we do this can we be true followers of Christ.

*Dear Father—Thank you for your Son, Jesus Christ, who daily shows us the way through His immeasurable sacrifice. In Jesus' name, Amen.*

# September 7

*James 1:27: Pure religion and undefiled before God and the Father is this, to visit the fatherless and widows in their affliction, and to keep himself unspoiled from the world.*

How can we keep ourselves "unspoiled" from the world's influences? We are bombarded by television commercials, e-mails that we don't have time to read, and noise pollution of all kinds. There are also movies, newspapers, magazines and books—many of which are not fit to be seen or read.

We should be ready to walk out of films that are filled with swearing and obscenity. We should refuse to be polluted by material that is sacrilegious. Often the public standard is so low that movies that receive good reviews and wide public acceptance fool us. And, we may not be aware until we watch these movies that they are irreverent and corrupt.

I recall an example of watching a television movie with friends. As actors began using the Lord's name or swearing, I felt a breeze go by me as a Christian friend quietly left the room. What a good example she set! I would like to be more discriminating than I am about the books I read and the movies I watch!

*Dear Father—Help us to be discerning about what we read and what we view. Give us pure hearts that we might better serve you. In Jesus' name, Amen.*

# September 8

*Colossians 4:2: Continue in prayer, and watch in the same with thanksgiving.*

*1 Corinthians 16:13: Watch, stand firm in the faith, be men of courage, be strong.*

Being daily connected to our Lord can work wonders in our lives. If we allow life's distractions or our work and busyness to keep us from alone times of prayer, we are cut off from His power, His miracle-working blessings and grace. The old saying, "If you are too busy to pray, you are too busy," is so true—I have learned over the years that the time I spend in prayer every day is indispensable to a good, peaceful day.

To pray and to be strong in our faith surely compliment each other. In order for us to stay strong in our faith and be courageous in facing life, we need to be rooted and grounded in prayer. Our constant communication, alone with God, is what revitalizes us. Prayer alone can rid us of the selfishness, pride, and impatience that are inborn in our sinful lives. Only prayer allows us to get rid of our guilt over mistakes of the past. It truly enables us to be strong, to be servants of the Lord, serving each other in love.

*Dear Father—Help me to be watchful, to stand firm, to live with a thankful heart, and to spend more time daily in quiet communion with you my God and my strength. In Jesus' name, Amen.*

# September 9

*Titus 3:8: This is a faithful saying, and these things I will that thou affirm constantly, that they which have believed in God's might be careful to maintain good works.*

It was so good to be back in Sherwood Oaks Christian Church, my church home, yesterday. We had an excellent guest preacher who spoke eloquently and movingly. He said that the primary need and function of the church should be only worshipping God. He elaborated that although evangelism, feeding the hungry and caring for the homeless are important, they will grow naturally out of the church that worships God.

In our personal lives, I believe the same principal applies. Our fundamental purpose, that will guide every other aspect of our lives, is to abide in God. He is the vine; we are the branches. Only by daily, sometimes lonely prayer and time with our Creator, can we be nourished by His strength, power, grace and forgiveness. Then we may be able to handle our duties, our relationships and work as He would have us do. Our good works should grow out of this prayer relationship as naturally as a gently flowing stream. He is our living water.

*Dear Lord—Help us, in your strength, to do those good works that you would have us do. Help us to remember that we are your hands and feet while on the earth. In Jesus' name, Amen.*

# September 10

*John 13:9: Lord, not my feet only, but also my hands and my head.*

Jesus set an example to his disciples. After washing their feet as a servant would, he asked them to do the same. Peter and the others were uncomfortable to have their Lord and Teacher washing their feet.

As a teacher, I believe Jesus is an example for me, too. It is all too easy to feel the authority of one's position, but it is so important to also identify a student's needs and insecurities. I can sometimes get involved in showing students how I think a musical passage should be fingered or played when that is not exactly what the student needed at that moment! Perhaps what would have been better was to encourage that student to keep striving with the old fingerings or to move on to another part of the piece.

It is also a challenge to be remain open to new ways of playing pieces, especially the ones I have played for many years. Truly, one needs to remain humble and keenly sensitive to each person's gifts.

Christ set an example of authority and humility that should always be our model as teachers, executives and supervisors of any kind.

*Dear Lord—Thank you for all the lessons you teach us. In Jesus' name, Amen.*

# September 11

*Matthew 6:10: Thy kingdom come.*

Today is the one-year anniversary of the terrorist attacks on September 11 that resulted in the deaths of almost 3,000 people. As all the commemorative services are televised, the sorrow and heartbreak of the victims' families and loved ones is hard to watch. My heart aches for them. Their losses and their pain will never go away in this lifetime.

I remember going for my morning walk between the planes even then already hitting and the towers falling. I was deeply troubled and felt our country might be even then already at war. Surely our country will never be the same again. No one will ever feel completely safe as we did a year ago. Tall buildings and airplanes will always remind us of our vulnerability to those who hate us.

But, the kingdom of God promises a place where every tear will be wiped away. Only His kingdom can overcome the pain and sorrow we experience in this life.

God is the same yesterday, today, tomorrow and forever. We are in His hands and He does not want us to live in fear. His kingdom is love. His will is peace and it is up to us to live in peace, love and harmony with every person we encounter.

*Dear God—Help us to build your kingdom here on earth. In Jesus' name, Amen.*

# September 12

*Zephaniah 3:2: She obeyed not the voice; she received not correction; she trusted in the Lord; she drew not near to her God.*

I enjoyed talking with other harp professors this summer, comparing experiences and discussing repertoire and harp matters in general. One of the most prominent French teachers said the one thing she cannot tolerate is a student who refuses to change, even after she has shown her what needs to be done—whether a faster tempo, different fingering or dynamics. She complained that such a student was a complete waste of her time and energy.

I have also experienced students like that. Although they want instruction, they don't want to make the effort to accept the changes suggested that will provide improvement. I, too, can be frustrated by such students.

But, aren't we sometimes like those students in our relationship to God? He wants us to lean on Him and trust Him in every area of our lives. Yet, we persist in keeping little areas to ourselves. We don't allow Him to correct those areas. Our disobedience is costly and hinders our growth and usefulness to God. We need His constant correction and we need to obey His voice—not next week or next month, but immediately.

*Dear Father—Help us to obey your commands and to accept your loving reproof, knowing you want our best always. In Jesus' name, Amen.*

# September 13

*Lamentations 3:26: It is good that a man should both hope and quietly wait for the salvation of the Lord.*

*Psalms 62:1: Truly my soul waiteth upon God: from Him cometh my salvation.*

It is another beautiful, clear fall day. The leaves are beginning to turn gold, crimson, and apricot.I am tired at the end of the busy week back at school. I had to get up for an early meeting to try to find new sources for funding for the USA International Harp Competition. But, the hymn "Great is Thy Faithfulness" came to mind as I looked out on the crisp fall day.  It is one of my favorite hymns.

God *is* so faithful. We have our ups and downs, struggles with aches and pains, and with relationships that wound us. But, God is always faithful. We only need to be patient and not lose hope.

The Bible repeatedly says that we should "wait patiently on the Lord." His timing is eternal; we are not in one time zone. A thousand years are as one day to Him!

*Dear Father—Help me to wait patiently for all that you have in store for me. In Jesus' name, Amen.*

# September 14

*Jeremiah 33:3: Call unto me, and I will assure thee, and show thee great and mighty things which thou knowest not.*

*I Kings 3:13: And I have also given thee that which thou has not asked.*

Sometimes we feel we have missed great opportunities: a house we did not buy that doubled in value within two years; a trip we did not take that those who did enjoyed tremendously; or even simply a telephone call we did not make.

I still regret arriving late at my teacher's tea in Paris. She had hoped for me, as her youngest student present, to be the one to pin on her medal, the Legion of Honor, which she received there that afternoon. I was so very timid and shy and I felt that I must not arrive too early!

But, God is watching over our fortunes, and He is in charge of our affairs. I think we should not be over-concerned about "missed opportunities." God knows so much better than we do what is best for us. His plans are all and more than we need.

Before we can even frame a request, God has answered it, often beyond our wildest dreams! Even situations that seem a burden and a cross to bear, He uses to mature us and give us increased strength and courage.

*Dear Father, Help me to leave every decision and every care in your hands. Thank you Lord for all your great gifts, beyond what I can imagine. In Jesus' name, Amen.*

# September 15

*Mark 10:38: Can ye drink of the cup that I drink of? And be baptized with the baptism I am baptized with?*

Many of my music students look at the success of some of their peers—winners of important competitions for example—and feel that they too deserve to have similar success. And many of them can and will achieve their dreams in due time.

But some do not realize the depth of sacrifice and dedication that is needed to win such a contest, the long and often painful hours of practice. Fingers that are blistered and bleeding are forgotten as they struggle to perfect each passage of long difficult programs. It is a life-style of constant sacrifice. One of my students who won an important contest, stayed up all night practicing before the final stage. But, she won!

Jesus' disciples, James and John, wanted to have the glory and honor they felt they deserved as followers of Jesus. He asked if they were ready to share in his suffering, the bitter cup of crucifixion which lay ahead. And when they agreed, Jesus said "you will drink the cup I drink." They would die as martyrs because they were His disciples. And they were to live lives of service, servants to all.

*Dear Father, Help me to understand that everyday you give me opportunities to serve others, to put aside my selfish desires, and be a servant. In Jesus' name, Amen.*

# September 16

*Isaiah 40:12: Who has measured the waters in the hollow of His hand, or will the breadth of His hand marked off the heavens? Who has held the dust of the earth in a basket, or weighed the mountains on the scales and the hills in a balance?*

God created us, God loves us and God helps us. These are three great truths by which we can confidently live.

The creator of the vast universe with its ocean depths, mountains and millions of stars in the heavens, also created the smallest forms of life—the acorn and the tiny ladybug, and us.

The wonderful spiritual, "His eye is on the sparrow, and I know He watches me," is such a meaningful and comforting song. Not a bird falls to the ground without His knowledge. This is the confidence that we have in Him. He cares for each of His creatures, we are precious to Him and He loves us with an unending love. His love is not dependent on our daily circumstances, it is constant.

We are not moving haphazardly at random through our lives. He has a plan for each of us. When we commit our lives to Christ, His Holy Spirit abides in us to guide and direct us in His ways. We have free will though, for He did not create us to be robots. Therefore, each one of us needs to come to Him, by choice. The most important choice of our lives.

*Dear Father, I worship you and honor you and praise you, my God and my Savior. In Jesus' name, Amen.*

# September 17

*Mark 10:43-45: Whomever will be great among you shall be your minister: and whomever of you will be chief, shall be servant to all. For even the Son of Man came not to be ministered to, but to minister, and to give his life a ransom for many.*

We can bring a servant's hearts to every aspect of our lives. If we do our work with an eye and an ear open to others' sorrows and needs, our work can become holy work and we can be used to comfort others and serve others.

I see every lesson I teach as an opportunity to be a positive influence in that student's life. I love to encourage them and to help them. It is a joy and a privilege.

I have an elderly friend who is in a nursing home, bedridden. Although her eye-sight is poor, even in this situation she still writes such sweet notes and letters to her friends and family. Writing is her special gift and she uses it even in her reduced living arrangement.

God has given us each unique gifts and He wants us to use them to serve others! Jesus gave His life for our salvation. He is our model as we seek to serve Him and all whom we meet.

*Dear Father, I pray that you will give me more opportunities to be of service to others. In Jesus' name, Amen.*

# September 18

*Psalm 25:10: All the paths of the Lord are mercy and truth unto such as keep His covenant and His testimonies.*

What incredible peace there is in knowing that we are placed where God wants us to be, walking in the paths He has set before us. What misery and absolute despair we experience when we do not have this peace. When you know in your heart that you are not where God wants you to be, nor doing the work He would have you do, that is truly torturous. There is no peace for the believer apart from being in God's will.

I believe God truly moved me to teach in Indiana. He opened every door and I felt it was absolutely His will that I move there. It was amazing to me that both my earthly father, my Dad, and my heavenly Father, both wanted me there.

Although we can all stumble and lose our way, this Psalm says <u>all</u> our paths will be under the umbrella of God's mercy and truth. If we truly belong to Him and obey His word, He forgives us our transgressions and mistakes, and gently guides us back to His chosen path for each one of us. Psalm 103 says "As far as the east is from the west, so far has He removed our transgressions from us. As a father has compassion on his children, so the Lord has compassion on those who fear Him."

*Dear Father, Thank you for your mercy and compassion. Help me to live in obedience to your truth as I study and spend time in your word. In Jesus' name, Amen.*

# September 19

*Jeremiah 42:2-3: Pray for us unto the Lord thy God...that the Lord thy God may show us the way wherein we may walk, and the thing that we may do.*

*Job 34:32: That which I see not, teach Thou me.*

I believe, with all my heart, that if we ask God for guidance in complete sincerity that He will show us the way we should go, and what we should do. God hears our prayers, and while we probably will not hear aloud an actual voice telling us what to do, He will make it clear in many other ways: sometimes by planting an idea in our minds during a time of prayer; sometimes by having a godly friend suggest a course of action; sometimes by arranging circumstances and opening doors in an amazing way. If we are seeking answers and open to His leading, we will know.  As I wrote yesterday, I am convinced and sure that God placed me in Indiana and intended for me to teach here and I absolutely felt his clear leading and direction.

I think we should remember that God is our loving Father and wants more for us than we can hope or imagine. "What human father, when a child asks for bread, gives him a stone?" How much more our heavenly Father seeks to care for us.

He wants to teach us and to show us His way. We need only to ask Him. Too often we blunder along, trying to go it alone. He is waiting for us to reach out to Him, always.

*Dear Father, Thank you for patiently showing us and teaching us. In Jesus' name, Amen.*

# September 20

*Psalm 31:20: Thou shalt hide them in the secret of thy presence from the pride of men: Thou shalt keep them secretly in a pavilion from the strife of tongues.*

It is true that as we are walking "with the Lord," that is, striving to live a holy life, He will protect us from the evil of gossip and the pride of man. I like the imagery of this verse, picturing a private wall around us where He keeps us safe from the daggers of tongues, of words that destroy or cut us down. Not that we are not aware of cruel words that may be said about us, but the hurtful words are deflected by the humility and gentleness of spirit in our secret place, under the wings of the Almighty.

Just as in performances, after a missed note or pedal, I urge my students to focus even more intensely on the passage that follows, feeling the music flow on, maintaining their equilibrium, not allowing themselves to be distracted. So it is with us. When hurts assail us, we can take refuge in the positive steps we live by —peace, love, gentleness, forgiveness, humility and kindness. Theses are our stepping stones towards a holy life.

*Dear Father, Thank you for showing us the way to live peaceful and joyful lives. Help us to share your love with others, who may not know you. In Jesus' name, Amen.*

# September 21

*Psalm 26:7: How excellent is Thy loving-kindness, O God! Therefore the children of me put their trust under the shadow of Thy wings.*

*Deuteronomy 33:27: The eternal God is thy refuge, and underneath are the everlasting arms.*

I drove to Chicago yesterday with a friend who is giving two recitals this weekend. We set out in light rain which soon became a downpour. We had to pull over for quite awhile and wait for the blinding rain to abate. It seemed impossible to go on.

Finally as we continued on our way, the worst of the storm seemed to pass over. My friend called her office and was told that tornadoes had touched down all around Bloomington and Indianapolis. In fact, had we left one hour later we would have been in the midst of the strong tornadoes.

We prayed before leaving for God's protection. Surely He protected us and spared us yesterday. His everlasting arms are always beneath us! As we drove home a few days later we were astonished by the terrible damage on our route, huge trees uprooted and homes destroyed.

And today, when I opened wide the drapes, His heavenly sunshine lit up the room. What a blessing to be safe at home.

*Dear Father, Thank you God for bringing us safely through yesterday's storm. I know that in the same way, you bring us through all of life's storms and trials. Thank you for your faithfulness, new every morning. In Jesus' name, Amen.*

# September 22

*Deuteronomy 30:14: The word is very nigh unto thee, in thy mouth, and in thy heart, that thou mayest do it.*

Just as we spend many hours a week on our physical well-being, so we should invest even more time on our spiritual growth. God desires our fellowship and quiet conversation with Him in the same way that I must spend many hours every day practicing for a recital.

We would not attempt to run a ten-mile race without months of daily training and preparation in the same way. Before we can aspire to true growth and spiritual depth, we need to be immersed in scripture. We need to be attuned to what God has already said in the Bible. We need to know what is meant by obedience to Him. We need to carry His spirit deep in our hearts and minds. Then we can aspire to Holy Communion with our Lord and our Savior.

I want to be a mature Christian. I want to be able to always explain clearly to others the reason for my faith. And I hope that people who know me can tell that I am a follower of Jesus Christ by my life and my countenance.

*Dear Father, Thy word have I hid in my heart, that I might not sin against thee. This is my prayer. In Jesus' name, Amen.*

# September 23

*Psalm 25:4: Show me Thy ways, O Lord; teach me Thy path.*

As we drove home last night after my friend's recital in Illinois, we were both amazed to see the moon, a deep orange in color, almost sitting on the horizon. It was amazingly low and seemed much larger that we had ever seen. Yet as we continued driving, it kept changing, and after two hours it went back to its usual color and rose high in the sky.

I was humbled as I was made aware of my ignorance about the moon, and what made for that special circumstance? Why so low, why so orange?

I am grateful that God answers our questions about His ways and shows us His path in the Bible. I imagine any good scientist could suggest a book explaining the moon's ways and answering my questions.

In the same way, the Bible teaches us about God. It clearly tells us that He sent His Son, Jesus Christ, to die for our sins. All we are asked to do is believe in Him and follow Him.

*Dear Father, Thank you for your word and for the freedom to study it. In Jesus' name, Amen.*

# September 24

*Psalm 139:18: When I awake, I am still with Thee.*

I wish I could wake up every morning like my little toy poodle, Baby. He is so happy in the morning, wagging his tail and eager to start the day. If a dog could smile, he does.

There are some days when it is hard to get up. Usually that is when there are difficult meetings or hard problems to face. But every day should begin with thanks to our heavenly Father, in gratitude for the blessings of sleep and rest, and appreciation for the new day ahead.

Our attitude upon awakening can set the tone for the whole day. One of my greatest joys is the wonder and peace of what I term a normal day. That is a day at home, with my usual afternoon lessons, morning practice, simple chores, meals to prepare and the comfortableness of being where God has placed me. Those days are like slipping into a pair of old soft shoes! I think, all too often, we take such days for granted, instead of savoring them.

*Dear Father, Thank you for the gift of this normal day. In Jesus' name, Amen.*

# September 25

*Deuteronomy 12:7: You shall rejoice in all that you set your hand to, you and your households, wherein the Lord your God has blessed you.*

How easy it is for us sometimes to take God's great blessings for granted. This is specially true when we are preoccupied with problems or work that absorbs our time and energies.

Our work too is such a blessing. In these days of so many serious lay-offs of workers and real economic uncertainty, just having work is a great good fortune, let alone work that one loves. A neighbor told me last evening that most American people have lost one-third of their savings this year, in the stock market. If we put our faith in our financial security, it may be a very fragile and shaky foundation.

One of my South American students told me of her parents' situation. They are living in a "cashless" society. They have enough to eat only by exchanging services, and getting the reward of some kind of coupons for work. But as she said, although their savings were wiped out, they have bread on the table, and most of all their loving family. What courage!

The blessings of God are love, joy, peace, kindness, gentleness and patience. These can never be taken away, regardless of the economy.

*Dear Father, Thank you for all the gifts, big and little that you give us. In Jesus' name, Amen.*

# September 26

*Psalm 23:4: Yea, though I walk through the valley of the shadow of death, I will fear no evil: for Thou art with me; thy rod and thy staff they comfort me.*

In reading the Psalms I often forget that David too was a harpist. Because of his outstanding talent, King Saul selected him, while still a boy, to come to the palace and play for him. The harp can be very soothing and beneficial to people who are suffering.

I was so touched to hear from a friend last night that she had taken one of my harp and organ CD's to the hospital where her sister-in-law lay dying. She said for two weeks they played it every day, and that it was all her sister-in-law wanted to hear. And before she passed away, she and her son came to know and to love Jesus Christ.

Many of my students take their small harps into cancer wards and play for the patients. It always seems to ease their suffering.

Christianity is the only faith that gives hope to the dying. In good times and in hard times, we depend only on our relationship to Jesus Christ.

*Dear Father, I trust you alone in the valleys and on the mountain top experiences of life. Thank you for never leaving me. In Jesus' name, Amen.*

# September 27

*Micah 7:8: When I sit in darkness, the Lord shall be a light to me.*

*Psalm 4:6: There be many that say, who shall show us any good? Lord, lift thou up the light of Thy countenance upon us.*

Yesterday, one of my dear students appeared troubled when she came in for her lesson. When I asked what was the matter, she broke into tears. One of her closest friends, a fine violinist, had been killed in a bicycle accident. As I tried to comfort her and share in her pain, I realized the fragility of our life here. We get up each morning never knowing what the day will bring, or even if it could be our last. For my student and her friends it was so hard to lose this wonderful violinist so suddenly.

We are truly "in the dark" about our earthly destiny. But to those of us who believe in Jesus Christ, we can have the blessed assurance of our eternal destiny. He who said "I am the Light of the World" is our light, our hope and our redeemer.

No matter how wonderfully blessed our earthly lives may be, the future spent in the presence of Christ is far better than anything we can imagine. So, although we may grieve and miss those we love who leave us, we can know that they are in a far better place.

*Dear Father, I pray for your loving comfort to be with the grieving students today, who have lost their friend. In Jesus' name, Amen.*

# September 28

*I John 3:18: My little children, let us not love in word, neither in tongue; but in deed, and in truth.*

*James 1:22: But be ye doers of the word, and not hearers only, deceiving your own selves.*

How easy it is to sit in an armchair and write about love – loving our neighbors as ourselves, doing unto others as we would have others do unto us. But it is another matter altogether to roll up one's sleeves and go out and truly help someone in need.

I had a meeting yesterday morning with university department chairs, which included a panel discussion about time management. It was apparent that we all share the problem of being overwhelmed by work, and that if we are to have leisure time at all, it too must be blocked out and scheduled.

Setting priorities and "To Do" lists were also recommended. Because our work lives are so intense, it was suggested we schedule first our times of relaxation and family times, then fill in the necessary work. I think we also need to schedule those times to call on shut-ins or write caring letters, or those loving activities will also be pushed aside by the ever-present pressures of work. It is hard to make wise use of our time. We need times of relaxation too. Unless we remain healthy in mind, body and spirit, we cannot be much help to others as teachers.

*Dear Father, Help me to better manage my time, so that I can "love in deed," and be a doer, not a hearer only! In Jesus' name, Amen.*

# September 29

*Matthew 5.8: Blessed are the pure in heart, for they shall see God.*

*Hebrews 12.14: Follow peace with all men and holiness, without which no man shall see the Lord.*

We have an awesome responsibility to be peacemakers, whether in our personal lives, our professional lives or as Americans. We must always try to follow and pursue peace with all men. We must always try to be part of the solution, not part of the problem.

Instead of reacting with anger or impatience, we must try to step back and try to defuse volatile situations. "A soft answer turns away wrath..." When we fail to respond gently, how badly we feel. And when we do manage to respond kindly, what a blessed feeling we can have, our hearts can truly feel lifted up.

What a great goal it would be, to have the innocence of a little child, seeing the good in others, and always hopeful and expectant of a happy outcome. We see good in others as we see others as being God's children and our neighbors.

*Dear Father: Help me to be a peacemaker today in every situation I encounter. In Jesus' name, Amen.*

# September 30

*Psalms 15.1, 2: Lord, who shall abide in Thy tabernacle? Who shall dwell in Thy holy hill? He that walketh uprightly and worketh righteousness, and speaketh the truth in his heart.*

How important it is for each of us to tell the truth, to simply be honest. We need to be honest not only to others, but also to ourselves. Sometimes we need to take an inventory of our life, what we are doing, and where we are going, and for how long? Is it possible that we are going frantically, full speed ahead, in the wrong direction for the wrong reasons? Have we set goals that are no longer valid or reasonable at this time in our lives? Are there different goals that may be more appropriate for us?

Truth, in the sense of taking an honest, hard look at ourselves, is necessary. God wants us to speak the truth, to live the truth, to know the truth——and then to walk in goodness and work in righteousness. He will guide us and help us to know ourselves if we commit each day to Him for His guidance and His truth. "And you shall know the truth and the truth shall make you free." John 8.32.

One of my goals has always been to draw closer to God so I don't become increasingly attached to the material world. It has been said that this life is just a preparation for the next, eternity. As we grow in depth in our spiritual lives, this should be a natural process..

*Dear Lord: I pray that you will help me understand my priorities, less attachment to things, and more wisdom in knowing your truth, In Jesus' name, Amen.*

# OCTOBER

## October 1

*Haggai 2.4: Be strong, all ye people of the land, says the Lord, and work; for I am with you.*

The Bible has many references to work. "If a man will not work, he shall not eat, respect those who work hard, be happy in his work, work as for the Lord, not for men."

Clearly work was important to God then, and it is today. I was touched to read in my church bulletin of several couples who, after they retired, went to seminary to train for Christian work. Instead of living a life of ease upon retirement, they chose to keep working, doing the Lord's work, in their case, to become missionaries.

We often are defined by our work, our self-respect dependent on it. Often people who retire are unhappy and lose their sense of self-worth.

The key is learning that whatever we do, we should do it as unto the Lord. He will direct our steps and our stops. He is the giver of all good gifts, including work. And He will equip us, give us strength, for the work He would have us do.

*Dear Father God: Thank you for giving us meaningful work. In Jesus' name, Amen.*

# October 2

*Psalms 19.3: I am resolved that my mouth shall not sin. (NIV)*

*Proverbs 10.9: When words are many, sin is not absent, but he who holds his tongue is wise.*

How easily we can fail in our resolutions not to enter into gossip or idle speculation or participate in criticism of our absent friend. We know what we should not do or say. "If you are talking about someone not present, say nothing that you would not say if that person were there."

Beyond that kind of talk, there is the failure to listen. I can easily get carried away recounting an experience and telling too much out of eagerness to share.

I remember my father telling us, when he was in law school he seldom spoke up in class. He said he was somewhat intimidated by those who were always zealous to talk. But it was Dad who had the highest grades, because he <u>listened</u> more than he spoke.

Silence is golden, especially when we cultivate quiet time with our Lord in prayer and meditation on His Word.

*Dear Father: Thy word have I hid in my heart, that I might not sin against Thee. In Christ's name, Amen.*

# October 3

*Matthew 7.1: Judge not, that ye be not judged.*

*Luke 6.41: Why do you look at the speck of sawdust in your brother's eye, and pay no attention to the plank in your own eye? (NIV)*

I get disgusted with myself for too easily finding fault. It is no excuse, but perhaps somewhat explained, by my having a perfectionist nature. I am surely a Type-A person, always trying to do more than can comfortably be done. My work as an artist-teacher requires a high standard of criticism although, hopefully, it is done with love and genuine caring for the student's best.

My work demands that I seek the highest possible standard for myself and my own playing, as well as for my students. This seems an integral part of my teaching and as such is acceptable. But when I try to impose my standards on others in areas that are not comfortable for them I can too easily hurt feelings or trample on another's pace of living. For example, I can want to have dishes washed and put away in a deep-seated need for order. Or, I can push a student to play a passage faster than is comfortable for them technically.

*Dear Father: My hope and prayer is that you excuse and forgive my all too human mistakes in these areas of living, and teach me to have patience and forgiveness for the weaknesses of others. I ask it in Christ's name, Amen.*

# October 4

*John 1.9: Be strong and of good courage; be not afraid, neither be thou dismayed: for the Lord thy God is with thee whithersoever thou goest.*

Because of a marked shortness of breath, I finally saw my doctor last week. She ordered all sorts of stress tests, pulmonary functions, X-rays and blood-work, which I had done yesterday. While everything apparently seemed fairly OK, I will only know the whole results in two weeks when I see my doctor again.

While I am trying not to be anxious, I do feel some fear. I have been blessed these many years with such good health. God has so wonderfully given me the needed strength and energy to be able to continue working. I must face the possibility of having my health inevitably go downhill. It is a hard thing to accept.

I know God will ordain each step and each change. So, I do not fear the future, for it is in His loving hands and I trust him.

*Dear Lord: I know that you never give us more than we can bear. Grant us the courage to accept whatever comes from your will for our lives on earth, and prepare us for eternity with you. In Jesus' name, Amen.*

# October 5

*Isaiah 35.4: Say to them that are of a fearful heart, be strong, fear not.*

God does not want us to fret about the future, a future which may not even be ours to experience. Our days are numbered and are in His hands.

God loves us and wants the best for us. My pastor spoke today about whether God wants happiness for us. While acknowledging that God does take pleasure in His people being happy – He made it clear that God most of all wants us to pursue holiness. Then perhaps happiness, like a butterfly, may alight on our shoulders!

Our culture encourages us to place such a high value on happiness. We think that this car or that dress or this job will make us happy – while none of these can really satisfy.

The only true, deep joy we can experience is in an abiding knowledge and relationship with Jesus Christ. He alone can bring us all we ever need of happiness; Jesus is all we need. The more totally we give ourselves to Him, the less fears and anxiety will have a place in our lives.

*Dear Father: We are strong in the knowledge of your love and we can live, free of fear, through Jesus Christ, our Lord - in whose name we pray, Amen.*

# October 6

*Psalm 27.13: I had fainted, unless I had believed to see the goodness of the Lord in the land of the living.*

*Genesis 32.12: I will surely do thee good.*

Today is Monday, the beginning of a new work week. As my mind touched on all I had to do today, I felt some unease.

After breakfast, I did my Bible reading and read about the goodness of the Lord. I breathed a sigh of relief. God will be with me today as He is every day, workdays or weekends.

And He will "do me good!" What a comfort to know the goodness of the Lord. We do not face life's pressures and difficulties alone. We have God's assurances and promises to sustain us and encourage us. We can face each new day with equanimity and peace, knowing His goodness surrounds us in all our circumstances.

*Dear Father: Thank you for your goodness and your faithfulness, which is new every morning. In Jesus' name, Amen.*

# October 7

*Galatians 4.6: And because you are sons, God has sent the spirit of His Son into your hearts, crying Abba, Father.*

It is a precious privilege to be able to call God, the Creator of the universe, Father, our Father. I am so thankful that in every circumstance I can turn to Him.

I can ask Him to forgive my sinful nature and to forgive each specific sin.

I can thank Him, day by day, for all His gifts to me and His mercy to me.

I can ask Him for patience to accept and submit to life's frustrations and difficulties.

I can seek His wisdom as I face problems too hard for me to solve.

I can ask Him to show me His will for my life, in specific situations and in the larger scheme.

Moment by moment, hour by hour, He is always present.

*The great hymn says it best: "Praise God from whom all blessings flow, praise God all creatures here below." In Jesus' name, Amen.*

# October 8

*Isaiah 12.12: Ye shall not go out with haste, for the Lord will go before you; and the God of Israel will be your reward.*

*Isaiah 28.16: He that believes shall not make haste.*

I am prone to setting goals for myself that are impossible to accomplish in the given time. Then I find myself rushing hither and yon, almost running through the house trying to tune a harp between waiting for my computer to bring up new e-mail. Then loading laundry between dressing for school. And heaven forbid that somebody phones me and puts even greater stress on my hurried time.

I read last week that we should never plan to do more than we can do with a calm and tranquil spirit. And today's scripture surely tells us that God does not want us to hurry. He wants souls at peace and one with Him, sensitive to His still, small voice, whispering words of encouragement and love. How can we hear Him when we live in turmoil, not to mention anxiety?

*Dear Father: Help me this day to remember to slow down, to be quiet and to draw from your deep and unfathomable peace and strength. In Christ's name, Amen.*

# October 9

*Joshua 24.15: As for me and my house, we will serve the Lord.*

As I approach the one year anniversary of my house burning, I give a lot of thought to my life and my future in my new house. I was very thankful to God for my old house, and I am very thankful to Him for the new house.

I have so often pondered why the house burned. I was holding Bible studies there, and using my time and energies to write this devotional book. I felt like I was serving the Lord there.

Now as I walk through the new house, I pray that God will use it for good. I know that I will serve the Lord with all my heart in my new abode as in the last.

I will have more space for guests, so I will try to live a life of greater hospitality, opening my home and life to others in a way I could not in my old house.

*Dear Father: We know that our houses are only our outer shell. It is the hearts that abide in them that count. May our hearts serve you and honor you at all times and in every place. In Christ's name, Amen.*

# October 10

*II Thessalonians 3.11: Now the Lord of peace Himself give you peace always, by all means.*

*Psalm 29.11: The Lord will bless His people with peace.*

I laid awake much of the night last night. I felt too tired to sleep, a strange and uncomfortable feeling to have when one is exhausted. But I was glad to have that time alone and silent to pray. I felt almost too tired to pray very coherently, but I just felt I was abiding in God, in his presence.

I had had three highly stressful days this week, necessitating long conference calls each evening on top of long work days. But I was so thankful to God for the resolution and peaceful outcome of the problem which was very serious.

Throughout the crisis though, I did feel God's wonderful, marvelous sense of peace inside, and I felt His wisdom speaking to me, helping smooth out and disperse the tensions that had arisen. I truly felt His Holy hand in mine.

*Dear Father: You do give us your peace, always, in all circumstances and by all means. Thank you Lord, in Christ's name, Amen.*

# October 11

*Numbers 11.1: And when the people complained, it displeased the Lord.*

It is so easy to complain, and when we do, I doubt that we ever think that our complaints are displeasing to God. If we did, we would instantly stop it!

From disparaging remarks about the weather to common complaints about physical ailments, our days can easily be filled with negativity.

Besides displeasing God, do we realize how our routine complaints can darken or shadow the lives of those around us? We become discouragers rather than up-lifters!

What a difference to be around someone who sees the glass half-full rather than half-empty! One person, with a happy smile and cheerful demeanor, can lighten the spirits of an entire roomful of people. Proverbs says "a happy heart makes the face cheerful" and "a cheerful look brings joy to the heart."

Are we spreading joy or are we creating depression and gloom?

*Dear Father: Help us today to be dispellers of gloom, and dispensers of cheer. In Christ's name, Amen.*

# October 12

*Ephesians 5.19: Singing and making melody in your heart to the Lord.*

*I Peter 3.15: Sanctify the Lord God in your hearts.*

I don't have a good voice and never received any training in singing. But I do love to sing, and often, while taking my daily walk, I have a song in my head and my heart. One of my favorites is "Oh What a Beautiful Morning." Once started, it is hard to stop. I deeply feel God's blessings as I sing and walk through the neighborhood, and I feel very thankful for His beauty in nature. Another favorite is "Only God can make a flower, only God can make a tree."

I notice that I sing more on bright sunny days with blue skies. It is harder when clouds fill the sky and rainy weather is coming.

Perhaps on cloudy days, I am more dependent on God, needing His joy, peace and strength to give me courage. Certainly weather should not determine the state of my heart. Rather it should be God in my heart that governs each and every day, and I pray that He will use me whatever the outside climate.

*Dear Lord: You are my sunshine and my song. Thank you Lord for loving me in every circumstance. In Jesus' name, Amen.*

# October 13

*Hebrews 6.11: We want each of you to show this same diligence to the very end, in order to make your hope sure. (NN)*

*II Thessalonians 3.3: But the Lord is faithful, and He will strengthen and protect you from evil. (NIV)*

God has promised to give us the strength to do the work He sets before us. He wants us to see through our duties and commitments.

I notice what a difference it makes when, before going to sleep, I check the next day's activities and prioritize what I need to do and when I will do it. Such a small thing can make a world of difference in not being caught off-guard with unexpected duties. Planning ahead can make for a much more peaceful and organized life.

In addition, when each day starts and ends in the Lord's presence, by prayer and reading scripture, we can know that wonderful "peace that transcends understanding." We can go to sleep and get up each day with hope in our hearts and trust in the Lord's protection.

*Dear Father: Thank you for the hope and protection you give us each day. Help us to do gracefully the tasks you set before us. In Jesus' name, Amen.*

# October 14

*Proverbs 8:32-36: Now therefore hearken unto me, O ye children: for blessed are they that keep my ways. Hear instruction and be wise, and refuse it not. Blessed is the man that heareth me, watching daily at my gates, waiting at the posts of my doors. For whoso findeth me findeth life, and shall obtain favour of the Lord. But he that sinneth against me wrongeth his own soul: all who hate me love death.*

*Romans 6.22-23: But now that you have been set free from sin and have become slaves of God, the benefit you reap leads to holiness, and the result is eternal life. For the wages of sin is death, but the gift of God is eternal life in Christ Jesus our Lord.*

Today I woke to gray, rain-filled skies and a change to cold weather signaling the end of warm fall days. Then I had an unsettling discussion with a friend which made the already gray day still darker and bleaker.

It is hard to pray and to write this devotion. But Lord, I know you are near during the gray days exactly the same as during sunny days.

I know that sin can so easily ensnare us and we can feel deep discouragement and a sense of failure. But the gift of God is eternal life, and hope. I need your wisdom when feeling so low. I know your love is always with me, giving me life and renewing my strength and courage.

*Dear Lord: We need the light of your love and peace during the dark times in our lives. Thank you for your faithfulness. In Christ's name, Amen.*

# October 15

*Psalm 40. 12-13: My sins have overtaken me, and I cannot see. My heart fails within me. Be pleased, O Lord, to save me: O Lord come quickly to help me. (NIV)*

*Psalm 40.1: I waited patiently for the Lord; and he inclined unto me and heard my cry.*

*Romans 6.14: For sin shall not be your master, because you are not under law, but under grace.*

At a gathering of prominent church clergy, in response to a question from the audience asking about how they personally refreshed their faith, they were all unanimous in replying, "we read several Psalms every day." In the Psalms, it is true, all of life is experienced, and the emotions the Psalm writers experienced speak to us in the same way today. The Psalmists' faith speaks to our hearts as we struggle against our own sins, grief and heartaches.

Just as the Psalmist cried for God to save him, we too need God's saving grace and power to overcome our sins, to change our ways, and to live victorious lives – outside our own selfish needs and ways.

I too have so often found great comfort in reading the Psalms, there are so many favorite verses that speak to me, Psalm 40 is one.

Jesus, by His atoning death, has freed us forever from weight of our sinful natures, and His grace permits us to live in freedom and forgiveness.

*Dear Father: Thank you for Jesus and for the forgiveness of our sins. We know, Lord, that we need your love and courage every day to protect us from ourselves. In Jesus' name, Amen.*

# October 16, 2003

*Genesis 32.10: I am not worthy of the least of all the mercies, and of all the truth, which Thou hast showed unto Thy servant.*

*Deuteronomy 33.37: The eternal God is thy refuge and underneath are the everlasting arms.*

We so often take for granted God's many mercies toward us. Then when the least problem or grief arrives, we want explanations. We take our happiness for granted, as though we have a right to it. Most of us in America live in comparative ease and comfort

People who live in chronic pain and suffering take their condition for granted and are thankful for the least easing of their suffering and count their blessings daily.

This morning got off to a hard start, with the phone ringing, the puppy crying and making a mess in the living-room, and I awoke with a nagging headache!

As I read this verse, I feel ashamed to have felt frustrated by such trivial matters. I feel God's love all around me, and I know He will make this a fine day, bright with promise and hope.

*Dear Lord: We are unworthy of all your wonderful blessings and opportunities. We thank you. In Jesus' name, Amen.*

# October 17

*I Samuel 15.22: Does the Lord delight in burnt offerings and sacrifices as much as in obeying the voice of the Lord? To obey is better than sacrifice. (NIV)*

*Exodus 14.13: Do not be afraid. Stand firm and you will see the deliverance the Lord will bring you today.*

Yesterday, one of my dearest students cried in her lesson. She has not won a contest, ever, though her playing is excellent. This fact had discouraged her greatly, but after calling her mother overseas, she went to a Christian bookstore and found some encouraging books. I comforted her during her lesson, and hope I was able to encourage her. We both feel sure God will use this disappointment for good. He has promised to be very near the broken-hearted. And instead of wallowing in self-pity, she turned to Him in perfect trust.

Godliness is the devotion of the soul to God. It is not simply doing things, even good things, or taking on additional duties. It is living in the presence of God, talking to Him and listening to Him. From this closeness comes the desire to hear Him and to obey His leading.

We have constant access to God, wherever we are or whatever we are doing. In addition, He speaks to us through the Bible, by the gift of the Holy Spirit abiding in us, and also through wise and loving Christian friends. We are not left in the dark to flounder helplessly, unsure of the path God would have us take.

*Dear Lord: Thank you for your faithfulness and for your Word. In Jesus' name, Amen.*

# October 18

*Matthew 5.20: Unless your righteousness exceeds that of the scribes and Pharisees, you will certainly not enter the kingdom of heaven.*

I believe God knows and blesses every effort we make to obey Him and to sincerely and diligently seek to do His will. He knows our hearts, and He also knows our frailties. When we fall short of attaining perfection,, which we will always do, we must confess it, not dwell on it, and resolutely strive to do better.

I think pride and hypocrisy were the faults that bothered Jesus the most in the lives of the scribes and Pharisees of His day, and I am sure when we exhibit those traits, they still bother Him today.

He is very near the humble and those with a contrite heart. When we acknowledge our weaknesses and give them to Him, we can be assured of His forgiveness and His gift of peace. While we will never reach perfection in this life, we will know it when we joyfully meet our Lord in heaven.

*Dear Father: Forgive us when we stumble. Grant us pure hearts and humility. In Jesus' name, Amen.*

# October 19

*Isaiah 48.17: This is what the Lord says – your Redeemer, the Holy One of Israel: I am the Lord your God, who teaches you what is best for you, who directs you in the way you should go. (NIV)*

There is such true, deep, blessed peace in knowing that you are where God wants you to be, doing what He has given you as a vocation.

I know many people who are drifting through life in a way, not sure what they should do or where they ought to be. Some of my students have been unsure if a career with the harp is right for them, or whether they should try another field even as protection if they are not able to get work after finishing school.

In such circumstances it seems we should do nothing, but simply wait for God's firm direction. If He wants us to wait, He will be responsible for our circumstances during the interim. When we trust Him for direction, He will not fail to provide it – but it will be in His perfect timing.

And it may well be that while we wait, He will teach us valuable lessons in patience, endurance, dependence on Him, humility and courage. For sure, we may be able to develop a suppleness of character and freedom from rigidity of our actions as we see ourselves as "on hold" by the Lord. He is always worth the wait, whether it be months or years.

*Dear Lord, our God: Thank you for caring about the details of our lives and for constant guidance. In Jesus' name, Amen.*

# October 20

*Romans 12.21: Be not overcome of evil, but overcome evil with good.*

When we are treated cruelly or unjustly, it is so easy for us to want to get even or retaliate. But the Bible and Jesus' teachings say the opposite is the way we ought to live. We are not only to "turn the other cheek," we are to actively pray for those who hurt us, and to try to be helpful and kind to them.

When I first returned to America after studying in France, I found it very hard to readjust to American ways. It was especially hard and discouraging for me to feel there wasn't a place for me in the harp world. All the teaching positions were filled, it seemed, and concert managers were very reluctant to engage a concert harpist. The field was not held in high regard at that time, or so I was told by many of them.

So, I struggled with discouragement. I felt misunderstood and unappreciated. We can combat such thoughts by prayer, and by focusing on things above. If our minds are stayed on God, on scripture, on good and pure things, we can overcome our own pessimistic tendencies. We all are sinners, falling so far short of imitating Christ. But to be focused on Him is to be our goal; He is our role model. He, who was without sin, paid for our sins and the sins of all mankind, so that we may be reconciled to a Holy God. Only Jesus can truly change our shortcomings and turn them to good!

*Dear Father: We thank you and praise you for your son, our Lord and Savior Jesus Christ. In His name, Amen.*

# October 21

*Genesis 17.1: I am the Almighty God; walk before Me, and be thou perfect.*

*Exodus 32.29: Consecrate yourselves today to the Lord.*

How right it feels to spend time in prayer and Bible study before launching into a new day. Yesterday, due to an unexpected emergency and some hard and difficult phone calls, I had to leave my devotions and I felt off-base all day because of it.

Today, I am back on track, and I am doubly grateful for this quiet time with the Lord. The weight of the world is so often heavy, I know I feel deeply the need for even more time spent in prayer to be a counter-balance to the pulls and cares of the outer world.

If we are to be a light to others, we need to drink deeply from God's Word, so that we will have the right words to comfort a hurting student, or to encourage a friend who is depressed, or even to be patient when confronted by anger. Our faith, to be living and active, needs constant nourishment from the Bible and time alone with our God.

*Dear Father: We consecrate this day to Thee. In Jesus' name, Amen.*

# October 22

*Luke 22.42: Father, if Thou be willing, remove this cup from me; nevertheless, not my will, but Thine, be done.*

*1 Thessalonians 5.16-17: Let the word of Christ dwell in you richly in all wisdom; teaching and admonishing one another in psalms and hymns and spiritual songs, singing with grace in your hearts to the Lord. And whatsoever ye do in word or deed, do all in the name of the Lord Jesus, giving thanks to God and the Father by him.*

Just now I have had to face up to some considerable delays about the house, and perhaps give up having green grass over an acre of brown dirt and mud until next spring. I am swallowing hard, and today must accept this and other delays like a good soldier. I must bury my will in God's will. This lesson will help so much and give me perspective about these momentary trials!

When we face hard situations, we must totally commit the outcome to God. Our will must be lost in His. As Christ prayed this prayer in the garden of Gethsemane, knowing the future held crucifixion, shame and humiliation, and the agony of the cross, even He asked if God would lift this decision. But He obeyed and "took the cup" his Father ordained for Him. And before His accusers, He stood silent.

We anguish over matters large and small, and we try to wiggle out of hard places and trials. And when events do not go as we hoped, we often complain bitterly and bemoan the outcome. Instead we should give thanks, in every situation, knowing it is God's will for us that the time.

*Dear Father: Thy will be done today and everyday of our lives. In Jesus' name, Amen.*

# October 23

*Psalm 143.10: Teach us to do Thy will; for Thou art my God: Thy spirit is good; lead me into the land of uprightness.*

In my prayer circle this week, we had a discussion of righteousness. It is used so frequently in the Bible to denote living a good, holy and godly life. In our society it is often derogatory, meaning a self-righteous and critical person.

Now this verse speaks of longing to be led into the "land of uprightness," which is similar, I think, to a land of goodness and godliness. It is sad to feel America is increasingly a country trying to remove influences like the Ten Commandments, and the words "under God" from the Pledge of Allegiance. Many churches refer to this period as post-Christian.

I think it is clear that to live a righteous and upright life, we need to acknowledge and give thanks and praise to God, our creator and creator of the universe. Then we must study His written word to be instructed how to do His will. The out-flowing of this will be a righteous life and ultimately, hopefully, an upright society.

*Dear Father: We pray for your blessing upon America. Lord, bless our lawmakers and justices and leaders as they choose ways that will honor or dishonor You. In Christ's name, Amen.*

# October 24

*Psalm 28.7: The Lord is my strength, and my shield; my heart trusted in Him and I am helped; therefore my heart greatly rejoices; and with my song I will praise Him.*

I have been so very tired this week. For perhaps the first time I have seriously asked myself if I should not keep working so hard, and consider retiring.

Although I love my teaching and the dear students, I am depleted when I can finally come home and rest.

The words, "The Lord is my strength," surely resonate in my soul. I do completely trust Him and totally rely on Him to be my strength. I am so thankful for all He has and is doing for me.

Yesterday a student cried as she recounted a terrible auto accident she had over the weekend; it left her car almost totaled, and with a large deductible to pay. She was so shaken and wondered to me how much more God would ask her to bear. She is a strong believer. I talked to her of His promises to restore what is taken from us.

Each one of us has special concerns and private griefs. If we bring them to Christ, He will renew our strength and protect us.

*Dear Lord: Thank you for the strength that you grant us every day. Help us to resolve to praise You every day for your great faithfulness. In Jesus' name, Amen.*

# October 25

*Romans 7.38-39: For I am persuaded that neither death, nor life, nor angels, nor principalities, nor powers, nor things present, nor things to come, nor height, nor depth, nor any other creature, shall be able to separate me from the love of God, which is in Christ Jesus, our Lord.*

I have been praying for it not to rain today. A bull-dozer is scheduled to grade my yard and spread top-soil so that it can be seeded and covered with hay. If it rains today, it may be too late to plant grass next week as cold weather sets in. I am so grateful that it is not raining yet this morning, and the work may go forward. I suppose in the greater scheme of things, this is a small matter, but it has become so important to me. I am so thankful that God's love encompasses even the smallest details of our lives, and I pray God will forgive me for attaching too much importance to something as mundane as a seeded yard!!

I wish I had thought of this verse to comfort my student yesterday after her car was wrecked. It is truly one of God's greatest encouragements and promises.

These words, which I have memorized several times, assure us that even in death, the love of God, through Christ, for us is with us. How much more His love will sustain us in our daily travails as we abide in Him.

*Dear Lord: Thank you for the incomparable gift of your love. In Jesus' name, Amen.*

# October 26

*Zechariah 9.12: Return to your fortress, prisoners of hope; even now I announce that I will restore twice as much to you.*

*Isaiah 30.7: Their strength is to sit still.*

We are so concerned with striving and doing and accomplishing. Even though we are facing hard assignments and worthwhile causes, God calls us to turn away from the world's pressures and wait upon Him.

I am almost always rushed and short of time in the morning. Of course, I can plan to pray and do my devotions later in the evening. But I have learned that taking time, early, for the Lord always pays rich dividends. I believe and have experienced that He does indeed double one's available time or allows me to achieve everything needed in half the time

I love to be still and experience His presence. As I commit the day ahead to His guidance, He fills me with peace and a sense of divine order. Spending time alone with our Lord is the best "investment" of time one can make. He is our strength and our hope for each new day.

*Dear Father: Thank you for listening to our prayers and for waiting for us to spend time with you. In Christ's name, Amen.*

# October 27

*II Corinthians 12.9-10: But He said to me, "My grace is sufficient for you, for my power is made perfect in weakness." Therefore I will boast all the more gladly about my weaknesses, so that Christ's power may rest on me. That is why, for Christ's sake, I delight in weaknesses, in insults, in hardships, in persecution, in difficulties. For when I am weak, then I am strong.*

When physical strength seems to falter, or problems weaken our inner strength to the point that we feel helpless and infirm, these verses are a great comfort. We can know that, when we are at the end of our spiritual and physical strength, God's almighty power is being perfected in us. He takes over and is best able to help us when we can no longer help ourselves.

It has been hard for me personally to realize that I don't have the same strength I used to have. Practicing takes more energy sometimes than I seem to have! It is humbling to not be able to do the things one once did so easily. In a way, the changes we experience in aging take a lot of courage.

If we truly learn this lesson, like Paul, we will be able to "delight" in hardships and difficulties that inevitably come into our lives. They will serve as lessons that may open us more fully to the grace and goodness and love of our great God and creator.

*Dear Lord: Thank you for the divine strength that you impart to us when we are weak. In Jesus' name, Amen.*

# October 28

*Jeremiah 29.11: For I know the plans I have for you, declares the Lord, plans to prosper you and not to harm you, plans to give you hope and a future.*

Whenever the immediate or long-term future looks bleak, we should hold tightly to these great promises of God. Even when we do not understand how good can come from a situation, we can know that God is working all things together for good. When our financial or work situations seem bleak, God is bringing about prosperity, when our relationships seem impossible and without hope, God is providing hope and with Him, all things are possible.

We should not cling to our ideas for they are possibly not God's will, for He knows the plan He has for us, and His plans will always be better than any we can even imagine. Certainly, before the fire happened, I expected to live the rest of my life in that house.

Yet, God has so richly blessed me in this new house, and provided for me in a way I could never have imagined. This has been an absolute revelation to me of His provision.

We can safely trust Him, and rest on His Word. Then His peace, which surpasses our understanding, will be ours.

*Dear Father: Thank you for your wise and loving plans for each one of us. In Jesus' name, Amen.*

# October 29

*Isaiah 48.10: See, I have refined you, though not as silver, I have tested you in the furnace of affliction.*

Affliction is never easy to bear, even when our faith is strong and we believe that God is refining us through our suffering and pain. If we bear the pain without complaining and allow God to work in our hearts, it changes us with our pride and our stubborn will, into someone malleable and useful to Him.

Sometimes nothing but tragedy and terrible affliction can get our mind off of our day-to-day self-absorption and turn our attention to our spiritual need of a Savior. In our pain we can hear His voice and as we lean on Him for comfort and solace, He becomes all we need. He wants us to be totally His, not just in church on Sundays, but in an intimate, close relationship. As my own physical strength seems to be waning, I find myself relying more and more on God's strength. When I find myself fretting about not being able to do something, I let it go and give it to Him to handle!

As we mature in our faith, we will see that He uses every circumstance of our lives to draw us to Himself. And we may even be able to count our afflictions as blessings from the hand of our loving Father.

*Dear Lord: Thank you for loving us and refining us in the furnace of afflictions. In Christ's name, Amen.*

# October 30

*II Timothy 1.14: Guard the good deposit that was entrusted to you – guard it with the help of the Holy Spirit who lives in us. (NIV)*

*The "good deposit" Paul refers to is "the pattern of sound teaching with faith and love in Christ Jesus" (verse 13).*

Would we not live and act differently if each day we were aware that we are the temple and abiding place of our Holy God? How important it is to remember that when we have accepted Christ as our Lord and Savior, His Holy Spirit lives in us, counsels us, comforts us and protects us.

Last night, in the space of one hour, I received two pieces of bad news, two blows, one after the other, involving students. I reeled with dismay and pain and also the awareness that I should not react to the events that were past and with which I had nothing to do, no action to take. After sleeping, I awoke with renewed pain – but quickly prayed about it and turned it over to God. I believe He does not want us to carry those burdens alone. He is always there to share our loads, and to help us face each day with His strength, wisdom and courage.

*Dear Lord: We pray that we may be acceptable vessels for your Holy Spirit and that You will help us guard preciously the sound teaching of our faith. In Christ's name, Amen.*

# October 31

*Genesis 5.24: Enoch walked with God, then he was no more, because God took him away. (NIV)*

*Philippians 4.6-7: Be anxious for nothing; but in every thing by prayer and supplication with thanksgiving, let your requests be made known unto God. And the peace of God, which passeth all understanding, shall keep your hearts and minds through Christ Jesus.*

There is a much loved old hymn that says, "O for a closer walk with Thee." I know that is what I long for and what I desire.

This day makes one year since my house was consumed by fire. One day it was there and my life was intact and I lived in peace and contentment. I was very thankful for my life and house which I felt God had blessed. Then, it was all "taken away." In the space of a few hours, 22 years of living were gone.

But God spared my life and my little poodle from the fire. He has taught me many things from that loss. Most of all not to rely on a house for happiness, or things we possess.

It has taken me several months to be able to start writing these short devotions again. I felt I needed the time to just receive comfort and wisdom from reading the Bible and *Streams in the Desert.* I needed spiritual nourishment before I could try to give my heart to writing for others.

One of my first purchases after the fire was a Bible, for I lost all of mine in the fire and felt so lost without them. And just last week, a dear former student sent me a beautiful new leather NIV Bible.

We, none of us, need material possessions in order to walk with God – spending time alone with Him in prayer is enough. Silence is all we need to have. And one day, like Enoch, we can know that He will take us away to be with Him.

*Dear Father: Until we are taken away, thank you for your faithful presence, day by day, as we lean on you for all our needs. In Christ's name, Amen.*

# NOVEMBER

## November 1

*Ephesians 3.14, 15: For this reason I kneel before the Father, from whom His whole family in heaven and earth derives its name.*

The Communion of Saints, the army of the living God, one church on earth and in heaven—we are all one vast body of believers. It has meant a great deal to me to meet weekly with three to four devout women to pray for each other's concerns and to study the Bible together. It is a wonderful joy to share our faith and very inspirational.

In my weekly performance class, when all the harp majors play for me and each other, there is also a sense of family, united by common interests and focused on encouraging each other to be the best harpists we can be.

In both cases, we are stronger in community than alone.

In our walk as Christians, communal worship is so very important. It is a reinforcement of our faith, and there is a great joy in praising and worshipping our Great God together.

*Dear Father: We are your children and we love to worship you as a family. Please help us to live worthy of your name. In Christ's name, Amen.*

# November 2

*Hebrews 12.1: Therefore, since we are surrounded by such a great cloud of witnesses, let us throw off everything that hinders and the sin that so easily entangles, and let us run with perseverance the race worked out for us. (NIV)*

My teachers were all so inspirational to me as a young harpist. I can still hear their words of encouragement and advice, and hopefully I can pass on some of their wisdom that I received from them to my own students. Music lessons are first an apprenticeship. Only after mastering the instrument's technical demands can one become an artist who can recreate the music by one's own unique gifts and musical personality.

I imagine our spiritual life can be an apprenticeship, too. As we study the lives of those faithful believers who are now in heaven, we are encouraged to also live our lives inspired by theirs. We can be greatly encouraged by their devotion and obedience. We can keep our eyes on Jesus, the author and finisher of our faith, until one day we stand before His throne. And like the "great cloud of witnesses" gone before us, be welcomed home!

*Dear Lord: Help us to run the race you have set before us, grant us the wisdom and perseverance to finish well. In Jesus' name, Amen.*

# November 3

*Ephesians 4.25: Therefore each of you must put off false-hood and speak truthfully to his neighbor, for we are all members of one body.*

In Ephesians 4.23-24: jus preceding this verse, Paul writes that we are to be made new in the attitude of our minds, to put on a new self created by God in true righteousness and holiness.

In our society, little "white lies" are often used to avoid hurting someone's feelings or to spare ourselves embarrassment. But a lie is still a lie and as such, it constitutes deception.

As Christians we must be sincere and practice transparency and sincerity in all our relationships. That does not mean that in critiquing a student's performance I need to stress what went wrong. In complete sincerity, I can focus on what was fine in their playing and urge improvement in troublesome areas, like steady tempo, better memorization, smoother phrasing, for example. We do not need to lie, nor do we need to deceive by false flattery. We should truthfully build up one another in whatever we do, for we are one body in Christ.

*Dear Father: Help us to be sincere and honorable in all our ways today. In Christ's name, Amen.*

# November 4

*Proverbs 15.1: A soft answer turneth away wrath; but grievous words stir up anger.*

*Jonah 4.4: Then said the Lord, Doest thou well to be angry?*

When I was a young teacher, I know that I tended to speak more directly to my students, not realizing the impact my words could have. Young people are so vulnerable, and my influence, as their teacher, was great. As I have more experience I try to be so careful with my words of advice and especially criticism. Above all, I try never to speak with anger.

Angry words can hurt for months after exchanged. We should try to forget them as soon as we can, instead focusing on the present with forgiveness in our hearts for the past.

It is easy to blurt out comments that hurt another. Hopefully, this is never done with deliberate malice, but simply being thoughtless or careless with our words can have the same effect.

Anger is such a draining emotion. Doctors say its effect on our bodies can be devastating, making us candidates for a heart attack.

Certainly one of God's great gifts is the ability to answer softly and humbly when one is baited with hurtful words. We know God wants us to always be peacemakers.

*Dear Father: Help us to be peacemakers in all our dealings with others today. In Jesus' name, Amen.*

# November 5

*I Corinthians 3.16,17: Know ye not that ye are the temple of God, and that the Spirit of God dwelleth in you? The temple of God is holy, which temple ye are.*

I have always kept an appointment book in which I keep track of my lessons, meetings and other duties. I would be lost without it and I wonder how some people seem to manage without one!

As I go about my daily responsibilities, teaching, shopping, cleaning, and doing all those routine chores, I am not consciously aware that I am the temple of the living God. He abides in us, and we should be aware of it all the time. This is quite an awesome responsibility.

Imagine walking with God and littering! Or gossiping, or using His name in vain! Or cutting in front of someone in line, or pushing in front of another car leaving the parking lot! Even worse, engaging in a heated quarrel with a friend, or watching a movie full of swearing and indecency.

If we truly practice feeling His presence with us, in the day-to-day moments of our lives, it should transform us into being His people, pliable and sensitive to His will. We can then truly be God's holy temple!

*Dear Father: Help us to fully realize your constant, indwelling presence with us. In Jesus' name, Amen.*

# November 6

*Psalm 145.19: He will fulfill the desire of them that fear Him; He also will hear their cry, and will save them.*

*Psalm 37.4: Delight thyself also in the Lord; and He shall give thee the desires of thine heart.*

When I first moved to Bloomington to teach at Indiana University, I bought an older house not far from campus. Even the realtor who sold me the house said I would probably want to move in a few years. But, I ended up staying in the same house for more than 20 years and remodeled it several times. I did sometimes dream of having a new house that would be beautiful inside and out, but never really expected that to happen. As I look back, now living in this beautiful new house, I marvel at God's goodness to me in granting this wish.

We often ask for things we think we ought to have, which in reality would not even be good for us or bring us peace and joy. God knows what is best for us, and we may not realize what that is. He will grant us our fondest desires, if they are in keeping with God's will.

But we can be sure of one thing, if we seek God and intimacy with Him, everything else will be secondary. We have the greatest provider and protector as our loving Father. He will not disappoint us, ever, and wants to give us more than we can ever dream of. As we walk in simple trust, our lives unfold according to His will, and what more can we ask or desire?

*Dear Father: Thank you for your loving provision; help us today to commit our way totally to thy care. In Jesus' name, Amen.*

# November 7

*Acts 26.19: I was not disobedient unto thy heavenly vision.*

*Joshua 24.24: The Lord our God will we serve, and His voice will we obey.*

When we know God's will in a matter and don't do it, we can expect to be chastised in some way. Direct obedience to God is the only path that will ever bring us peace, joy and contentment.

In the harp department, when we assign orchestra repertoire, we expect each harpist to listen to a record of the work, and to learn the harp part perfectly before going to the first rehearsal with orchestra. Since sight-reading difficult orchestra parts is very hard, being prepared avoids difficult rehearsals and being embarrassed in front of the whole orchestra by a conductor. Recently two students thought they could by-pass all that early preparation. Sadly they have not done well at rehearsals and have embarrassed themselves repeatedly. I have had to "chastise" them both for so poorly representing our fine department.

God has given us rules to obey that will bless our lives if we follow them. When we disobey, we will often pay a much heavier price than a gentle rebuke. Often, shattered and broken lives are the result of sinful disobedience.

*Dear Lord our God: Help us to live in complete obedience to your will. In Christ's name, Amen.*

# November 8

*Hebrews 10.9:  Lo, I came to do Thy will, O God.*

*Psalm 143.10:  Teach me to do Thy will, for Thou art my God.*

It is a cool but clear Saturday morning.  I am grateful for a respite after a very busy week.  Even though I have to go back to school for one lesson and a recital, it feels blissful to know I will have some free time today.

I actually look forward to clearing my desk, catching up on bills and returning some phone calls.  These small "duties" can sometimes seem burdensome, when one is so busy.

God is a God of order.  Even though we sometimes are confused or in situations of conflict and stress, we know that His will for our lives is orderliness, not chaos; peace, not turmoil; faith, not doubts; clarity, not confusion.  We cannot be light in a dark world if we are living lives of conflict and turmoil.  We must constantly seek time alone with Him, to heal and clear up the stress in our lives and know His will for us in each situation we face.

*Dear Father:  Please show us your will for us today and everyday.  In Christ's name, Amen.*

# November 9

*Ephesians 5.1,2: Be ye therefore followers of God as dear children; and walk in love, as Christ also has loved us, and given Himself for us as an offering and a sacrifice to God.*

I try to maintain a healthy routine of walking two miles almost every morning. When the weather is too hot or like today, too cold, I go to the shopping mall to walk. I especially enjoy seeing parents with their children, whose faces are bright with anticipation of a shopping spree!

I picture us as God's beloved children. We can face life, secure in His presence, and joyfully anticipate the remainder of our days by His side as we follow Him through the valleys and peaks of our lives.

To me, to walk in love is to be filled with Christ's love toward all creatures, not just those who are loving to us. God wants us to be like Christ, who was wholly good and if we want to know what God is like, we only need to look at the character of Christ. He is forgiving and loving, and we may trust Him perfectly.

*Dear Father, our God: Help us to walk in love today, for you are love. In Jesus' name, Amen.*

# November 10

*Acts 17.28: In Him we live and move, and have our being.*

*Psalm 139.7: Where can I go from your Spirit? Where can I flee from your presence? (NIV)*

The last four weeks of this fall semester have been unusually intense. They also are going by rapidly, perhaps because of so many recitals and recital hearings.

I am very grateful to have stayed well, even amidst the additional activity of building the new house. I have felt God's protection during these past months – truly in Him I have been living and walking! Today I will meet all morning with the decorators to finalize color schemes and furniture fabrics. It is a very exciting and happy time. I imagine one is privileged only once in a lifetime to build a house from the ground up, and also completely furnish it with new things. Because of the fire, I don't have any furniture and have even been renting what I have!

As I contemplate the move and the many changes, I think of Psalm 139. 8 and 10. "If I make my bed in the depths, even there your hand will guide me, your right hand will hold me fast." The Lord will go before me and knows "my heart" and "my anxious thoughts" (v. 23).

*Dear Father: We are very thankful that wherever we go, you are with us and you are guiding us. In Jesus' name, Amen.*

# November 11

*Colossians 1.10,11: Walk worthy of the Lord unto all pleasing, being fruitful in every good work, and increasing in the knowledge of God; strengthened with all might, according to His glorious power, into all patience and long-suffering with joyfulness.*

Patience and long-suffering are not attributes we associate with our "right-now" society, much less to endure them with joy!

As a teacher I often forget that some of my students, who sometimes seem to not make good progress as I hoped for them, will blossom and be fruitful after they leave school. The lessons that have been learned will bear fruit with patience and maturity. I have seen it to be true in over fifty years of teaching.

My role is to persevere with patience, dutifully teaching technical and musical principles that are enduring, and entrust the results to God. In my own life, He has strengthened me and given me these gifts that I may be fruitful. His power and grace enables us to do those duties He places before us with endurance and long-suffering with joy!

*Dear Father: Thank you for your patience with us and your faithfulness, new every morning – even on a grey, dreary November day. In Jesus' name, Amen.*

# November 12

*John 9.4: I must work the works of Him that sent me, while it is day; the night cometh, when no man can work.*

*Exodus 5.14: Wherefore have ye not fulfilled your task?*

The Bible teaches us that one day we will all stand before God for judgment. Surely one of our greatest sins is our ability to procrastinate, to put off doing those tasks set before us that we know we should do. Sadly, not doing them promptly and with good will also robs the whole day of joy, for the undone tasks keep calling us and pricking our consciences. How much better to simply do each chore, perhaps the least pleasing first, so that the mind and heart are free to embrace another and yet another.

I believe this kind of discipline is healthy, and grows us into maturity, physically and spiritually.

Right now I am wrestling with the need to lose weight and exercise more vigorously. It is often painful and depressing to have to work harder physically than is comfortable, and then to come home after work, hungry and tired, and eat very sparingly. But I know that greater good will come, perhaps sparing me diabetes and high blood pressure. Moderation in what I take in and stepping up my pace are hard to do, and I pray for God's strength to give me the necessary will power.

*Dear Father: We need your wisdom and encouragement to do those tasks you ask us to do. In Jesus' name, Amen.*

# November 13

*Psalm 94.12: Blessed is the man you discipline, O Lord, the man you teach from the law. (NIV)*

*Jeremiah 10.19: Truly this is a grief, and I must bear it.*

I believe I am feeling the Lord's discipline these days. Faced with the threat of pre-diabetes and high blood pressure and possible heart problems, I am finally finding the strength to moderate my eating habits in a serious way. It is not easy or pleasant, but God may be sparing me a heart attack. His law is moderation, and I was not obeying it – and there is always a price to pay for that! His laws are always for our good and to protect us, even from ourselves. So, I know what I am going through, hard as it is, is a blessing.

Dieting, although difficult, is not grief. Losing everything in the fire was grief, but even that does not approach the pain of losing a loved one. Such heart-wrenching sorrow can only be endured by the grace of God. Thankfully, we never have to carry such burdens alone. The Bible teaches us that He is very near the broken-hearted.

*Dear Father: Teach us to give all our burdens over to you and leave them with you. Thank you for loving us enough to send Christ to die for us. In His name, Amen.*

# November 14

*Isaiah 44.21,22: Remember these things, O Jacob, for you are my servant O Israel. I have made you, you are my servant, O Israel, I will not forget you. I have swept away your offenses like a cloud, your sins like the morning mist. Return to me, for I have redeemed you.*

There is a cold grey mist this morning. How apt to watch it lift and see clear blue skies replace it, just as God wipes away our sins and forgives us. Yesterday, I am afraid I spoke impatiently and insensitively to a friend who is going through hard trials. I tossed and turned in the night, regretting my hasty words. I prayed that God could make that situation right. To read today's scripture was such a comfort. When I was able to tell my friend how sorry I was for my impatient remarks, it was such a relief to have her forgiveness.

We do not have to live with regrets and disappointments for ourselves or others. God's grace and mercy toward us is "from everlasting to everlasting." He remembers each of us and He knows each of us, for He made us. We are His servants, and He is with us each moment of each day. Yesterday's mistakes are swept away like today's morning mist.

*Dear Father: Thank you for your forgiveness and for your cleansing power. In Jesus' name, Amen.*

# November 15

*Isaiah 41.10: Fear not, for I am with you; be not dismayed, for I am your God. I will strengthen you and help you; I will uphold you with my righteous right hand.*

Misunderstandings, loneliness and pain can actually cause us to physically ache. When we add to that mix fatigue and cloudy skies filled with rain, depression can overwhelm us.

This Saturday morning I feel all those emotions, and I wonder how I can face this day. Like a child I would love to go back to bed and bury myself in my comforter. I think part of my problem is the constant work on the house, so many decisions to make, and never feeling really free to just relax.

However, I feel courage creeping into my spirit as I read these steadfast words in Isaiah.

I would like to slip my hand into God's right hand, and rely and draw strength from Him. He will see me through this day, one hour at a time, as I rely on Him. He can turn my sad heart into a quiet, still place of His peace.

When surrounded by darkness, He is truly the light of the world.

*Dear Lord: Thank you for being our light and our comfort. In Jesus' name, Amen.*

# November 16

*Isaiah 26.3: Thou wilt keep him in perfect peace, whose mind is stayed on Thee; because he trusteth in Thee.*

As I prepare for a concert, my mind is truly concentrated on the music I will perform. I play it over and over in my head, picturing every note and every pedal movement. In bed at night, I often find myself playing through wholes pieces instead of sleeping. The mental preparation for a performance is the most important part. The music is always in my mind.

I compare that mental work, to staying focused in a similar way on God. We need to seek His serenity and shun those thoughts that trouble or vex us. Anxieties and worry and depression can darken our very souls and have no place in our relationship to Him. Even our faults should not trouble our calm; He forgives them, and we too should move beyond them in tranquility of spirit. We should allow nothing to "ruffle our feathers"! If we commune with our tranquil and holy God, keeping Him uppermost in our thoughts, He will impart His peace to us.

*Dear Father: Thank you for the gift of your "perfect peace." In Christ's name, Amen.*

# November 17

*Psalm 145.2: Every day will I bless Thee, and I will praise Thy name for ever and ever.*

*Proverbs 16.3: Commit they works unto the Lord, and thy thoughts shall be established.*

Before I got out of bed this morning, I mentally ran through the day ahead: An all-morning university meeting, two calls concerning the house, the safe arrival of a baby boy to one of my married grad students and to get a gift for her and call at the hospital, plus four hours of lessons all afternoon.

I prayed for God's presence and committed each item to Him, asking for His guidance. Then I got up, fed the dear dogs and started the day.

To my amazement, today's verses concerned exactly that which I had just done. I am always deeply impressed with how the Bible is relevant to our every circumstance. Whatever we face in life, the wisdom of our great God is there for us to study and ponder and act upon.

Every day is a good day, a new chance to serve Him and abide in Him.

*Dear Lord: We praise you every day for giving us life and for blessing after blessing. In Christ's name, Amen.*

# November 18

*1 John 4.13: We know that we live in Him and He in us, because he has given us his Spirit. (NIV)*

The next verses in 1 John 4.15 are, "If anyone acknowledges that Jesus is the son of God, God lives in him and he in God." Belief in Jesus is the only doorway to the heaven on earth of abiding in God and He in us, as well as to life eternal.

This is not a popular stance to take in this seemingly post-Christian era. The world does not want to hear about Jesus. Society demands more and more tolerance, without concern whether it is biblically correct. The world only cares if we are politically correct and that we not step on any toes.

1 John 4.4 says "the one that is in you is greater than the one who is in the world," referring to the spirit o Satan. Everyone "that does not acknowledge Jesus is not from God." These are hard words for unbelievers, and they are hard words for believers who are often accused of intolerance.

But for those of us who believe, what a comfort to know God is in us and with us. The old song, "What a friend we have in Jesus, all our sins and griefs to bear, what a privilege to carry, offer everything to God in prayer," is so true.

*Dear Father: Thank you for the gift of your Holy Spirit. In Jesus' name, Amen.*

# November 19

*James 1.26: If any man among you seems to be religious, and bridles not his tongue, but deceives his own heart, this man's religion is vain.*

*Psalm 39.1: I said, I will take heed to my ways, that I sin not with my tongue.*

Nothing depresses and upsets me more than when I say things that hurt others. I know that I would not say such things if I were not reacting in frustration or fatigue to a situation. Silence is truly golden, and I often wish I could take back words spoken in anger or impatience.

Over and over in the Bible we are told of the power of the tongue for good or evil. We are taught to "bridle our tongues, to not be provoked to anger or to provoke others to anger." Sometimes we strive to be honest and frank with others, but that too is no excuse for blurting out thoughtless and unkind words.

Only God's grace and the inward prompting of the Holy Spirit can enable us to use our words to build up each other in love. And also, only God's assurance of forgiveness when we sin with our words can enable us to face each new day with humility and courage.

*Dear Father: We pray for your forgiveness for the sins we commit by thoughtless words, and ask you to protect us from sins of the tongue today. In Jesus' name, Amen.*

# November 20

*Hebrews 10.36: You have need of patience, that, after you have done the will of God, you might receive the promise.*

The more hectic or confusing our circumstances, the more we stand in need of patience, one of God's greatest gifts. We need to not only develop patience towards others who may frustrate us, but with ourselves, when we let ourselves down.

Teaching young musicians requires one to be patient. When a student is beginning a piece like the *Danses sacrée et profane* by Claude Debussy or the Impromptu for Harp by Gabriel Fauré and playing very slowly to learn the notes accurately, my patience is usually tried. But, it is important to allow the painstaking, slow work until all the notes are in place.

Sometimes, the patience I show as a teacher can so easily give way to frustration in my personal life, perhaps because of the fact that I am exhausted from being patient all day! But, surely each student deserves the opportunity to learn a piece from the beginning, slowly, with correct notes and fingerings. And our professional frustrations should not spill over into our personal and family lives. But this takes more of God's strength to realize and live out.

In all cases, the will of God is for us to patiently endure whatever befalls us and He will give us a "crown of righteousness."

*Dear Father: Help us to be patient in all circumstances. In Christ's name, Amen.*

# November 21

*Matthew 4.4: Man shall not live by bread alone, but by every word that proceedeth out of the mouth of God.*

*Luke 12.15: A man's life consists not in the abundance of the things he possesses.*

I have gone through the devastating losses of the fire, where I truly was left with the clothes on my back and all my treasured belongings were swept away. I can attest that during the bleak weeks where I adjusted to the losses, I was warmed and comforted by dear Christian friends, and although I did not understand why God allowed the fire, my faith was always strong.

Thanks to God, the insurance company was very fair and has enabled me to build a new house, and replace and restore many material possessions. So I have known what it is to be without and then to have abundance of things again.

It is so very true that only a close personal relationship to God is the primary important necessity of our lives. To live is Christ! He is all we really need, and the one person we cannot do without. We will all leave this earth with nothing, except our faith.

*Dear Lord: We appreciate all your material blessings to us. Blessed be your Holy name. In Christ's name, Amen.*

# November 22

*Matthew 6.8: Your Father knows what you need before you ask Him. (NIV)*

*Matthew 6.33: Seek first the kingdom of God and His righteousness, and all these things shall be added unto you.*

Even though our great God knows what we need and what is best for us, He wants our prayers. He wants us to lay our every burden at His feet in prayer and communion with Him.

I look forward to spending a quiet week in the quaint little chalet village in Pine Mountain, Georgia. I will spend Thanksgiving with dear friends who also have chalets there. I keep a harp locked in my owner's closet so I can even practice while here. It will be wonderful to have "time out" to recharge my batteries for the last two busy weeks of school before Christmas break.

I am so grateful to God for this time and my heart is filled with such deep thankfulness for all His blessings, and for His enabling me to have the necessary energy and strength for this semester's teaching, coupled with the house building.

*Dear Father: At this blessed Thanksgiving time, what comfort it is to lay our cares and burdens aside, and to just worship and praise you. In Christ's name, Amen.*

# November 23

*Proverbs 4.11: I have taught thee in the way of wisdom; I have led thee in right paths.*

God has implanted in each of us a conscience, a strong sense of right and wrong. Even in primitive tribes, this is found to be true.

But God's wisdom is a precious gift. I was so blessed to grow up in a godly home with godly parents. Our church was a small missionary Presbyterian church, Gloria Dei. Dad was an elder and Mother was superintendent of the Sunday School. I taught one of the young 3rd grade classes each Sunday and conducted the junior choir. This was an important part of the fabric of my life. Even while I was studying in France, I taught Sunday school at the American Church in Paris.

However, in spite of this wonderful background, I still made many wrong decisions, and still make unfortunate choices. The Bible says we all have sinned, and that is surely true of my life. And we are never really free of continuing to make mistakes as long as we walk this earth!

Only by God's grace and mercy, assured of His divine forgiveness, can I face the future and not live in regret over the past and my many mistakes. He can make all our paths straight and imbue us with wisdom to make godly choices.

*Dear Lord: Forgive us for our foolish ways and wrong choices and grant us your wisdom for today. In Jesus' name, Amen.*

# November 24

*Psalm 31.24: Be of good courage, and He shall strengthen your heart, all ye that hope in the Lord.*

*John 14.27: Let not your heart be troubled, neither let it be afraid.*

It rained heavily here all night long, but it was such a warm rain and, snug in the cozy chalet, it felt like a blessing. Up north the first snows were starting.

It was so good to sleep ten hours last night, a true, deeply refreshing rest. Today is a holiday and friends will join us on a shopping spree on Thanksgiving.

As I listened to the rain in the night, I prayed for a long time, the kind of open-ended prayer, pouring out all my concerns and cares to God. It was so good not to need to be rushing, but to have all the time in the world to talk to Him.

And this morning, I feel a new courage and hope, as the psalmist said, "Our God is a God of peace, and He imparts it to all those who call upon him." Secure in the knowledge of His love, we can face the unknown future without fear.

*Dear Father: Thank you for the gift of your peace and courage, for today and all of our tomorrows. In Jesus' name, Amen.*

# November 25

*Deuteronomy 21.8:  And  the Lord, He it is that doth go before thee; He will be with thee, He will not fail thee, neither forsake thee: fear not, neither be dismayed.*

I am facing some big decisions, about the my long term future. I am so grateful for the assurance that God will go before me, and be with me and never fail me.  I do not need to fear the future, even though I cannot see it clearly.

I am convinced that God will provide the guidance and the right timing as I commit my future to Him.  I love to pray in the night when there are no time constraints, even if I end up drifting off to sleep.

It is so wonderful to have these precious vacation days here in this tranquil small town.  It is also nice to have these dear Christian friends to enjoy it with me.  Yesterday we did "shop 'til we dropped." Then, it was such fun to go to lunch in a quaint little restaurant and antique shop nearby. For someone like me, who hardly ever has time to shop, it was really fun!

*Dear Father:  We thank you for your faithful presence in vacation times and work times.  In Jesus' name, Amen.*

# November 26

*Genesis 28.15: Behold, I am with thee, and I will keep thee in all places whither thou goest.*

When we travel to Europe or Asia, and ponder the vast universe and endless skies it can be hard to imagine God keeping track of us. Even more, that He is with us as we travel, and goes before us, wherever in the world we go.

Likewise, when we drive on crowded highways, what a comfort to know that God is with us there too.

On a much, much smaller scale, I try to keep track of my students and former students, following their travels and successes, remembering them in my prayers as many marry and have children of their own, or begin new jobs.

How much more our Heavenly Father watches over His beloved children, and is able to be everywhere at once, holding us up with His strong right hand, preventing us from stumbling into sin, strengthening our resolve, and always, always "in our corner" sustaining us and enabling us to strive for holiness.

*Dear Lord: Whether on an airplane or on a busy highway, thank you for your holy presence and protection. In Christ's name, Amen.*

# November 27

*Psalm 115.12: The Lord hath been mindful of us: He will bless us.*

Although rain is predicted today throughout the southeast, when I woke this Thanksgiving morning, it was still clear. After a light breakfast, I was able to complete a long walk around the lake. In anticipation of a turkey feast with friends, I needed the exercise.

God hears our innermost thoughts and desires, He is mindful of us, His creatures, and is aware of our every need. He desires to bless us. What an incredible promise, "He will bless us." It doesn't say that He might bless us if we are especially good or if we follow His commandments. He will bless us, even perhaps in spite of ourselves, for it is His will that will prevail. Our role is to honor and praise Him, to thank Him for His great love for us. No matter our circumstances or what adversities we face, the God of the universe is mindful of them, and He will bless us.

*Dear Father, our great God: Thank you that you are aware of each of us and that you are blessing us each day. In Jesus' name, Amen.*

# November 28

*Jeremiah 31.3: Yea, I have loved thee with an everlasting love; therefore with loving-kindness have I drawn thee..*

What a blessing it was to celebrate Thanksgiving with dear, close friends. Two sisters who are superb cooks, created such a loving feast for us all to enjoy. They have been so kind to include us in their family holidays on many occasions. My brother and his family live mostly in California and we are rarely able to spend holidays together.

The human love that God has placed in our hearts is a pale, faint reflection of the love God has for us. The Bible says God has made us in His image. Jesus came to earth as a man and experienced all of human emotions. There is nothing we have experienced God is not aware of.

Our love should model itself after Christ's love for us. His was never self-seeking, but was rather self-sacrificing. It is easy for us to love others who love us. How much harder it is to love those who are unloving and unkind to us. It is truly hard to love someone who has hurt us, and then to completely forgive them. We need courage to do that, and great humility. Pride is the opposite of that. We need to put our pride away as we seek to show love in even the most difficult circumstances we face.

The Bible teaches that we are to consider all others as more worthy and deserving than we are. That takes a truly humble and loving heart. Such a heart is a gift from God.

*Dear Lord: Help us to get rid of pride in our lives, that we might learn to be humble and loving servants in every situation we face. In Jesus' name, Amen.*

# November 29

*2 Chronicles 29.11: My son, do not be negligent now, for the Lord has chosen you to stand before Him and serve Him. (NIV)*

Winter has come gently to the Midwest this year. The temperature dropped from seventy degrees to thirty-eight degrees overnight as I headed home from Georgia. Small patches of snow dotted the hills of Tennessee and the out-skirts of Bloomington.

The re-entry is always tiring, and this time was no ex-ception. I went to the new house even before unpacking, to see the changes, always a thrill. Beautiful white pine trees had been planted and mulched in the backyard, and dogwoods and small bushes had been transplanted in the front. And the kitchen cabinets are all installed! It is all so wonderful that I can hardly contain my excitement.

This Christmas will still be spent in the rental house, so I will decorate a tree and hopefully be able to have a class party here next week. Most of my Christmas decora-tions were lost in the fire, so there is much to be done in preparation.

As I face the last two weeks of the semester, I pray to "not be negligent," and to share with my students the joy of Christmas. I pray for the peace and joy of sharing Christ to reign in my heart, and to not allow the business of the sea-son to take away from their important lessons and recitals. It is such a special time, and I want to be ready for it!

*Dear Father: Thank you for the joy of Christmas. Use us to help others during this special and sacred time. In Christ's name, Amen.*

# November 30

*Psalm 42.5: Why art thou cast down, O my soul? And why art thou disquieted in me? Hope thou in God; for I shall yet praise Him for the help of His countenance.*

*2 Corinthians 4.8: We are troubled on every side, yet not distressed.*

It was so good to be back home again and to go to my church this morning. My minister preached a sermon on Jonah, which was very meaningful. He pointed out that we cannot hide anywhere from God, from His will, or from His love. Jonah tried to hide and disobey God, but even in the depths of the sea, God found him and saved him and gave him a second chance to obey Him.

We should never lose hope, no matter what our circumstances. God does not forsake us or forget us. He is always waiting for us and longing for us to return to Him.

When we know His will for our lives and still refuse to do it, we are truly in great peril. He loves us and does not want disobedience and sin to separate us from Him. But if we ask Him, He will deliver us from ourselves and our sinful ways. We can truly praise Him and rest in His forgiveness and salvation.

*Dear Father: Thank you for giving us second and third and unending chances like you gave to Jonah. In Jesus' name, Amen.*

# DECEMBER

## December 1

*I Corinthians 13.4: Love is patient, love is kind, it does not envy, it does not boast, it is not proud. (NIV)*

Having lived through the devastation and heartbreak of my fire, when I read about other families who lost their homes to fire I feel much more compassion than I did when reading of such misfortunes before. We should always view others' mistakes or failures with mercy and compassion. We should never be entertained by news of someone's mistakes or misfortune. There, but for the grace of our loving and compassionate God, go we.

We all have sinned; we all have failed at some time or another; we all fall so short of living holy lives. We, as believers, should be the last to ever judge someone else. The Bible also warns that we will be judged the same way we judge others.

On the other hand, we should be the first to rejoice at others success or good news. Envy should not to be a part of our make-up at all. We must be content with our own lot and not compare ourselves or our lives to someone else's. I know this is not always easy, especially when we feel slighted or see someone undeserving placed over others more deserving. But, our hope should always rest in God's ultimate justice and His perfect love. He alone knows what is best for us, each one of us. Our job is to be non-judgmental and to rest in His divine will.

*Dear Father: Help us today to refrain from judging others and to be brave with our own disappointments, trusting everything to your love and care. In Christ's name, Amen.*

265

# December 2

*Romans 2.1: You, therefore, have no excuse, you who pass judgment on someone else, for at whatever point you judge the other, you are condemning yourself, because you who pass judgment do the same things.*

Today, at the university, there are student evaluations of every class. The students "grade" their teachers, and it is a humbling experience to have the "tables turned." Students can decide if a teacher is enthusiastic about teaching, is available to them, is well-organized, has good speaking ability, is knowledgeable about the subject matter and many other topics. They then give the teacher a rating based on their experience.

Isn't it true that the shortcomings we criticize in others are often our own weaknesses that we don't want to acknowledge? We all can be prone to be slow in responding to needs around us, when we could ease someone else's suffering or hurt. We can have times when because of sheer laziness and selfishness, we turn a deaf ear to someone whose cares we could lift.

We know that God sees our slights and we will be judged – using probably the same yardstick by which we judge others. We want to live faithfully and honestly as we try to imitate our role-model, none other than Jesus Christ.

*Dear Father: Help us today to live up to your standards, being non-judgmental and being loving in all our relationships. In Christ's name, Amen.*

# December 3

*Romans 15.13: Now the God of hope fill you with all joy and peace in believing, that ye may abound in hope, through the power of the Holy Ghost.*

We often refer to situations as being "hopeless." Certainly I felt pretty hopeless after the fire. Financial reversals can bring people to the edge of despair. Some fund-raising for charitable purposes can seem staggering and almost impossible or hopeless to achieve. I have struggled for many years to raise the necessary funding for the USA International Harp Competition. It is easy to sometimes feel overwhelmed and without hope and courage for the task!

For those who do not place their faith in Christ, life can truly be without hope. Our only source of hope, even until our last breath, is God. With trust in him, no situation or person is ever truly without hope.

As we turn over every problem and concern to God in prayer, we can experience His peace and joy in the midst of our greatest hardships and His power can rescue and transform the worst difficulties and most "hopeless" situations.

*Dear Father: Thank you for giving us hope for today's challenges. In Jesus' name, Amen.*

# December 4

*I Timothy 6.11: But you man of God...pursue righteousness, godliness, faith, love, endurance and gentleness.*

*I Timothy 6.12: Fight the good fight of the faith. Take hold of the eternal life to which you were called.*

During the busy last days of school with the pressures of Christmas parties for the students, cards and gifts to tend to, how greatly I need this quiet time alone with God. The peace He gives us at such times alone seems to prepare me for specially hard and hectic days.

I know we should not whine nor complain about the work with which God has blessed us, and that we are so fortunate to have. But, this passage from Timothy inspires me to pursue His qualities of godliness, with love and gentleness and endurance, as I go about my duties even when tired and discouraged sometimes.

We must be good soldiers, persevering with courage when the going gets tough. I am so thankful to be surrounded by wonderful colleagues and dear students, all who buoy me up as we share our work together.

*Dear Father: Thank you for the blessings of this Christmas season. Help us to make time to be alone with you to recharge our batteries. In Christ's name, Amen.*

# December 5

*I Peter 5.10: And the God of all grace, who called you to His eternal glory in Christ, after you have suffered a little while, will himself restore you and make you strong, firm and steadfast. (NIV)*

*Isaiah 7.4: Take heed, and be quiet; fear not, neither be faint-hearted.*

As I write this morning, the cold rain is turning gently into snowflakes falling softly on the shrubs outside the window and transforming the scene into a winter wonderland. So God's powerful love and grace can transform our lives and make us new creatures, as beautiful in His sight as this softened, snow-covered landscape.

I have seen in my own life, and in the lives of my students and friends, how disability and suffering can soften and mold character. I believe God allows some suffering and heartache and heartbreak into our lives so that we learn to lean more completely on Him. The more self-sufficient we feel we are, the more God-deficient we may be. For God to mold us into strong, faith-filled Christians, He may first need to strip us of our self-reliance. When we are hurting and depressed, then His power and strength can restore us, in the measure to which we open ourselves to Him.

*Dear Father: Forgive us for being often so self-reliant, trusting in our own abilities. Transform us according to your will, and mercifully cover our mistakes, today and everyday. In Christ's name, Amen.*

# December 6

*Psalm 48.14: This God is our God forever and ever: He will be our guide even unto death.*

*Proverbs 3.26: For the Lord shall be thy confidence.*

It is good to stop and quietly ponder—in what do we put our trust, in whom do we place our confidence. When I think of the new house being built, I trust my builder to do things correctly. And when I think of my work as a professor in a state university, I trust the university to be reliably strong, dependable and trustworthy for my job security. When I think of relationships, I realize that at some time or another, even our closest family members or friends can disappoint us or let us down. Even great institutions and giant corporations that seemed invincible can fail: think of the Enron scandal! And I have had the incredibly hard experience of losing my beloved house that seemed so safe for so many years.

Truly, we can lose everything this world has to offer. The only person who will never ever fail us is Jesus Christ. The better we know Him, the better we will know the living God. He is our confidence. He will guide and protect us when all else fails. He even protects us from ourselves. We can never know the hundreds of evils He has kept from us, or the many, many times He has spared us great bodily or spiritual harm. Truly He is our trustworthy, reliable, dependable, loving God, forever and ever. He alone is worthy of our complete trust.

*Dear God, our great Creator: Thank you for loving us and guiding us in this life. You are unchanging and we can trust you totally in every circumstance. In Jesus' name, Amen.*

# December 7

*Job 22.21:  Acquaint now thyself with Him, and be at peace.*

*Isaiah 54.13:   All thy children shall be taught of the Lord, and great shall be the peace of thy children.*

As parents or grandparents or teachers, the greatest gift we can give to our children, grandchildren or students is a reverent knowledge of God.  No other learning experience we can offer them can compare with that.  If they can develop a personal relationship with the Lord and receive the gift of faith in Jesus Christ, they may experience lives of  incomparable  peace and deep satisfaction.

No material gift can ever compare with knowing Christ.  Nor in my case, as important as it is to teach my students wise musical considerations, I only hope that my students know what is <u>most</u> important to me – my faith in Christ and sharing it.  I pray that my life will be used to impart love and that precious spark and seed of faith in God, so that they too may trust Him with their lives.

A former boyfriend, whom I had not talked to for over thirty years, called me.  He said he had used my dedication to the harp as a role model in raising his four children!  He also said that he had used my example hoping to inspire them to succeed in their chosen fields.  I was dumbfounded to hear that, and replied, "It was my faith in God, like a deep river, flowing through my very soul that was my "raison d'etre," my reason for living and the source of my life as a musician.  I realize how we can give a wrong impression to others unless we pinpoint our faith in Christ as the focus and inspiration for all we do.  It  was a real lesson for me!

I am so grateful to have had such a loving Christian home, parents who were such strong believers.  They too have served as role models for me as I look back on the kind of gentle, holy life, caring and thoughtful of others, that they exemplified.

*Dear Father:  Help us to be more forthright in giving credit to Christ for our successes and achievements.  Thank you for the strength you bring to all we endeavor in our lives.  In Christ's name, Amen.*

# December 8

*Ephesians 1.3: Blessed be the God and Father of our Lord Jesus Christ who hath blessed us with all spiritual blessings.*

*II Corinthians 6.10: Sorrowful, yet always rejoicing; poor, yet making many rich; having nothing, and yet possessing everything.*

It seems our society is always seeking happiness in some form or another. Wealth, material possessions or shallow relationships outside of marriage substitute for spiritual peace and joy It has been called the "me" generation, what feels good to me, what I want, regardless of the pain or suffering that it may cause others.

God's gift to us is a spiritual centeredness and contentment, whether our circumstances are pleasant or sorrowful. In fact, sorrow itself can bring out the best in us if we accept all as coming from God's hand. Acceptance of our lot in life and contentment in it is a blessing. Of course we can and should do all we can to improve our circumstances and make changes that are helpful, healthy and wise. If we have lost a job, we can surely seek other employment while accepting the loss as part of God's plan for our lives and trust that He may have something far better prepared for us!

Merging our will with His will, that is a state of blessedness and a cause for rejoicing, no matter what happens to us.

*Dear God and Father: Thank you for giving us always a reason to rejoice, because of Christ, your Son, our Savior. In His name, Amen.*

# December 9

*Psalm 32.6: Therefore let every one who is godly pray to you, while you may be found; surely when the mighty waters rise, they will not reach him.*

*Philippians 4.6,7: Be anxious for nothing; but in every thing by prayer and supplication with thanksgiving, let your requests be made known unto God. And the peace of God, which passeth all understanding, shall keep your hearts and minds through Christ Jesus.*

Yesterday, I was swept by a rare depression. The hopeless and helpless feelings threatened to totally engulf me. I felt so low, and my whole life seemed a mess. All the good and fine things in my life seemed to disappear in my mind, leaving only loneliness and despair. Out of that darkness, with my heart so heavy, it was very hard to even try to pray. As I walked toward school to start a long teaching day, I sent a quick prayer to God: "Lord, please use this depression to help me be more sensitive to others when they may be hurting like this."

Mercifully he granted me respite from this dark depression during the day, and I was able to teach my dear students whole-heartedly, totally forgetting my own pain. And by evening, I felt only God's amazing grace!

God's promises to deliver us from the floods or tempests. He does not tell us that we won't have any storms, only that He will be with us in them.

*Dear Father: Thank you for your mercy and deliverance from despair and depression. In Jesus' name, Amen.*

# December 10

*James 5.11: Behold, we consider blessed those who have persevered (NIV).*

*Hebrews 12.7: If you endure chastening, God deals with you as with sons.*

Today was the last masterclass of the semester. I found the courage to have the whole class here in this small rental house for a pizza party afterwards. With just two more days of teaching and one recital, Christmas break begins. During this break, God willing, I will be moving into the new house. I am simply over-awed imagining it! To be back home again in own yard, at last, seems a miracle!

Our capacity to endure pain and suffering is surely a mark of character. We should at least <u>aspire</u> to accept all suffering with dignity and grace, if we realize it is coming from God's hand. We cannot always succeed in this. Pain is never pleasant, and really, we never know exactly how much we can bear. But, if we grow through it and can be content within it, we may emerge stronger, humbler and more pliable.

God has said He will never give us more to endure than we can bear. Because we are His children, "the sheep of His flock," we are and must be totally dependent upon Him. And like a good shepherd, He will at times discipline us and for our own good, turn us in a different direction than the one we are taking.

All change can be bewildering and discomforting. Aging is in itself a series of experiences where we feel increasingly diminished in our physical strength and well-being. It is not easy to realize our bodies just don't work the way they used to! However, I believe God compensates us for our new weaknesses by granting us greater wisdom, peace and contentment.

*Dear God: Thank you for loving us like your sons and daughters, and for disciplining us because you care for us. In Christ's name, Amen.*

# December 11

*I Chronicles 4.10: Oh that Thou would bless me, and enlarge my territory! Let your hand be with me and keep me from harm so that I will be free from pain.*

*Exodus 23.25: You shall serve the Lord your God, and He shall bless thy bread and thy water.*

These words from Chronicles are the prayer of Jabez, which have become very famous because of a successful book based on it. This prayer covers everything we need—God's blessing and God's protection—over every area of our lives.

Today is my last day to teach for one whole month. It will feel good not to be so divided between my work at school and all that must be done for the new house. Also, I can be free to plan for Christmas, gifts and cards to be sent, and the joy of celebrating Christ's birth. This year so many of my foreign students will stay in Bloomington for Christmas, and I hope to have them spend that day together with me.

I know the Christmas vacation will pass quickly. But I hope to savor every moment of every day. I pray for God's peace and his harmony and grace to reign in my heart and to radiate out to others. Perhaps never before have I felt so blessed by His incredible goodness.

*Dear Father: I echo Jabez's prayer and pray for your blessing and your grace with us in this special Christmas season. In Christ's love, Amen.*

# December 12

*Psalm 40.8: I delight to do Thy will, O my God: yea, Thy law is within my heart.*

*Colossians 3. 16,17: Let the word of Christ dwell in you richly in all wisdom; teaching and admonishing one another in psalms and hymns and spiritual songs, singing with grace in your hearts to the Lord. And whatsoever ye do in word or deed, do all in the name of the Lord Jesus, giving thanks to God and the Father by him.*

It is not enough to simply do our duty; we are to do it cheerfully, not as martyrs but as servants. I so often repeat the verse, "God loves a cheerful giver." He also loves a cheerful "doer." Complaining, whining and reluctance can spoil the most kind act. If we do loving things in an unloving way, one can cancel out the other.

If we know God's will, it should be pure joy to us to do it. Sometimes though, we mistake what is His will. Filling and crowding our schedules during the Christmas season until we drop with fatigue, or becoming very tense and pressured, cannot be pleasing to God. We need to spend time with Him and slow down from our schedules so as to enjoy His peace and gentleness of spirit.

I really pray for a patient and unhurried attitude this Christmas. I resolve right now not to attempt more in each day than I can do with good spirits, and with a peaceful mind and heart.

God wants <u>us</u>, not our good deeds. He wants us to spend time alone with Him.

*Dear Father: May we take delight in celebrating Jesus through Christmas and every day. In His name we pray, Amen.*

# December 13

*Psalm 90.12: So teach us to number our days, that we may apply our hearts unto wisdom.*

*Luke 12.2,31: Seek ye not what ye shall eat, or what ye shall drink, neither be ye of a doubtful mind. But rather seek ye the kingdom of God; and all these things shall be added unto you.*

Today is the first day of Christmas vacation. Snow is predicted. The house is all decorated, out-of-town gifts are ordered and sent; now, all that remains is doing Christmas cards! I am so very thankful for these precious weeks and this great gift of free time.

We know that God never wants us to worry or to have doubts, yet we so often carry those needless and wasteful burdens. If only we would trust Him more. Each day, when we awaken, we should resolve to do our best with that day's duties, and commit them to God. Anxiety and worry should not be given a haven in the hearts and minds of believers.

As I look back at the difficulties and choices I have faced in my life, most of them were not at all worth the anxiety I experienced over them. Worrying did nothing but make me miserable. As I grow older, I feel so strongly the need to live wisely, valuing and appreciating each day and not borrowing trouble from tomorrow or yesterday.

*Dear Father: All of your gifts are precious. Help us to appreciate them fully, everyday. In Christ's name, Amen.*

# December 14

*Galatians 6.14, 16: May I never boast except in the cross of our Lord Jesus Christ through which the world has been crucified to me, and I to the world. Peace and mercy to all who follow this rule, even to the Israel of God.*

In this Christmas season when we can so easily be preoccupied with getting just the right gifts for those we love and decorating our homes with beautiful decorations and colorful trees, these verses stand in stark contrast. We are often so proud of all our acquisitions and we do indeed boast about them, perhaps only to our closest family and friends.

But we should never forget that <u>all</u> we have is a gift from God. His mercy and blessings are indeed our only reason to boast. We base our entire hope for eternal life on the birth, crucifixion and resurrection of Jesus Christ. The world's attractions should be less and less appealing to us – or else are we so little different from people who have no faith or belief in Christ?

We are to be "new creatures" in Christ – like the beautiful blanket of fresh snow that fell last night on our Bloomington landscape. And just now, as I write, comes the news that Saddam Hussein has just been captured, marking a new beginning for Iraq and a possible help and resolution of the conflict there. I pray that our brave soldiers can come safely home soon.

*Dear Father: Help us to put Christ first in our lives. Everything else should be a distant second! In His name, Amen.*

# December 15

*Psalm 116.7: Return unto thy rest, O my soul: for the Lord hath dealt bountifully with thee.*

*Hebrews 4.3: We which have believed do enter into rest.*

The Lord has indeed dealt bountifully with me in this hard past year. As Christmas approaches and the time to move into the new house draws ever closer, I am so deeply thankful that I cannot find words to express it.

The insurance agent just called again and has been so generous and fair in every way. They will pay the moving expenses and even additional storage until the carpentry is really finished.

I know that the work of moving will be hard and tiring, but this time, unlike moving into the rental house, it will hopefully be the last move. I have such a sense of peace, that I will be entering into God's rest, into His will and plan for my life. In trusting Him and committing the future to His divine plan, my faith has been so rewarded, beyond my wildest dreams.

I pray that God will use this house and use me for good to those in need around us.

*Dear Father: You have dealt with us with grace and mercy and compassion beyond anything we deserve. You are our great God, and the giver of all good gifts. In Jesus name and with thankful hearts, Amen.*

# December 16

*Psalm 139.2: You perceive my thoughts from afar. (NIV)*

*Psalm 19.12: Who can understand his errors? Cleanse Thou me from secret faults.*

Our thoughts can often show us to be petty and silly creatures. Even when we try to control our minds, thoughts of self-centeredness and even anger can surface involuntarily. I have found myself, even in the midst of prayer, wondering about some small detail of home furnishing or other practical, unimportant problem. I am embarrassed to interrupt communication with the Creator of the universe with such silliness and pettiness.

Philippians 4.8-9 provides one of the finest portraits of what our inner thought-life should be like: "Whatever is true, whatever is noble, whatever is right, whatever is pure, whatever is lovely, whatever is admirable, if anything is excellent or praise-worthy – think about such things…and the God of peace will be with you."

What an antidote to unlovely thinking. If we look outward from a base of such inner beauty and peace and loving thoughts, we may become the people God intended us to be.

*Dear Lord: Forgive our many faults and shortcomings. Please rule in our hearts and our minds through Jesus Christ. In His name we pray, Amen.*

# December 17

*Galatians 5.22: But the fruit of the Spirit is love, joy, peace, patience, kindness, goodness, faithfulness, gentleness, and self-control. (NIV)*

*John 15.8: This is my Father's glory, that you bear such fruit, showing yourselves to be disciples. (NIV)*

Yesterday I met with four friends for our last Bible study-prayer meeting until after the New Year. These times of study, prayer and sharing have been a real source of strength and encouragement.

When I think of these dear friends, I am so aware that each definitely shows the indwelling fruit of the Spirit. Each has shared their private sorrows and trials, never in a complaining way, but rather to show how God has provided for them, and is providing for them.

There is a sweetness in Christian fellowship that is a beautiful thing to experience. I often feel unworthy to be among these women, who truly are saintly. There is an aura of holiness about them. Their goodness, kindness, gentleness and self-control are so very evident. Their lives have borne great fruit, and they are truly disciples of God.

*Dear Father: May your Spirit in us bear fruit today, that our love for You be evident in all we do today. In Christ's name, Amen.*

# December 18

*I Timothy 4.10: We trust in the living God.*

Today when I woke up and looked out the window, a soft gentle snow had blanketed the neighborhood. The fields and trees are all covered and it is a beautiful sight.

In a similar way, the living God softly and gently covers our weaknesses and mistakes. When we stumble through hard times, the valleys of our lives, He uses those experiences to mature us and to equip us for the sorrows and storms in our lives. He comforts us so that we may be able to comfort others.

God is a living force and power. He is always wanting an intimate, personal relationship with us. The more we trust Him and the greater our reliance upon Him, the more we enable Him to release His power in our lives.

I relate this in a way to my teaching. The more a student asks of me and probes for my advice and suggestions, the more I am able to help him or her. As students mature and search for deeper understanding and knowledge, the more I can work with them on a deeper level of music-making.

I believe God can help us more when we turn to Him for help in every area of our lives, opening ourselves to Him more and more fully, committing everything to Him.

*Dear Father: We trust you this day to guide and direct us in all we do and say. In Christ's name, Amen.*

# December 19

*Isaiah 33.2: O Lord, be gracious unto us; we have waited for Thee.*

*Psalm 39.7: And now, Lord, what wait I for? My hope is in Thee.*

These days before Christmas seem to be going by so very fast. I want to savor them slowly, not rushing anything—the cards, the gifts, the Christmas trees, the wrapping, the parties and all the preparations for Christmas. Yesterday, there was a coffee with neighbors, and it was so nice to meet a whole group of neighbors that I had never before had a chance to meet..

Last night the Indiana University School of Music celebrated the eightieth birthday of Menahem Pressler, a world-famous pianist and colleague and neighbor of mine. I sat next to him and was moved by the touching and deserving tribute to this great artist. So many wonderful pianists among his former and present students came to play and honor him.

I hope and I trust in the Lord that He will direct my path as I face the whole process of aging. I hope that He will enable me to age gracefully, walking in His wisdom and accepting the inevitable changes with humor and understanding. I hope that I can give increasing wisdom and knowledge to my students, and that they will also come to know Him, and have this faith in Christ as the most important ingredient for their spiritual and professional lives.

*Dear Father: Our hope is in You; your peace and your wisdom are what we need and wait for. In Jesus' name, Amen.*

# December 20

*Matthew 10.19: Take no thought how or what you shall speak: for it shall be given you in that same hour what you shall speak.*

*James 1.5 If any of you lack wisdom, let him ask of God, that giveth to all men liberally, and upbraideth not; and it shall be given him.*

*Colossians 1.10: That they might walk worthy of the Lord unto all pleasing, being fruitful in every good work, and increasing in the knowledge of God*

How often I put off making a hard phone call about something I cannot do because of my schedule, or with news that will not be easy or happy for the recipient. I stew about such calls and procrastinate as long as possible making them. Then, when I finally find the courage and make the call, I am almost always utterly amazed by the other person's kindness and understanding of my call. Afterwards, I wonder what on earth I feared!

I wish I could remember these pleasant interchanges and never again waste time and energy in worrying and dreading such calls. God oversees all these details in our lives and I should trust Him to give me the wisdom to handle them appropriately. He will give me the right words of explanation, and He will govern their response. And if by chance, I am met with something else, at least I will not have wasted worry and spent anxious hours in vain!

If we commit our words to God's divine editorship, we have no need to fear another's response!

*Dear Father: Help us today to live victoriously secure in the knowledge that in everything we fear, You are with us. In Christ's name, Amen.*

# December 21

*Isaiah 40. 28-29: Do you not know? Have you not heard? The Lord is the everlasting God, the Creator of the ends of the earth. He will not grow tired or weary and His understanding no one can fathom. He gives strength to the weary and increases the power of the weak. (NIV)*

During the Christmas season, it is easy to become exhausted, trying to do too much. All the extra work of shopping, wrapping gifts, putting up decorations, baking, preparing for company, all are placed on top of our normal routines. And during this hectic pace, we can lose sight of the real meaning of Christmas.

I looked at the faces of tired shoppers – and I came home aching with fatigue myself yesterday. Today I can hardly move!

These verses from Isaiah are comforting. God never grows tired or weary. He is able to increase our strength and bolster our weakness. He forgives our sins. He takes away our guilt. Every prophecy in the Bible has been true. The Creator of the universe, our holy, everlasting God came into the world as a small baby. He it is whom we celebrate at Christmas. He is our savior, our "up-lifter," who takes away the sins of the world, and our aches and pains too!

*Dear Father: We are so thankful that Jesus came into our world and experienced everything we experience. Give us strength today for those tasks before us. In Jesus' name, Amen.*

# December 22

*Isaiah 8.17: I will wait upon the Lord, that hideth His face from the house of Jacob, and I will look for Him.*

It is so hard to wait and to summon up our patience when every fiber of our being longs for action, resolution, results, and conclusions.

In these days before the big move into the new house, as workers come and go (mostly go) leaving quantities of finishing work undone, my anxiety deepens. While much is done, so much remains undone. So many details fill me with a nameless kind of dread and worry. I awoke this morning feeling a depression coming over me. I prayed fervently for God to restore my peace of mind. I know, deep down in my heart, eventually everything will come together, but right now it seems like flood waters that may overwhelm me and threaten to engulf me.

But one thing I know for sure. I <u>must</u> only look to Jesus. I know He is the answer to all my problems. I ask Him to take away my impatience about the work to be done and my unnecessary desire for too much perfection in the construction details. As I bow at His feet, in humility and with thanksgiving, the house recedes in importance, and I can look only to Christmas and celebrating the birth of my Lord and my Savior.

*Dear Father: Forgive our impatient clamoring. Come into our hearts, Lord Jesus, and dwell there today and always. In Christ's name, Amen.*

# December 23

*II Timothy 2.3: Thou, therefore, endure hardness, as a good soldier of Jesus Christ.*

*2 Corinthians 1.3,4: Praise be to the God and Father of our Lord Jesus Christ, the Father of compassion and the God of all comfort, who comforts us in all our troubles so that we can comfort those in any trouble with the comfort we ourselves have received from God.*

When I lived in France, I often heard people say I offer my pain or my discomfort to the Lord. I have always felt this was a beautiful way of looking at hardships and I think this is similar to today's verse, the way Christ would have us view those times of great misfortune or pain.

It is easier to "endure hardness" if we feel we are doing it for Christ's sake. If we are doing something that seems selfish or only benefiting ourselves, without a higher motive or good, that is much harder, I believe.

Yesterday, my spirits lifted as I taught private lessons to two dear students. That was my reward for the day. Work is a wonderful antidote to depression. Also being with other people who were working so hard to get the house finished cheered me.

By day's end, although physically very tired, really exhausted, I no longer felt on the verge of tears. And having experienced God's great comfort and powerful uplifting presence, I felt enabled to actually cheer up a friend later in the day. It seemed a perfect example of Corinthians 2.3-4. God comforts each of us so that we may be equipped to comfort others in their need.

*Dear Father, and God of all comfort: Help us to endure the suffering that you allow in our lives, as your good soldiers and servants. In Jesus' name, Amen.*

# December 24

*Colossians 1.12: Giving thanks to the Father who has qualified you to share in the inheritance of the saints in the kingdom of light. (NIV)*

I find myself remembering my dear parents, during this Christmas time, and how good and kind they were. Looking back, it always amazes me how they worked long hours putting up the Christmas tree and laying out and wrapping countless presents for us, my dear brother and me – only after we were sound asleep on Christmas Eve. They did all that so that we would not lose faith in Santa Claus during those early childhood years. Throughout their lives, my parents were always giving to others, visiting the sick, taking widows out to dinner, and taking flowers from our garden to everyone. They remain such an example to me, of putting others needs before their own, and doing it so gracefully

Now, I <u>know</u> they are both in heaven, and are sharing "the inheritance of the saints." What a wonderful example they were of godly living. I marvel at all the good they did around them. But most of all, they honored Christ. Everyday they read the Bible and the devotional booklet, *The Upper Room.* It was a tradition that they continued throughout their lives. .

I am so grateful for them and for the inspiration of their example.

*Dear Father: May we qualify to share in the great inheritance of the saints in heaven. In Christ's name, Amen.*

# December 25

*Ephesians 3.17-19: I pray that you, being rooted and grounded in love, may be able to comprehend with all saints what is the breadth, and length, and depth, and height, and to know the love of Christ, which passes knowledge, that you might be filled with all the fullness of God.*

"Come, thou long expected Jesus" is a much loved hymn of faith. I feel moved by those words when Christmas day finally arrives, bright with expectation. I have always hoped that loved ones will be happy with the gifts given. Tonight, especially, I hope that the meal preparation for the students will go smoothly. But, most of all, I pray for the peace and love of Christ to be in my heart all day. I pray that I might feel a special closeness to Jesus today, as we celebrate His birthday.

Unfortunately, I already got upset this morning because Baby, the puppy, started the day by tearing through the house, dragging a roll of toilet paper gleefully in his mouth which extended into three rooms! It is hard to feel inner peace at such moments!

But, I thank God that I can be at home with my dogs and friends and not alone in some other corner of the world. I remember being alone in Paris on Christmas Day as a student, waiting for a call from my parents which never came because circuits were busy; no cell phones in those days! This is a blessed Christmas day, for sure.

*Dear Lord: We celebrate your birth today with all the hope and love which You brought into the world. In your name, we give thanks, Amen.*

# December 26

*Philippians 4.7: The peace of God, which passes all understanding, shall keep your hearts and minds through Christ Jesus.*

*Colossians 3.15: Let the peace of God rule in your hearts.*

*Isaiah 26.3: Thou wilt keep him in perfect peace whose mind is stayed on Thee.*

The day after Christmas, what peace to wake up to a completely free day, with no plans at all other than to write some thank you letters and call some special friends and family members.

The Christmas party for the class went very well. The students were happy and spirited and we all ate and talked until after 10 p.m. It was midnight before the dishes were all cleaned and put away. It has always been my preference to completely clean up right after a big party, even late at night, so that when the next day begins I don't have to cope with cleaning up. Dirty dishes are always harder to clean the next day, emotionally and physically!

The sun is shining and the sky is blue, and temperatures are in the high 40s. I know I will soon need to start packing boxes and organizing the big move to the new house.

For today, I will let the peace of God flow over and through me. Putting all cares away, I am going to rest and abide in Him.

*Dear Father: Thank you for these precious times of respite from work and cares. Help us to use them to draw near to you. In Christ's name, Amen.*

# December 27

*Galatians 4.7: So you are no longer a slave, but a son; and since you are a son, God has made you also an heir. (NIV)*

We have the great privilege of calling God, Abba, or Father. He wants us to have an intimate, personal relationship with him, to bring our problems and our praise directly to Him. We don't need any intermediary.

I awoke feeling very foolish. After getting up in the night to take the puppy out, I restlessly tossed and turned, stewing over all the details of moving in almost one week. I wished I had spent that time in prayer instead. How much more helpful that would have been!

I determined that this morning I would simply write down all those concerns. Then perhaps tomorrow I would sleep more peacefully.

Of all the many tasks and duties we all face daily and hourly, the dearest and most essential use of our time is the time we spend alone with our Father, listening and praying. It is a privilege, not a duty. He is always waiting for us and He longs for us to simply spend time with Him in prayer.

*Dear Father: Thank you for always being there for us, at every moment. In Jesus' name, Amen.*

# December 28

*Hebrews 13.20-21: Now the God of peace make you perfect in every good work, to do His will, working in you that which is well-pleasing in His sight.*

*Titus 3.1: Be ready to every good work.*

How timely that our present First Lady, Laura Bush, and President Kennedy's daughter, Caroline Kennedy were guests on a talk show this morning discussing good works, volunteerism, and patriotism. Both are actively involved in visiting hospitals and teaching and helping disadvantaged children. They are living out Hebrews 13.

The Bible teaches that we are to serve God by serving and helping those in need. Dr. D. James Kennedy pastor of Coral Ridge Presbyterian Church in Ft. Lauderdale, Florida also did a program last night about the enormous influence for good Christianity has had. Because of Christ, schools and hospitals were built, and all kinds of charitable works were instigated. The Salvation Army, the Red Cross and all the other faith-based services were founded because of biblical teaching. Many people, myself included, are not aware of the enormous influence for good that Christianity has had in the world throughout the ages.

"If you have done it unto one of the least of these, you have done it unto me." Those words uttered by Christ have inspired millions of workers to devote their lives to services to people in need. Doctors, nurses, our military pastors, cooks, builders, teachers – all these are "ready for every good work." What they do is surely "well-pleasing" in God's sight.

*Dear Lord: Give us the vision and courage to see the work you place before us and to do it for you. In Christ's name, Amen.*

# December 29

*Philippians 4.8: Finally, brothers, whatsoever things are true, whatsoever things are honest, whatsoever things are just, whatsoever things are pure, whatsoever things are lovely, whatsoever things are of good report – think on these things.*

*Proverbs 23.7: As he thinketh in his heart, so is he.*

Our whole mental outlook is governed by our "thought-life." If we allow poisonous thoughts, anxious or jealous thoughts to take root in our minds, they can truly even make us physically ill.

The opposite is also true. If in our minds we plant and nurture happy and thankful thoughts, cheerful and beautiful memories, these can keep us in good health and at peace. We all need to police our thoughts and remain free of unhappy and depressing ideas, to firmly replace them with good, healthy and honest thoughts.

In teaching memorization techniques to my students, I urge them, before recitals, to mentally review every note and every pedal of their entire program. This can definitely help to assure them of a smooth and confident performance.

In a similar way, I want to be able to mentally review the things from my life that are beautiful, good and happy, so that my "repertoire" of thoughts is always a solace to me, and not a pain. And there is no greater comfort than to memorize scripture and to be able review mentally those great words of faith and encouragement found in the Bible.

*Dear Lord: As we fill our hearts and minds with your words, there will be no room for angry or anxious thoughts. Keep our minds healthy and holy today. In Christ's name, Amen.*

# December 30

*Jeremiah 10.23: I know, O Lord, that a man's life is not his own: it is not for man to direct his steps. (NIV)*

*Isaiah 45.13: I will direct all his ways.*

I believe it is a good thing as a new year approaches, to reexamine our life and our priorities in the light of eternity. In other words, which of our life's priorities have eternal value?

If we start by looking at our physical attributes and material possessions, it is easy to see that we will lose some of our physical health and looks as we age. And since losing my house to fire, I realize how ephemeral our material possessions are. Even as I pack and prepare to move into a lovely new home, I worry that I am far too preoccupied with that!

So, what I understand more with each passing year, that it is only the imprint we leave on other lives that may endure, and the values we instill in our children, and in my case in my students. We can share with others our love of God and how He has blessed us. Our <u>spiritual</u> health and vigor become the most important priorities in our lives, far beyond our physical well-being. As we trust God to direct our ways, we can face the future without fear, and we can try to help those around us to do the same.

*Dear Father: You know all our thoughts and our often foolish ways. We stumble and fall as we try to make our way through life. Help us to relax and allow you to direct our steps, day by day. In Christ's name, Amen.*

# December 31

*Philippians 3.13-14: Forgetting those things which are behind, and reaching forth unto those things which are before, I press toward the work for the prize of the high calling of God in Christ Jesus.*

New Year's Eve! The end of one year and the chance for a new beginning! A chance to forget our mistakes and trials and look with hope upon an open-ended new year, bright with promise and new possibilities. So many of us make resolutions to start a diet or to exercise more and then a few months later resume our old habits.

My little teacup poodle puppy, Baby, suddenly took ill two nights ago. He began twitching and moving his head from left to right in constant movement. He seemed to hear things on all sides. I rushed him to the vet, but he could find nothing wrong. He slept normally last night and today. I am so grateful, he seems almost normal again. I feared he had eaten some pill by mistake that caused symptoms of acute anxiety. I fell asleep praying for Baby, for he had been lost to me yesterday, in a world of his own.

Are we not often like that, so caught up in our worries and cares that we are blind to the world around us? We can become so lost in our own worries that we are insensitive to the people around us, who may desperately need our attention and our compassion. Only Christ can answer our concerns and help us care for those around us, yesterday, today and forever!

*Dear Father: Thank you for granting us a new year. May we live it under the direction of your loving guidance, and may all we do serve to praise and honor You. In Christ's name, Amen.*

# January 1

*Psalm 84.7 11: They go from strength to strength. The Lord God is a sun and a shield; the Lord bestows favor and honor; no good thing does He withhold from those whose walk is blameless.*

*Mark 4.26-28: A man scatters seed on the ground. Night and day whether he sleeps or gets up, the seed sprouts and grows, though he does not know how. All by itself the seed produces grain – first the stalk, then the head, then the full kernel on the head. (NIV)*

Jesus, speaking in the simple language of a parable, compares the kingdom of God to the quiet and persistent growth of a seed, growth brought about by divine power, not human effort. As we relinquish our wills to God, we are filled with His divine strength and power. Nothing is impossible for Him to do and accomplish in our lives.

It is so fitting to begin a new year as I prepare today to begin moving into the new house and rebuild the life which was splintered after the fire last October a year ago. I ask the reader's patience as this past year's writings are half before the fire happened, with a long hiatus in the middle, and then the remainder after that event.

I place my trust in God and his mighty power and divine plan to be able to use this book in some way to encourage others.

*Dear Lord: We commit our plans and dreams for this New Year unto your tender care. In Christ's name, Amen.*

# January 2

*Psalm 121.8: The Lord shall preserve thy going out and thy coming in from this time forth, and even for evermore.*

*Psalm 90.1: Lord, Thou hast been our dwelling place in all generations.*

Today I am beginning the move into my new home and I thank God for the strength and protection he has given me through this difficult time. The cleaning crew has done the windows and floors and bathrooms. While still a lot remains to be done, the actual moving in can now begin. As I write this, I am surrounded by boxes filled with the rather meager belongings purchased since the fire. Instead of four truck-loads of books, I have only three rather small boxes full. But, I am rather amazed at all I have accumulated in just one year. The boxes for my music have arrived, and I can finally start to put that huge collection back in order, most of which is covered with soot and terrible smells, but still precious to me for the markings on the scores.

Today's verses, God-inspired, as is all scripture, are perfect to encourage me for these days ahead to remind me in such an inspirational way that God is with me in every task, however large or small, especially as I prepare this new dwelling place. God has been my strength throughout this year, and all my life He has been so faithful and merciful to me. He alone gave me the courage to rebuild the house, and I trust Him alone to preserve it.

*Dear Father: We ask your blessing upon all the changes in our lives, both big and small, and thank you for your constant encouragement. In Christ's name, Amen.*

# January 3

*Deuteronomy 33.25: As thy days, so shall thy strength be.*

*Matthew 6.34: Sufficient unto the day is the evil thereof.*

How appropriate was Deuteronomy 33.25 for today! I got up early, setting the alarm so that I might have time for these writings, and still be ready for the "big move." I had not counted on phone calls (one all the way from Bulgaria!) and when four strong young men arrived at 9:30 to help move, I was not totally ready, to say the least!

Nevertheless, I hastily dressed and started making feverish trips back and forth from here to the new house! The four movers were great. What seemed to me as insurmountable loads disappeared into their van, with no problem! With all of the closets emptied out, it was the moment for my two new beautiful gold concert harps to be moved to their new home! Computer, fax machine, copier, music stands, furniture – all are now safely in place in the new house. Electricians and electronic people worked alongside us all day. I've never seen so many wires and attachments! Still, so many things are unfinished. One of the hardest was not having my clothes closets installed yet, or linen closets, no pantry shelves or towel racks! It made the unpacking very frustrating, as much had to stay in boxes.

But, God is good, and He gave me the strength to lift and carry and unpack until late tonight. His strength is always sufficient when we falter.

In view of His great blessings and the gift of this new house, I cannot think of anything bad tonight. I am just totally exhausted and totally happy and thankful!

*Dear Lord:  Thank you for giving us the necessary strength for today.  We trust you for the same strength tomorrow.  In Jesus' name, Amen.*

# January 4

*Proverbs 11.2: When pride comes, then comes disgrace, but with humility comes wisdom. (NIV)*

*I Peter 4.8: Above all, love each other deeply, because love covers over a multitude of sins. (NIV)*

I could hardly move this morning, my arms, legs and back rebelling against all the lifting and packing and unpacking of yesterday!

It is such a good feeling to know that all the clothes, books and furniture are now in the new house. Unfortunately, however, my shoes for church were not moved during the rush of packing the cars, so I shall have to stop by the rental house on the way to church to get them..

Perfectionism is also a hard thing to overcome. Many sinful habits are hidden in the desire for complete order. We can want everything picked up and put away, and that may be uncomfortable or not usual for others. In general, it is more important to have peaceful relations, than a perfectly ordered house! It is hard to find the right balance between the good and normal desire for order and not nagging others around us to achieve it.

I think love can overcome many sins – sins of selfishness, wanting one's own way. If one loves another deeply, it is natural to want their happiness over your own. Rather, their happiness is your happiness. Also if they are sad and hurting, how can you, as their friend, be happy?

*Dear Lord: Grant us hearts attuned to the needs of others, take away our prideful ways and fill us with your love, acceptance, patience, and humility. In Christ's name, Amen.*

# January 5

*Ephesians 5.27: To present her to Himself as a radiant church without stain or wrinkle or any other blemish, but holy and blameless.*

*I Peter 2.5: You also, like living stones are being built into a spiritual house.*

I woke at 2:30 this morning, my mind playing over the many details needing to be done today, to turn off the newspaper delivery here in the rental house, to remember paintings still hanging on walls and to bring the phones. There are still so many things to be moved.

Then I stopped and thought, this is precious time I can spend in prayer. I decided just to meditate on "Be still and know I am God." It calmed me! I prayed for several friends going through hard times, I felt at peace and was able to stop worrying about the coming day's work.

I know that God wants me to be quiet more, to be less busy running and doing and achieving. His will would be for me to spend more time with Him. I pray that this new house may be used by Him, that it will truly be a spiritual and Spirit-filled house. I hope that it may be useful and helpful to students and friends.

Tonight, I will sleep for the first time in the new house! My brother Sandy and his dear wife Janet will arrive from California to help with the many chores of getting settled. What a happy day lies ahead!!!

*Dear Lord – This is truly the day the Lord has made! I am so very grateful and give thanks for it. In Jesus' name, Amen*

# January 6

*James 1.5: If any of you lacks wisdom, he should ask God, who gives generously to all.*

I was not able to write this on Tuesday. The morning started with the puppy needing to go out at 5 A.M. I had trouble figuring out even how to open the door, and outside it was icy and eight degrees! Then I was awakened again at 7 A.M. and then never stopped until I fell into bed at midnight! I felt like I was in the center of a hurricane. Between plumbers, carpenters, electricians, telephone company, cable service, computer, movers, closet installers, painters, all feverishly finishing their work, I never stopped. It seemed everyone needed something from me, all day long!

But, it was wonderful to have my brother and wife here, even just to hold the dogs! The house is lovely and everything is going to be simply wonderful, but right now, there is so much to take in and get used to!

Everyone though, seems to agree that it was wise to build this house on my old lot, and I know that surely that wisdom came from God. After the fire, when I had to decide what to do, where to go, I totally committed the whole situation to Him, and I felt and now I know, that it was He who clearly guided me from beginning through completion. So, I will forever be thankful to Him for this great new beginning.

*Dear Lord: You are a God of great wisdom and incredible generosity. We thank you and praise you. In Jesus' name, Amen.*

# January 7

*Ephesians 1.19: ... and His incomparably great power for us who believe. That power is like the working of His mighty strength.*

In church Sunday, my pastor asked us all to start a journal, listing God's blessings to us each day. Because of the move, I have not yet been able to start, but I feel every day, as I do my devotions and write, that I am keenly aware of God's blessings to me.

Today, the sun is shining and there is a light covering of snow on the yard. What a joy for me to look out on this acre and a half of my beloved yard once again, with its tall, stately pines and evergreens and expanse of lawn! It truly feels like home and always will to me.

The dear dogs have to get used to the yard again. First, because of rain, then bitter cold, they have not been able to be trained for the invisible fence I had installed for their safety. They are so small and cold, and they refuse to be coaxed to walk along the border of the fence. Also, the yard was reconfigured when the old house was demolished and the new foundation was laid. I too need to get used to so many new things.

Today, I will have the joy of practicing for the first time on my new harps in the new music room, which was designed for them. And last night, I used the new ovens, microwave and dishwasher, for the first time. I am so grateful for every single aspect of this new home.

*Dear Father: Thank you for every new beginning you so graciously grant us. In Jesus' name, Amen.*

# January 8

*Galatians 6.10:  As we have therefore opportunity, let us do good unto all men.*

*Hebrews 13.1:  Let brotherly love continue.*

Opportunities to help others may be missed if we become self-absorbed and look inward rather than outward. There are so many people who need to be comforted or uplifted in some way.  We need to stand ready to lend a hand or an ear at any time.

Time is so important, and we need to use it wisely. During the stress of moving, it has been hard to make the time to answer e-mails with care and consideration. I have had to spend so terribly much time and energy with the house and moving that I look forward to leading a more stable, normal life again.  I want to be able to look outward, to help my students, and to be hospitable about sharing time with others.

Christmas break is drawing to a close and soon school will start up again.  I pray that I will be ready!

*Dear Father:  Help us to be ready for each opportunity you give us to be helpful and kind to all whom we meet.  In Christ's name, Amen.*

# January 9

*II Chronicles 31.21: And in every work that he began in the service of the house of God, and in the law, and in the commandments, to seek his God, he did it with all his heart, and prospered.*

*John 6.28: What shall we do, that we might work the works of God.*

This was my first night alone in my new house. I had the full responsibility of my puppy, and his house training, of the kitchen and all the new appliances, the plasma TV with its complicated remote control, the new computer that I barely know how to use, and the security system that I don't understand at all! I have so much to learn! My brother and his wife were such a great help in making these big adjustments – but they left last night, and I am now "on my own."

I suddenly felt very alone. After playing with Baby, the puppy, I went to the harp and practiced. I have deeply missed my normal daily practicing. It just wasn't possible during the past few weeks. I found it very comforting to settle into my practicing routine. I felt back in tune with God's will for me.

I believe that God has a plan for each of our lives and we need to try to live in tune with the gifts He has given us. Then we should do it with all our heart. Our God-given gifts then become His holy work.

*Dear Lord: Help us today to do our work as unto God, with all our hearts. In Jesus' name, Amen.*

# January 10

*Psalm 63.3: Because Thy loving-kindness is better than life, my lips shall praise Thee.*

*Luke 17.32: Whosoever shall seek to save his life shall lose it; and whosoever shall lose his life shall preserve it.*

I am grateful for this final weekend before the start of classes. I have worked so hard physically with moving that I feel I must rest and recharge my batteries now. Baby and I are alone now in this big house and it feels a bit overwhelming.

But it feels so good too to have a really quiet time to read my Bible and write this morning. And I look forward to a long, peaceful practice at last!

I am so grateful to God for the miracle of this beautiful new home. His loving-kindness to me has been "better than life." I want to share this joy with everyone I meet.

One thing I look forward to is spending more time reading the Psalms and letting those words of praise soak deeply into my soul. In these happy days, my heart feels so full of thanksgiving, and the Psalms seem more meaningful to me than ever.

*Dear Father: Your loving goodness is life to us and we thank you and praise you. In Jesus' name, Amen.*

# January 11

*Psalm 31.7: I will be glad and rejoice in Thy mercy; for Thou hast considered my trouble; Thou hast known my soul in adversities.*

As I sit in front of the fire this cold January morning with Baby on my lap, I cannot help but think back to one year ago. It was then that I decided, after much prayer for guidance, to build a new house. The blackened shell of the old was still standing, a terrible eyesore and heart-breaking reminder of the loss that was so hard to bear. As I contemplated living in a rental for a year, and all the hard work of building, it seemed it would take too long a time, at my age, to live like that.

God knew all my sorrow and pain, and He knew that a year later I would indeed be living in this beautiful new home, truly a dream house with every convenience. God knew the plans he had made for me, and they were better than I could even imagine.

I feel so known and loved by Him. There is no thought or worry or suffering that I have experienced that was unknown to Him. Even to providing me with this dear little new puppy.

He gave me hope throughout this long year. It is no wonder that I am so very thankful to Him.

*Dear Lord: We are in awesome wonder before your mercy and everlasting goodness. Thank you, Father. In Jesus' name, Amen.*

# January 12, 2003

*(First after the fire)*

*Psalm 19.14: Let the words of my mouth, and the meditation of my heart, be acceptable in Thy sight, O Lord, my strength and my redeemer.*

This verse from Psalm 19 is truly my prayer today. The writing of this devotional book stopped abruptly on October 31 when a raging fire devastated my home, burning the last six weeks or more of my work, including the books and Bibles sitting on a table together.

In the following weeks which became over two months, I struggled with many doubts and depression, and I could not seem to start writing again. I also did not have the book of the scriptures I was using, or the copies of the earlier devotions until this week. Fortunately, most of the devotions had been removed from the computer's hard drive and safely copied by a friend onto a CD, but I did not find that until January 10.

It was a time of great confusion and soul searching. I wondered how and why God had allowed this terrible event to happen. I never stopped trusting Him, but it was a deep hurt I carried inside.

Then, walking the beach one day in Florida, I realized that God had saved me from the fire! I cried as I felt His love surrounding me. I thought of how I would feel if I was unfairly blamed for something I did not do. A missionary friend also had cautioned me that Satan loves to get into such matters, encouraging us to be bitter and blame God. That thought was very comforting to me also. Then in sorting through hundreds of boxes with a dear friend who came from California to help me, I found one of the months of hand-written devotions I had thought burned in the fire! I thanked God and took courage. When that same day I found the CD, I knew that I could once more start writing these devotions.

I pray that God will again bless my efforts, as I search to apply His truth to my life and share this goodness and mercy with others.

*Dear Father: I am grateful to once again spend this quiet time with You. Thank you for giving me this new beginning. In Jesus' name, Amen.*

# JANUARY

# January 13

*James 4.11: Speak not evil one of another, brethren.*

*Ephesians 4.31: Let all bitterness, and wrath, and anger, and clamor, and evil speaking, be put away from you, with all malice.*

If we are to guard our tongues from speaking with bitterness and anger, we must first guard our thoughts. Dissension and malice begin first in our minds.

We need to take every negative thought "captive," and not allow bitter or evil ideas to take root in our minds. Like weeds in a lovely garden, we must uproot them as soon as they appear or they will grow rapidly and spread. We can transform our minds by filling them with precious Bible verses that can work like a cleansing lotion, and fill our hearts with the sweet aroma of love, forgiveness, kindness and goodness.

I find nothing more helpful than memorizing verses of scripture, which can be recalled when I struggle with painful or hurtful thoughts. We can renew our minds by dwelling on the good in others and erasing and forgetting the disappointments or hurts of the past.

God is good. I believe that with all of my heart. He wants us to experience His peace that passes all human understanding.

*Dear Father: Thank you for showing us the way, and giving us the recipe to dwell in peace and love with everyone around us. In Jesus' name, Amen.*

# January 14

*2 Samuel 15.15: Thy servants are ready to do —whatso-
ever my lord the king shall appoint.*

As I sit trying to pray and begin writing, the phone has been constantly ringing with important calls that I need to take. I think how hard it is to change direction and do what God appoints us to do, moment by moment.

I particularly seem to schedule more than I can possibly do in a given time, and then experience frustration when interruptions disturb an already overcrowded work period. I know this is not God's will for me. When I find myself too busy, I need to slow down, be quiet and relax. The work will always be there. And who knows what opportunity I may miss to hear a friend in need of encouragement, or to help a colleague by being there, or even simply to recharge my batteries?

As servants of Jesus Christ, we need to be available to do whatever He appoints us to do, whenever He chooses. That is our highest calling and it supersedes all others. So when I am determined to finish sorting a pile of bills or answer new e-mails, I must realize my priority is not to finish my tasks but His.

*Dear Father: Help me to put aside my tasks whenever You call me. In Jesus' name, Amen.*

# January 15

*I Thessalonians 4.3: For this is the will of God, even your sanctification.*

To know and to do God's will is the deepest and most important task of our lives. We should constantly ask ourselves, "Are we fulfilling God's purpose for our lives? Are we claiming His power? Are we seeking in every way to draw closer to Him?" He hears our prayers and He wants to teach us.

I know as a teacher how my heart lifts when a student comes to me in a lesson and admits a problem and asks for my help with it. Just this week a freshman asked for help in memorizing a difficult contemporary piece. It was a joy for me to provide her with tools and methods to help her understand the process of memorization and to see her grasp it and understand it.

In the same way, I believe God rejoices when we admit and confess our failures and problems to Him. He is waiting patiently for us to turn them over to Him. And He is more than able to forgive us and renew our courage.

*Dear Father: Thank you for teaching us and growing us in holiness. In Jesus' name, Amen.*

# January 16

*2 Thessalonians 2.16,17: Now our Lord Jesus Christ, himself, and God, even our Father, which hath loved us and hath given us everlasting consolation and good hope through grace, comfort your hearts, and establish you in every good word and work.*

I awoke this morning to hear that a friend's beloved 15-year-old dog had died after fighting to survive kidney failure for almost a year. I grieve with her as I know her pain will be deep. I wrote her a card and, as I wrote, I prayed that her faith will bolster her, and that God will comfort her in this loss.

Truly, when we suffer such heartache, there is only the love of friends and the consolation and comfort of God which can help us and ease our pain.

January 16 is my mother's birthday. Although she is surely in heaven now, I will always think of her and celebrate her in my heart on this day. I am so thankful to have been raised by such a godly mother. She started every day, all her life, with prayer and Bible study. This was such an important example to me and continues to be a model for a happy and fulfilling life.

*Dear Father: You are with us, in all the important events in our lives, both happy and heart-breaking. Thank you for your divine hope and comfort. In Christ's name, Amen.*

# January 17

*I Peter 4.12,13: Beloved, think it not strange concerning the fiery trial which is to try you, as though some strange thing happened unto you; but rejoice, inasmuch as you are partakers of Christ's sufferings.*

How fitting these verses from I Peter are, after I have lived through a true trial of fire. I continue to believe that resignation and complete acceptance of the will of God do ultimately lead to rejoicing. As I trust Him to bring good out of the "fiery furnace," I am led to closer fellowship with my Savior, Jesus Christ.

There is something about the destruction wrought by fire that is so awesome. Whole rooms were left without any roof and in some others; it was as if no furniture had ever been there. Everything had melted into the floor.

But, I am aware that I had perhaps too many material things in my life. Surprisingly, I had tried to get rid of many things last summer, and had just cleaned almost every drawer and cupboard in the house. But I still know I had too much. Now, having lost so much, I hope to live more simply, using and needing far fewer things, and therefore less burdened –certainly a reason for rejoicing!

*Thank you, dear Father, for every trial You allow to befall us. May each of them bring us closer to Thee. In Christ's name, Amen.*

# January 18

*Deuteronomy 26.11: Thou shalt rejoice in every good thing which the Lord thy God hath given unto thee.*

*I Thessalonians 5.16, 17: Rejoice evermore. In everything give thanks for this is God's will for you in Christ Jesus.*

I have a vivid picture of God's blessings flowing from heaven to us, like a strong beam of sunlight, and our thankfulness to Him flowing in a similar way up to Him. This is how God created us. He loves us with a never ending love, and as His beloved children our natural response is continuous thankfulness.

We should never change and never stop praising God and thanking Him. All else in our lives is secondary. I so often worry or fret over work not yet finished or my house not in order. I even get upset because I have not emptied the dishwasher before breakfast! These daily tasks are always with us and they will get done. I should just appreciate the fact that I have dishes and a dishwasher and a house that needs cleaning. These are all precious gifts!

So, first of all, let us give thanks for every good and perfect gift with which He has showered us.

*Dear Father: We thank you and praise you for each new day. We face each day secure in your love and your protection, no matter what may befall us. In Christ's name, Amen.*

# January 19

*Psalm 105.3: Let the heart of them rejoice that seek the Lord.*

*Nehemiah 8.10: The joy of the Lord is your strength.*

I have always admired those believers who have re-nounced all earthly wealth and possessions and entered a mission field or a convent or monastery, there to live solely for God. We live in such a consumer-oriented society, yet many of our products are poorly made and need to often be replaced. We are inundated with ads for the latest PCs, TVs and gadgets, none of which will give us lasting happiness.

It is not easy for believers who live in this world to simplify our focus and live for God. The accumulation of possessions is always with us. Even after losing nine-tenths of my possessions to the fire, a year later I am amazed to have already accumulated so much!

I really long to live a simpler, less cluttered life, with my joy to be found in the Lord, in spending time with Him, listening to Him, and taking my strength and direc-tion from Him. He is sufficient for all our needs. But He is not easily found in our fast-paced lives. We can be so oriented toward work and achievements. Jesus says, "Seek ye first the kingdom of God and all these things shall be added unto you." For sure, seeking God first is the key to a joyful life.

*Dear Father: I want to seek you with my whole heart. In Jesus' name I pray, Amen.*

# January 20

*Psalms 149.4: For the Lord takes delight in his people, He crowns the humble with salvation.*

Three retired harpists, colleagues and dear old friends of mine, were recently honored by the American Harp Society for their many years of service to the harp community. All three raised families while they continued to have outstanding professional careers. And, then in addition, they gave of their time and energies to the profession, making enormous contributions to the harp world. I think they are wonderful role models for young harpists today. They exemplify giving back to our profession in order to benefit others.

It is easy to be so busy with our own careers that we forget those young artists who have not yet achieved financial stability and recognition. I believe nothing is more rewarding than to be in a position to help others.

In a similar way the great saints of the Bible inspire us by their faith and courageous lives of obedience. They help us to be steadfast in our faith, and we can rest in the sure knowledge of our salvation through Jesus Christ.

*Dear Father – Help me to be a light that others may look toward for inspiration and encouragement, In Jesus' name, Amen*

# January 21

*Isaiah 40. 30,31: Even the youths shall faint and be weary, and the young men shall utterly fall; but they that wait upon the Lord shall renew their strength; they shall mount up with wings as eagles; they shall run and not be weary; and they shall walk and not faint.*

These verses are among the most often quoted in the entire Bible. I think it is because we all have experienced times of great fatigue, and discouragement. Aging is not an easy process. A friend is fond of saying, aging is not for sissies!

I recently was told that I would soon have diabetes if I did not alter my diet and exercise much, much more, and do so more vigorously. I have been trying to do it, walking farther and even riding a stationery bike evenings. I realize that it is my own individual responsibility to take care of my body and my health.

As I have shed some pounds, I have been aware of renewed energy. I am very thankful to have been warned in time to avoid, hopefully, serious physical complications. I have felt God's hand in giving me the courage and will power to make needed changes.

*Dear Lord – Thank you for renewing our strength, even as we do face growing older and seeing our physical bodies slow down. In Christ's name, Amen*

# January 22

*Hosea 6:3 Then shall we know, if we follow on to know the Lord*

*James 1:5 If any of you lacks wisdom, he should ask God, who gives generously to all without finding fault, and it will be given him.*

I often warn my students that after they have played a piece by memory for several months or years, that they should always continue to go back and look at the music to be sure they are still being accurate. It often happens that we can overlook many details of the score as we play it more and more our own way!! We can easily forget what the composer actually intended.

Even devout Christians must never think they know the Bible so well that they no longer need to study it. It is our single, most important task, in order for us to know God and to obey Him. While much of our knowledge of God will only be made clear in heaven, He has given us a road map for life in the Bible. Reading and studying it represents our best chance to grow and mature in our faith.

As I encourage my students to constantly refer to the musical score, even after they have studied a piece for several years, so we must always refer to the Bible, to be sure we are not depending on our own thoughts instead of relying on His will for our wisdom.

*Dear Father – I pray that you will reveal yourself to me as I daily study your word and listen for your voice speaking to me through the pages of the Bible. In Jesus' name, Amen*

# January 23

*Isaiah 58.10,11 If you spend yourselves in behalf of the hungry and satisfy the needs of the oppressed, then your light will rise in the darkness and your night will become like the noonday. The Lord will guide you always.*

There have been so many disasters lately, floods, hurricanes, famines, and cruel civil wars. Charitable giving has been stretched to the hilt as the needs throughout the world and here in America have been urgent. Most of us have never gone hungry or lost our homes or been forced to live in abject poverty. We, who have been blessed with so much, need to share generously with those in need, wherever it may be.

Probably one of the greatest lessons in my life has been my understanding of God's principle of tithing. We are to give the first ten percent of our earnings to God's work, our church for sure, and other Christian and humanitarian ministries. I have learned that one cannot "out-give" God! When we put Him first, He blesses us richly.

It is hard to know how much we ought to give and when we have given enough. There are so many fine Christian organizations, one wants to help them all. I feel particularly that while I cannot have the strength or ability to travel overseas or to tend the ill or homeless, my responsibility is to give financially to those who are called to do the hard, physical work.

*Dear Lord – Thank you for blessing me financially so that I may use my resources and gifts from You, to help others. In Jesus' name, Amen*

# January 24

*Psalms 16.7: I will bless the Lord, who hath given me counsel.*

*Romans 12.11: Not slothful in business; fervent in spirit; serving the Lord.*

When I began writing these devotions, I foolishly imagined that it would only take one year to complete, writing one a day. It has now been over three years and I am still working diligently to finish them. In addition to the interruption of the fire, I have had constant trouble getting each month in order, often discovering missing days, or even whole months which seemed to have mysteriously disappeared!!! It has certainly given me a healthy respect for writers!

I have discovered that this is a larger project than I initially believed. But I have felt God's leading and counsel as I have plodded on, finishing month after month, then editing and correcting mistakes. I always feel so badly when I reread passages that seem to be holier than thou in feeling, or worse, that don't seem to even make sense!! But, as I read the Bible and work on each day's thoughts, I have felt a real growth in understanding, and I know that in God's time, it will be finished. My admiration has grown so much for the great saints and missionaries who have written so eloquently of their faith and sacrificed so much to do it.

*Dear Father – Grant me the wisdom and patience to finish this task which is before me, In Christ's name, Amen*

# January 25

*John 13.17:* *If ye know these things, happy are ye if ye do them.*

*James 4.17:* *Therefore to him that knoweth to do good, and doeth it not, to him it is sin.*

Many times, I have been tempted to stop writing these devotions and give up. Yet, as I have prayed about it, it has always seemed that the right thing to do is to keep going. I rarely have felt good about quitting, whether it be in leaving one of my university positions, (at one time I was teaching in 4 different schools at the same time), or in continuing the USA International Harp Competition, (a constant source of work raising the necessary funds accompanied by frequent discouragement), or in learning a new piece that was uncommonly difficult. Somehow, I have believed that when it is time to stop, the Lord will let me know. Meanwhile I will keep working.

Writing these devotions has been a very humbling experience for me. I know that God can somehow use my weaknesses to show his strength. It is my hope that these words may serve as an encouragement to those who may read them, not through my ability as a writer, but through the power of Christ who can transform the words and make them shine with His power and love.

*Dear Father – Thank you for giving me the opportunity to write. I pray that you will transform these words, and that they may be acceptable to You, and that you can use them in the lives of others. In Christ's name, Amen*

# January 26

*I John 3.2: Dear friends, now we are children of God, and what we will be has not yet been made known.*

*Romans 11.33: O the depth of the riches both of the wisdom and knowledge of God! How unsearchable are His judgments and His ways past finding out!*

I admired my teacher, Henriette Renié, so very deeply. I respected her musical advice completely. Her wonderful ear amazed me. As a young woman, she used to go to string quartet juries and wrote four-part dictation, for entertainment, something I found to be extraordinary. Her musical intelligence was incredible. Best of all, she believed in God with her whole heart and being. What a role model she was for me!

But if I think of the wisdom and depth of God's omnipotent power, all human wisdom pales in contrast. We can never understand the unsearchable will of God. But we can seek after holiness. We can earnestly pray, without ceasing, to know His will and to do it. We can pray to be channels of blessings to others.

It may well be that in this life we will never understand what God has in mind for each of us. But one day, perhaps only in heaven, we will know and we will understand. What an incredible joy that will be!

*Dear Father: Your ways are unsearchable, but we know you love us and care about each one of us. Thank you for this great love which is beyond our understanding. In Jesus' name, Amen.*

# January 27

*Isaiah 57.15: For thus saith the high and lofty One that inhabiteth eternity, whose name is Holy: I dwell in this high and holy place, with him also that is of a contrite and humble spirit, to revive the spirit of the humble, and to revive the heart of the contrite ones.*

I am surprised to find it more difficult to write these devotions after the fire than before it. Perhaps it will take some time to get back into the rhythm and flow of writing again. I had imagined that experiencing weeks of such grief would have given me much to say. Instead, I feel a sort of numbness, inhibiting any expression, like experiencing a death.

Certainly, I have been troubled by the loss of my home because much of my security was there. But I am learning that wherever one abides, that becomes home, and I am grateful beyond words for the haven of this dear rental house. As I gaze at empty bookshelves, I know that less can be more. The Lord weeded out much that I was carrying in excess baggage by the fire. Although many old treasures were lost, He made space for newness of life.

I think we all need to be constantly aware of our inability to live holy and righteous lives apart from the grace of God. Humility is one of our gifts from God, enabling us to live contrite and sincerely remorseful lives. He has promised to be very near to the broken-hearted.

*Dear Father: You are Holy and You are my great God. You revive my spirit and lift me up and I am very thankful. In Jesus' name, Amen.*

# January 28

*Psalm 145.16: Thou openest Thine hand and satisfiest the desire of every living thing.*

*Psalm 34.9: O fear the Lord, you His saints: for there is no want to them that fear Him.*

God knows our every need, and many of them of which we are not even aware ourselves. But He wants us to ask Him and seek Him. Then will we find Him and all the blessings He is waiting to pour out upon us.

It is so true that we often do not know what we should ask for, for we do not always know what is best for us. We ask for health, a good job, a good marriage, or peace of mind. The Bible says, "Seek ye first the kingdom of God, and all these things will be added unto you."

After the fire, I hardly knew what to do or what to ask God to do for me. I struggled with knowing whether to try to rebuild or to rent or to buy a new house. Probably the only thing I really had to do, and I did it, was to seek His will.

The beginning of wisdom is the fear of the Lord. Some people do not like to feel fear; they prefer to think only of God as the loving, merciful Father. However, He who created the universe is too awesome for us to imagine, and we should stand in awe of Him and worship Him.

*Dear Father: We do stand in awe of you. Thank you for showering us with your blessings, day by day, You are so faithful. In Jesus' name, Amen.*

# January 29

*Isaiah 41.13: I the Lord will hold thy right hand, saying unto thee: I will help thee.*

*Psalm 17.7: Show Thy marvelous loving-kindness, O Thou that savest by Thy right hand them which put their trust in Thee.*

It is natural for us to fear change, to worry about our future, especially as we ourselves show the inevitable signs of aging. It seems every few weeks I see a new wrinkle, or feel a new ache or some difference in some part of my body.

But God wants us to trust Him, one day at a time. He saw us safely through all our yesterdays and He will see us faithfully through our tomorrows. He will either protect us from suffering or He will uphold us with His strong right hand and give us the needed strength to bear it.

We do not need to live in fear because we have His wonderful assurances. He saved me from the fire that took my home, and now He is giving me comfort and hope to build a new life. He is faithfully guiding me in finishing these devotions.

*Dear Father: Thank you for your all-powerful right hand that holds us up and prevents us from falling. Your loving kindness is so wonderful. In Jesus' name, Amen.*

# January 30

*Psalm 139: 9, 10: If I take the wings of the morning, and dwell in the uttermost parts of the sea; even there shall Thy hand lead me, and Thy right hand shall hold me.*

This morning was bitter cold. I went to the burned-out wreck of my old house and met the demolition people who arrived with large trucks and bull-dozers. A dear neighbor came with a camera to take pictures which would help us remember that day.

We peered into the burned interior one last time, and I even retrieved an artificial tree that was lying unburned out in the snow! Two boxes of old photos stored in the attic have been left behind in the garage by the salvage company. Singed photos of former summer classes smiled out at me as a friend put them in her car trunk.

We waited nervously while gas, water and electric companies arrived to check if the utilities were all shut off.

Then as the signal was given to the driver of the bull-dozer, we gasped as he lunged his machine at the garages and they at first resisted and then broke open and crumpled in. It was such a violent upheaval. His huge fork dug into the roof, recently new, and tore huge holes into it, until it too collapsed.

I left for school then; I truly was overcome with emotion. It was very hard to witness the destruction, again, of the house I had lived in so happily for so many years.

*Dear Father: I need you right now, Lord, more than ever to uphold me during this turbulent time of change. Thank you Lord. In Jesus' name, Amen.*

# January 31

*Proverbs 3.6: In all thy ways acknowledge Him, and He shall direct thy paths.*

*Psalm 23.2: He leadeth me.*

Today I meet with the designer who is drawing up plans for my new house. With the help of a good friend, I have given him a rough sketch of the house floor plan I would like. Now, we need to make many difficult decisions about the placement of rooms, and the exact location of the new house on the old lot emptied by the demolition team.

I am truly excited about building a dream house from scratch! I always hoped one day I would have the thrill of building and designing a new house. But I never dreamed that such an opportunity might happen because of fire!

My over-riding prayer is for God's will to be accomplished. "Unless the Lord build the house, its builders labor in vain." I pray that God will bless the endeavors as I go forward in faith, not without much trepidation!

*Dear Father: I ask for your direct and specific guidance as I go forward with these plans. Lord, please make them your plans. May this new house begin in prayer and be truly a house of the Lord. In Jesus' name, Amen.*

# February 1

*Romans 15.5: Now the God of patience and consolation grant you to be like-minded one toward another, according to Christ Jesus.*

*James 1.4: Let patience have her perfect work.*

Yesterday afternoon I drove by my old house. The house itself is totally gone. There are just huge piles of wood, stone, dirt and rubble. Even the crawl space has already been cleared away leaving just bare dirt.

Although I felt great sadness over what was gone and all the happy memories in that house, I felt a new hope surge in me. I looked at the beautiful pine trees and the spacious empty lot, and I imagined a lovely new home soon to be erected there. It felt somehow cleansing to have the black, charred ruins gone. But I also felt anxious to get settled again as soon as possible.

God is so patient with us. And He asks us also to be patient, with others and with our own desires and wishes. He is always wanting the best and highest for our lives. Our role is to wait upon Him, to live in obedience to Him in every way that He makes clear to us. In return He gives us every possible blessing.

*Dear Father: Thank you for each fresh, new start; each day is new, and we thank you for the many opportunities you give us. In Christ's name, Amen.*

# February 2

*I Thessalonians 5.14: Now we exhort you, brethren, warn them that are unruly, comfort the feeble-minded, support the weak, be patient toward all men.*

Almost every evening I catch myself sighing at my desk as I turn off my computer. I bemoan my inability, or so it seems to me, to ever be finished with work. Daily there is more than I can possibly do. It is a rare day that I manage to answer all the e-mail, clear my desk of bills and letters, and am able to feel relaxed and at peace. And time to practice the harp seems almost squeezed out altogether, unless I do it first thing in the morning.

I have been advised by friends to hire secretarial help, and I am seriously considering that. But so much of my work would take longer to explain to someone else than if I just did it myself.

There are many friends and colleagues that I long to reach out to and invite for a dinner or get-together – but even that seems to be an effort, when I have so little free time.

I know I am not alone in feeling these frustrations. It seems to be so prevalent in our society as a whole. God wants us to live our lives, giving ourselves away for others, with patience and consideration to all. Writing letters of recommendation, visiting a house-bound friend who is ill, making time for other friends in need -- these are very important parts of the very fabric of our lives. We need to make time for them.

*Dear Father: Give me patience with my own unending work. Help me to see your hand guiding me in these chores. In Jesus' name, Amen.*

# February 3

*Psalms 139.23, 24: Search me, O God, and know my heart; try me, and know my thoughts; and see if there be any wicked way in me, and lead me in the way everlasting.*

No matter how we try to keep our hearts and minds on a high and noble level, we are constantly pulled down by the world's intrusions and by our own sinful and selfish natures and ways.

We have no secrets from God. He knows our every thought before we think it. Above all, He longs for us to spend time with Him, seeking His will. We can listen in the quietness for His urgings which speak to us through the Bible. But it is hard for God to be heard if we keep filling our schedules to the brim, leaving no free time for Him.

Sometimes I feel as if God takes a gentle eraser and rubs out and blots out the sinfulness in our lives. I know I need His cleansing forgiveness on a daily basis. Only then can I feel at peace and can live free of guilt over past and present failures or mistakes. Because of Christ's forgiveness we can be freed to live positive, hopeful and constructive lives.

*Dear Father: Thank you for the incredible gift of your forgiveness, and for keeping us "on track." In Jesus' name, Amen.*

# February 4

*James 3.2: If any man offend not in word, the same is a perfect man, and able also to bridle the whole body.*

*Psalms 141.3: Set a watch, O Lord, before my mouth; keep the door of my lips.*

I think the hardest part of self-control is our rush to speak. It is so hard to refrain from speaking our mind, when we think we are right! When we are hurt or treated unfairly, we want to lash out in our defense, sometimes hurting the offender as well and aggravating the situation.

Between people and between countries, words can so easily escalate into hostility and to out and out war. Accusations and recriminations fly back and forth. Probably the hardest words to utter are "I'm sorry" or "Please forgive me." These are the only words that seem to be able to restore peace and harmony.

Jesus is a role model for us to emulate. When accused falsely by the priests and Pharisees, He remained silent, not even defending himself from the threat of death. We need to learn to turn the other cheek and not to retaliate in word or deed. But that is very hard to do when we are hurting.

Even though we will often fail to control our emotions and hence our words, how very rewarding to our relationships if we can master this art.

*Dear Father: Let the words of my mouth and the meditations of my heart be acceptable in Thy sight, O Lord, my strength and my Redeemer. In Jesus' name, Amen.*

# February 5

*Psalms 106.3: Blessed are they who maintain justice and who constantly do what is right.*

*Job 11.15, 16: Thou shalt be steadfast, and shalt not fear: because thou shalt forget thy misery, and remember it as waters that pass away.*

The fear and misery of the fire recede with each passing month. While for several weeks I would re-live the moment when the fire alarm woke me and I saw smoke coming under my door, these nightmares have been blessedly absent for the past few weeks.

God has been so good to me in providing for my needs since the fire. The insurance people have been fair and the worst of the time-consuming paperwork is over. God has blessed and protected me continually, and I am very grateful.

I have trusted God from the beginning to bring good from the disaster, and He has been so faithful to do it. The rental house is warm and comfortable and is beginning to feel like a real home. New house plans are being drawn right now and a builder is standing by, ready to start constructing a new house on the old lot. And I have felt the love and support of a world-wide community of colleagues and former students.

*Dear Father: Thank you for your faithfulness; how great Thou art. In Jesus' name, Amen.*

# February 6

*Proverbs 29.25: Whoever putteth his trust in the Lord shall be safe.*

*Psalms 57.2: I will cry unto God most high; unto God, that performeth all things for me.*

Part of trusting God is believing that we are exactly where He wants us to be and where He planned for us to be, from the beginning of time.

Often people live with guilt, regretting past choices and decisions, and continuing to live in the past. God is all powerful and all forgiving. He can move us anywhere, at any time.

If we feel "stuck" where we are, we can at least be thankful and accept that God has placed us there and that He will "perform all things" that we need, exactly where we are. He will also keep us safe.

We, as a nation, are grieving the loss of the astronauts in the space shuttle Columbia this week, and feeling the terrible pain of their dear families. Truly, this is a time for crying unto God, and putting our trust in Him. As the commander of the shuttle said to his pastor before he left on the mission – "If this does not work out, you will know I've just gone a little higher." His faith surely was a great comfort to his family.

*Dear Lord: We trust in you during hard times and good times, knowing that you will be with us and protect us. In Jesus' name, Amen.*

# February 7

*Jeremiah 7.23: Obey my voice, and I will be your God, and ye shall be my people; and walk ye in all the ways that I have commanded you, that it may be well with you.*

Sometimes I have procrastinated making a phone call or doing a task that feels hard or uncomfortable to do. It has always caused problems and made me feel anxious and out of sorts. To obey God by doing our duties is to approach Him, to draw near to Him. If we are not obeying Him, in so far as we know His will for us, we are separated from God. We will not be at peace.

Many times we fail to hear God's voice and we feel like a rudderless ship. But we do not need to ever feel cut off from His voice. In scripture He has given principles and directions for virtually every area of our lives. His will should be made clear to us if we trust Him and turn our lives over to Him.

He has promised to be with us, and give us the strength and courage to do the hard things we face in life and He is faithful. His way may sometimes be very difficult, indeed, it may be very painful often, but He also has promised that it will go well for us and he will never leave us. Ultimately, His way is the only way to live at peace.

*Dear Lord: We want to be your people. Please continue to speak to us so that we may not walk in darkness, but live in your presence now and forever. In Jesus' name, Am0en.*

# February 8

*Psalms 23.2,3: He leadeth me beside the still waters. He restoreth my soul. He leadeth me in the paths of righteousness for His name's sake.*

There is no substitute for habitual communion with God. Daily reading the Bible and studying and searching there for God's wisdom needs to be a constant in our lives. Then when the floods (and fires!) come, our souls are nourished and we have the strength and courage for whatever trials beset us. We can be like a giant oak tree with roots that go down deep into the earth, with our deepest strength being grounded in our faith in Jesus Christ.

He is more than sufficient to carry our greatest burdens, our disappointments, our private grief. We must turn all of these troubles completely over to Him, not trusting in our own abilities, but solely leaning on Him. That is when He can be our total sufficiency.

When we fall, He will pick us up and restore us; when we lose our way, He will lead us and guide us. His gift to us is the peace that surpasses all understanding.

*Dear Lord: Please hear our prayer, forgive us our sins and restore our brokenness. By your strength make us into strong and courageous people. In Christ's name, Amen.*

# February 9

*Matthew 25.25: I was afraid, and went and hid thy talent in the earth; lo, there thou hast what is thine.*

The story of the talents is so compelling today. God expects us to use the abilities He has given us, whether they be great gifts or very humble and simple ones.

I think we often deprecate the different gifts we have, believing they are not important, or even that our efforts are never perfect enough or worthy enough to be used by God. So, out of fear or pride or something from our past, we "bury" or safely try to "hoard" our talents.

This parable teaches us that God does not honor this kind of behavior. He expects us to invest ourselves in His kingdom, to share all we are and all we have with those around us in need. We are never encouraged in the Bible to hold back, or to "invest" timidly. When we do give fully of ourselves, He promises to bless our every effort. We must learn to live and give courageously.

*Dear Father: Help us to go forth today with renewed courage and hope in our hearts, trusting You to use our efforts and to increase them beyond what we can imagine. In Christ's name, Amen.*

# February 10

*Isaiah 25.9: We have waited for Him, and He will save us; this is the Lord; we have waited for Him; we will be glad in His salvation.*

How hard it is to wait patiently for anything in our chaotic lives. Yet impatience is the opposite of peace. If we could only learn to be patient with ourselves, we might then be able to be more patient with others.

Sometimes we are like backseat drivers. It is so tempting to want others to move at the pace that we find comfortable, especially if they seem too slow. We find it hard to adjust to another person's tempo.

When a student is playing a piece too slowly, I need to urge the student to play faster, within the proper interpretation of the composition. It can also happen that a student is playing a passage too fast, rushing through phrases, which is even harder to correct sometimes.

God may well want to urge us in the same way. But I suspect He would urge us to take a slower tempo. He wants us to spend more time with Him, and He wants us to be at peace, not always rushing about, achieving. He wants us to live with space in our lives that only He can fill.

*Dear Father: We commit this day to you. Grant us the patience to wait for your prompting, and to spend time alone with you. In Jesus' name, Amen.*

# February 11

*John 17.4: I have finished the work which Thou givest me to do.*

*Mark 14.8: She hath done what she could.*

Jesus prayed at Gethsemane before He was arrested and crucified. He accepted God's will and His plan for salvation, and Jesus knew that His earthly walk was finished. He obeyed unto death.

Earlier in Mark, we read the story of the woman who poured expensive perfume over Jesus' head. The disciples rebuked her and said it was a waste. But Jesus defended her, and said she had done what she could, and whenever the Gospel would be preached throughout the world, she would be remembered by that act.

I urge my students to memorize their pieces as soon as possible because of the freedom it will give them to play with more ease and technical facility. Then they can concentrate totally on the strings and the interpretation, not looking back and forth at the music stand. Many resist memorizing and put it off, and their work suffers because of it.

Do we realize that our work, whatever it may be, can be done as to the Lord? The simplest task, if done perfectly with all our hearts and without anxiety, can be a gift to Him. If we dedicate our efforts with love to Him, He will enable us to complete our work and He will bless it and multiply it.

*Dear Father: Help us to finish those tasks that you have given us to do. In Jesus' name, Amen.*

# February 12

*Psalms 68.19: Blessed be the Lord who daily loadeth us with benefits.*

*I Timothy 6.17: Nor trust in uncertain riches, but in the living God, who giveth us richly all things to enjoy.*

It is not yet the middle of February and the newspaper reports over 28 inches of snow, a record for Bloomington. The snow is overwhelming for the road crews who must clear the roads and salt them. But inspite of the problem, I love to thoroughly experience all four seasons here!

I almost slid into my neighbor's yard last week on the way to school! The students seem to take the extremely cold weather in their stride, although many have had the current cruel flu bug. I am very grateful to have stayed well so far this winter, even though I am constantly exposed to students who are ill with colds or the flu.

The snows have been especially beautiful this year. God's handiwork is awesome. He has lovingly planned each season and each has special blessings. These cold winter days are perfect for getting major indoor tasks accomplished. And it is exhilarating to bundle up in boots and walk in the snow. Baby specially loves to romp in the snow and is so comical as he is almost buried in the depths of the snowbanks and I have to rescue him.

God truly gives us rich blessings to enjoy in every season.

*Dear Father: Thank you for blessing us every day with your amazing creativity in the world you have made for our enjoyment. In Jesus' name, Amen.*

# February 13

*Acts 21.14: The will of the Lord be done.*

*2 Samuel 15.26: Behold, here I am. Let Him do to me as seemeth good unto Him.*

Since the fire, I have done so much thinking about the will of God. It was, I think, natural that I would have trouble believing God would have deliberately wanted me to lose my house and harps and belongings in such a devastating way. My heart hurt over it for weeks and months.

Even during the sad and painful period when I grieved the loss, I trusted God to bring good from it. And I am beginning now, three months late, to see so many good things. Neighbors have been helping me with the details of designers and buildings. The insurance company has been so considerate and fair in making a rapid settlement, enabling me to build soon. God seems to be bringing everything together to enable me to move ahead and build a beautiful new home.

I believe this has been a new lesson for me in God's will, and a letting go of my own plans and letting Him do "as seemeth good" to Him.

*Dear Lord: You are all knowing and all powerful. May your will always be done, and we give you all the praise. In Jesus' name, Amen.*

# February 14

*I Corinthians 7.32, 25: I would like you to have no con-
cern...that ye may attend upon the Lord without distraction.*

*1 Peter 5.7: Cast all your care upon him, for he careth
for you.*

It is so important to spend time alone with God in
prayer. It is during that time alone with Him that we can be
daily refreshed in His presence. There we can rid ourselves
of yesterday's burdens and prepare for today's unknown
challenges.

He does not want us to carry our anxieties alone. He
would have us turn over every care and concern to Him.

When students come to me with problems or cares, I
am so happy to be able to help them and to alleviate their
anxieties. I can imagine in a similar way, how pleasing it
may be to our great God when He too lifts our burdens and
grants us relief from some anxiety.

In these days of terror alerts, when our whole world is
anxious, it helps to know that God is still in control. While
He will not perhaps prevent evil people from attacks, He
will be with us to face whatever happens. Meanwhile, He
tells us to "cast all our care" on Him.

*Dear Father: Thank you for caring for us and sharing all
our concerns today. In Jesus' name, Amen.*

# February 15

*James 2.8: If ye fulfill the royal law according to the scripture, thou shalt love thy neighbor as thyself, ye do well.*

*Luke 12.30,31: For the pagan world runs after all such things, and your Father knows that you need them. But seek his kingdom, and these things will be given to you as well.*

Errors of omission or errors of commission can exist side by side in our busy lives. Thoughtlessness is often the key to both in many cases. However, pure selfishness, wanting our own way, can also be the root cause of many lost opportunities to be helpful to someone in need. It is sometimes hard to put aside our goal-driven self-interests and truly focus on the needs and desires of those around us. Many times we can be most thoughtless of those who live with us. Because we can grow so accustomed to many of their needs, we can tend to not consider them always important. If we truly love our neighbor as we love ourselves, including the "neighbors" we live with, there should be plenty of love and thoughtfulness to go around!

In my harp class I try to foster a spirit of love and cooperation, as opposed to rivalry and competition. No matter what the outcome of their careers, the students will have happier lives as they make friends with future colleagues from around the world. Sometimes it seems that my class is a small United Nations! Almost anywhere my students travel in the world, they will usually find a classmate from here.

*Dear Father: Help us to think, with love, before we act today, and to say and do those things which will help and uplift those around us. In Christ's name, Amen.*

# February 16

*I Chronicles 28.9: And thou, Solomon my son, know thou the God of thy father and serve Him with a perfect heart, and with a willing mind; for the Lord searcheth all hearts, and understandeth all the imaginations of the thoughts: if thou seek him, he will be found of thee: but if thou forsake him, he will cast thee off for ever.*

It is rare that by performing great feats we best honor God. We serve God best, I think, by our small daily and even hourly sacrifices, done with willing and holy hearts and minds. If we set our minds on things that have eternal value, not focusing on this world, we may then be able to surmount the petty arrogances and grievances than can so easily disturb our peace of mind.

A heart that is constantly willing to put aside selfish desires and seek to help those around us must be pleasing to God. A thoughtless and careless heart, immersed in one's own sensitivities, not considering the needs of those around us, must grieve God.

I often feel that my students need me sometimes to take time during their lessons, to hear what is troubling them and to know I am sympathetic to their cares. This time of caring may be far more important than hearing their work. Afterwards, they may be able to play the lesson material with a lighter heart.

We must not assume that those around us are just fine and that they don't need help, but always strive to be open to hearing need and hurt in those we love. Then God can really use us in the lives of others. He will help give us the words of comfort and solace they need.

*Dear Father: Help us to serve you with willing and open hearts and minds. In Christ's name, Amen.*

# February 17

*James 1.2,3: My brethren, count it all joy when ye fall into diverse temptations or trials, knowing this, that the trying of your faith worketh patience.*

Patience is surely one of the greatest of God's gifts to us. Acceptance of our own weaknesses and foibles and those of others is a sign of maturity.

As a teacher, I am keenly aware of the different gifts of my students. Some are quick, excellent sight-readers, and learn very easily. But the race is often not won by the one who is the fastest! Others who learn very slowly usually play with a more beautiful tone quality, and their memorization, because taking longer, is perhaps deeper, so that in the final analysis, they may play more beautifully and artistically, with greater depth and confidence. The audience or public who hears these young artists is completely unaware of the difference in their learning time nor is that important to them. They simply experience the final result.

It takes patience to work with people who proceed at a different "tempo" than our own. God will give us patience as we ask Him for that help. As a teacher, patience is one of the most important traits I need in order to encourage and guide a student wisely.

*Dear Father: Thank you for the gift of patience. In Jesus' name, Amen.*

# February 18

*Psalms 119.71: It is good for me that I have been afflicted, that I might learn Thy statutes.*

*Lamentations 3.32: But though He cause grief, yet will He have compassion, according to the multitude of His mercies.*

It never feels good to be afflicted with painful trials, troubled relationships, and other similar problems. We can react with anger, hurt, bitterness and resentment. Or we can turn the problem over to God, asking Him for His instructions. The Bible speaks to every condition of our human hearts. If we earnestly seek God's answers, we will find them; and in the process, we will experience God's healing hand.

Sometimes a student has prepared a piece of music, memorized it and played the notes with technical accuracy. But what may often be missing are details written clearly in the score, but overlooked during the process of memorizing. As we go back and make note of the composer's instructions, a *ritardando* here, a *crescendo* there, a *diminuendo* here, or an accent there – the piece takes on a completely new life and is transformed into the composer's original vision.

So it is in our lives. As we study God's word and really understand His ways and how He wants the best for us, our lives too can be transformed by His power. He cares about every detail of our lives.

*Dear Lord: Teach us your will for our lives. Today may I grow in understanding your will and be open to changing the details of my day to day walk. In Jesus' name, Amen.*

# February 19

*John 4.34: My meat is to do the will of Him that sent me, and to finish His work.*

We can often disparage our work, feeling that those tasks set before us are not important. However, in God's eyes, nothing is insignificant, and the smallest duties may be very important in the development of our character.

The key is doing everything "as unto the Lord." We should do the next thing, that is, the chore or assignment before us, with all our hearts, never with resentment or ill-will.

Some of my lessons may be less than inspiring, but I always want to search for ways to help the student rise to a higher level of performance. I especially try to be sure that the repertoire I assign my students is within their musical and technical capabilities and is therefore appropriate. That can help to assure good results.

In the same way, I believe God places lovingly before us the tasks He would have us do, not giving us burdens too heavy for us to bear, or work that makes us miserable. The work He gives us to do, He will enable us to finish.

*Dear Lord: Help us to finish today those tasks you set before us. In Jesus' name, Amen.*

# February 20

*Romans 14.13: Let us not therefore judge one another any more; but judge this rather, that no man put a stumbling block, or an occasion to fall, in his brother's way.*

*Luke 11.52: Ye enter not in yourselves, and them that were entering in, ye hindered.*

In Luke 11.52, Jesus was chastising the Pharisees. Not only were they hypocrites, but they were stumbling blocks, preventing others from believing.

During this winter season with unusually heavy snow and bitter cold, I have found myself lamenting the weather to my students more than once as I struggle with boots and umbrellas and briefcase – I realize even such criticism of the weather can dampen another's spirits, and I know we should try to spare others this kind of complaining attitude.

How much worse it is to ruin a friend's happy attitude through disparaging remarks due to our own bad mood or frustrations! As a teacher, needing to make necessary corrections, it is a great responsibility to do so in an encouraging way, so as not to dishearten a student, and hopefully show them an easier way uncritically. In either situation, our feelings should not adversely affect anyone.

In our families and our work lives, how important it is to not bring home our moods of discontentment or irritability lest our gloom infect those about us, and we unwittingly spoil another's joy and peace. Our families need our support and encouragement. We need instead to seek our own comfort from God.

*Dear Father: Help us today to spread cheerfulness, encouragement and hope with all those we encounter. In Christ's name, Amen.*

# February 21

*Matthew 7.11: If ye then, being evil, know how to give good gifts unto your children, how much more shall your Father which is in Heaven give good gifts to them that ask Him.*

God answers our prayers sometimes by withholding from us what we desire. Sometimes He delays in giving us our desires, and we may often need to wait for years. But we always believe that He hears us and wants for us more than we can imagine, beyond our dreams.

We cannot know the future, nor can we know that sometimes what we want is not right for us. Our loving Father, in His infinite love and mercy, keeps from us what may harm us, even if at the time we are disappointed. And who knows how many calamities he may have spared us that we knew nothing about!?

Often a student asks me if she can play a piece that is actually far too advanced and difficult for her to play well. I must then search for other repertoire more suited to her development. And ultimately, when she has the necessary technical and musical skills, she will be able to play the work she longed for, and then she will play it wonderfully.

This reminds me of the plans God has for us, plans that are best for us, plans to help us and give us hope and a bright future.

*Dear Father: Every good and perfect gift is from you. Thank you for the plans you have for us. In Jesus' name, Amen.*

# February 22

*Philippians 4.6: Be anxious for nothing, but in everything by prayer and supplication, with thanksgiving let your requests be made known unto God.*

An attitude of thanksgiving seems to me to be the key that God uses to shower us with His blessings. When we have thankful hearts without anxiety, it leaves us wide open to receive blessings from the Lord.

However, when we hang onto our fears and worries, it seems to prevent or hinder our receiving help from the Father.

In the same way that a swimmer in trouble must relax and not struggle in order for a lifeguard to rescue them, so we must cease to struggle about those problems that cause us anxiety. We must totally release them and entrust them absolutely to our loving Father.

Students sometimes tense up in performances and, instead of helping them, it will lead them to produce tight, harsh sounds and have memory problems. Only when they relax and allow their fingers to remain supple will the tone quality be warm and beautiful and the music flow naturally.

Lives that are trusting in God, secure in His loving and faithful promises, will also radiate beauty and joy around them.

*Dear Father: Help us today to release to you all our anxieties and cares, loving and trusting your care for us. In Jesus' name, Amen.*

# February 23

*I Chronicles 19.13: Let the Lord do that which is good in His sight.*

*Psalms 33.22: Let Thy mercy, O Lord, be upon us, according as we hope in Thee.*

All week I have been anxiously watching the weather predictions, fearing another major snowstorm that might make travel to Indianapolis dangerous or impossible. There is a fund-raising event for the USA International Harp Competition this afternoon. I am expected to speak and our gold medalist is expected to perform. Last evening my worst fears were realized, and today everything is blanketed in five inches of snow, with another big storm due early today. But now, the worry is over and I know what to do and can take action. In this case, I need to hire a limousine to take the harpist and me up to Indianapolis and back.

The problem is solved and now I can release everything and trust in God's provision. Our worries and anxiety do not accomplish anything. It is wonderful to know that God is in charge, and doing what "is good in His sight."

*Dear Father: Thank you for your provision, always so much better than we can imagine! In Christ's name, Amen.*

# February 24

*John 16.33: These things I have spoken to you that in Me you might have peace. In the world you shall have tribulations; but be of good cheer; I have overcome the world.*

Leaders of countries have hard choices and decisions to make when confronted with natural disasters and man-made ones. Hopefully they pray about the lives they influence so greatly and rely on Godly advice.

We all have choices to make, whether to allow injustice or unreasonableness that enter our lives to shatter our calm, or to bear such situations with equanimity. It is hard to be cheerful when we read of such terrible catastrophes as the genocide in Africa or the suffering after the tsunami in southern Asia. Wars, which include "collateral damage" of the deaths of innocent civilians, cause heartbreak in countless lives.

I think we must pray for these situations, first of all, and then we should also pressure our elected representatives to take action to alleviate the suffering involved where it is possible.

Jesus knew suffering, and when He spoke of tribulations He knew what the future held, for Him and for the world in that regard. He has promised to overcome the evil in this world and I trust Him to do it.

*Dear Lord: Thank you for your promises of peace, which we may not experience in this world, but only in eternity with you. In Jesus' name, Amen.*

# February 25

*Isaiah 43.1: But now thus saith the Lord that created thee, O Jacob, and He that formed thee, O Israel: Fear not, for I have redeemed thee, I have called thee by thy name; thou are mine.*

It is awesome to realize that the God who created the universe cares for me personally. He is always with me, loving me and aware of my every thought, word and deed. Also, He protects me in times of great danger.

These verses in Isaiah are among my favorites in the whole Bible. A little further on, in Chapter 43, it continues, "When you walk through the fire, you will not be burned; the flames will not set you ablaze." (Isaiah 43.2)

Many people, hearing about my home burning down, exclaimed how wonderful that I was not at home – not knowing that I *was* in it, and at home that night! By God's mercy, I woke up and was able to get out unharmed. So this verse has special meaning and significance to me.

God's love is ever present within and around each one of us. We become aware only afterwards of the many circumstances from which He has saved us, or spared us, and sometimes we are never aware of all He does on our behalf!

*Dear Lord: We are unable to grasp the magnitude of your love, but we observe it daily in the beauty and wonder of your universe and our safe-keeping. Thank you for your Word and for revealing yourself to us in it. In Jesus' name, Amen.*

# February 26

*Psalms 145.18: The Lord is nigh unto all them that call upon Him, to all that call upon Him in truth.*

*Psalms 34.4: I sought the Lord, and He heard me, and delivered me from all my fears.*

This week I needed to convince a student to give up working toward a contest. The music required was much too difficult for her, and the time spent on one or two pieces all year could be put to much better use learning several pieces more suitable for her level. This was not an easy decision for me or for her.

I think God watches over us, much more closely than a caring teacher. He does not want us to stumble, but sometimes He has to send us trials in order to get our attention and to bring about needed change in our lives. He wants us to have no other "gods" but Him. He wants us to depend on Him alone, relying on nothing else and no one else. Our role is simply to trust Him.

It is sad to be with someone who is suffering from remorse and living in regret. God is so close to the broken-hearted and only longs to provide comfort and healing. But, it seems at some point acceptance is necessary. He wants us to ask Him for help in complete faith and trust. His timing is not ours, and His answers too can be very different from what we think we need.

*Dear Father: We know you hear us when we call upon you. Thank you for answering every prayer and grant us the trust to accept your will in the circumstances of our lives today. In Jesus' name, Amen.*

# February 27

*Psalms 37.3: Trust in the Lord, and do good; so shalt thou dwell in the land, and verily thou shalt be fed.*

There are some students who are content to take my advice about fingerings or repertoire, and there are others who question many fingerings and suggestions. Many times the difference is made clear when they experience the fingerings or play the repertoire up to tempo and see that they may be needlessly complicating a passage that could be simple. Other times, I become convinced and accept that their own fingerings are fine. I believe there are many different ways to achieve good results and I need to constantly strive to keep an open mind to change and differences.

Sometimes it seems that we complicate our lives needlessly. What should be easy and effortless, we make difficult and exhausting. If we truly trust God in all the big and small issues of our lives and set our hearts and minds on doing each day what is good and right, God will provide for us, all and more than we need. We need to accept that His ways are not our ways, and learn from His ways, which unlike me as a teacher, are perfect!

*Dear Father: Thank you for providing us with work and making our work meaningful. In Jesus' name, Amen.*

# February 28

*I John 4.7: Beloved, let us love one another, for love is of God; and every one that loveth is born of God, and knoweth God.*

*Isaiah 26.3: Thou wilt keep him in perfect peace, whose mind is stayed on thee; because he trusteth in thee.*

Love truly conquers all. Every day may be lived in perfect peace if love is dominant in our lives. If we look at some of the hard problems that we must often face, through the lens of loving eyes, the problems may almost disappear. Many artists, myself among them, have had to face the jealousy of colleagues.

Selfishness and bitterness cannot take root when our hearts are filled with love. They cannot exist side by side. In the music world, there can often be heard stories of great rivalries and jealousies among artists of renown. And there are also so many wonderful stories of artists helping each other. I know in my life, I owe much to colleagues who helped me along the way.

Jealousy and envy cannot stand in the face of love. The absence of love is the cause of most unhappiness in the world. Love is one of God's greatest gifts to us. Now abide faith, hope and love, but the greatest of these is love.

Love of God is love of good. If God's love abides in our souls, we will see the good around us, and we will be spreaders of good around us.

*Dear Father: Help us to be a source of love to everyone we meet today. Thank you for Jesus who exemplified love in giving His life for us. In His name we pray, Amen.*

# March 1

*Matthew 6.25: Take no thought for your life, what ye shall eat or what ye shall drink, nor yet for your body, what ye shall put on.*

If we really are honest with ourselves, most of our worries and anxieties are about future events or circumstances. In this sixth chapter of Matthew, Jesus tells us in no uncertain terms that we should not worry about tomorrow, and should only live one day at a time.

God knows of our every need and does not ask us to carry more than one day's burden. And we are to live fully in the present, not regretting the past or borrowing fear and anxiety about the future. So many potentially joyful and productive moments in the "here and now" are lost because of these wasted emotions.

When my graduate students worry about their future in the precarious music world, which is natural to do, I urge them to be prepared to go wherever there is a need for them and gain as much practical experience as they can. There is always room in our field for excellence, and if they are superb musicians they will eventually succeed. It is true even for those who are not at the top of the class. If my students truly love their work and do not get discouraged, they will be successful. Probably the most important thing is perseverance – to "stay the course" and not give up hope.

God is in charge of our destinies and He will provide for us.

*Dear Father: Thank you for carrying our burdens of the past and future. Thank you for this day's opportunities. In Jesus' name, Amen.*

# March 2

*Hebrews 13.16: But to do good and to communicate for-get not: for with such sacrifices, God is well-pleased/*

*I John 3:11: For this is the message we have heard from the beginning, that we should love one another.*

I try to walk about two miles a day in the indoor mall. Because the winter has been so cold and we have had so much snow, the mall is really the only place to be able to walk. Hundreds walk there daily, and I see the same faces with regularity. Although mostly total strangers, many smile and wave hello as they pass, and it always lifts my heart. Others plod along, never making eye contact nor appearing to notice anyone else.

It is such a small thing to smile, but it is like a "ray of sunshine." I think we should always be ready to offer a smile and a greeting. We never know what heartaches and pain those we pass may be carrying. Most are surely lonely, as I am often, also.

We feel sometimes that we need to do great things for the Lord, make great sacrifices or gifts. But really, it is in our small gestures of kindness, simply loving someone, that pleases God most.

Our lives can become so self-centered. As we adhere to schedules, we leave little time to help a friend or to make a caring phone call. We need to remember that foremost we are to love one another.

*Dear Father: Help us to show your love to everyone we meet today. In Jesus' name, Amen.*

# March 3

*Psalms 119.60: I made haste, and delayed not to keep Thy commandments.*

*James 4.14: Ye know not what shall be on the morrow.*

I believe that procrastination is one of Satan's greatest tools to tempt the believer to put off doing one's duty or help someone in need. It is true that we often think, I will do thus and so tomorrow or next week or even this evening—and then something happens and the circumstances change. We have forever lost that opportunity to do what is right and good.

My father used to tease my mother by calling her "Miss Right Now." Mother never put off something God placed on her heart to do. I wish now that I was more like her and not prone to delay some phone calls, for example, that need to be made.

I watch my students and see some who put off memorizing their music until the last minute and others who memorize right away. The latter, of course, play with greater freedom and fluency sooner, and also can learn larger quantities of music faster.

If we are living a life committed to following God's directions, we should make haste to do what He places before us.

*Dear Father: Help me today to do the large or the small tasks that you put before me. In Christ's name, Amen.*

# March 4

*II Corinthians 4.6:   God who commanded the light to shine out of darkness, that shined in our hearts, to give the light of the knowledge of the glory of God in the face of Jesus Christ.*

*Isaiah 53.4: Surely, He hath borne our griefs and carried our sorrows.*

We all seek to avoid troubles, sorrow and grief. I am always very thankful for an ordinary day – one without a sudden crisis or heartache. However, the Bible says, "Fix your eyes upon Jesus." Learn from His life. He was "a man of sorrows and acquainted with grief." If we are to imitate Him, we cannot shun sorrow but instead we should learn from it, embrace it, open ourselves to it. We should forget ourselves and live in sacrificial love.

Each step we take in that direction draws us closer to God, who did not spare His own Son but gave Him as a ransom for many, for us.

Today I am taking a friend to the hospital in a few minutes to undergo what we hope will be minor surgery. A hospital is  full of suffering people and I pray that my friend's procedure will go smoothly and easily. I know everyone that is in surgery or who knows someone in surgery prays for the same. Yet, sometimes God allows illness and death to claim those we love. In such times of sorrow, we can only be thankful that Jesus experienced all these emotions and He will be our guide when we walk that dark valley.

*Dear Father: We look to Jesus for a role model in all that we face. Be with us today. In Christ's name, Amen.*

# March 5

*I John 3.3: And every man that hath this hope in Him purifieth himself, even as He is pure.*

If we aspire to live holy and pure lives, we must take time to listen to God's quiet urgings. We cannot hear Him if we are constantly doing and achieving, even if we are busy doing His work.

As we quiet our minds and meditate on a favorite hymn or verse of scripture, we can come into His presence. We will not hear an audible voice, but spirit will speak to spirit and soul will speak to soul,. We will not only be refreshed, but also purified.

Sometimes, in preparing a new piece of music, I will spend hours just playing it through many times. But the most important work is when I am silent and am contemplating the score, searching for its meaning, studying the composer's indications to better understand the interpretative guidelines that are sometimes not clear. The "play-throughs" are important too, as without them there would not be the freedom and ease of performance.

But isn't this like our lives? We must, of course, be out and about our work---whatever we do for a living. But, to understand the real meaning of our lives, we must spend time alone with our Creator---seeking His guidance, reading His words to us in the Bible, praying for His forgiveness and thanking Him for His great love and faithfulness.

*Dear Father: Thank you for this new day. May we spend much of it close to Thee. In Christ's name, Amen.*

# March 6

*Isaiah 32.2:  The shadow of a great rock in a weary land...*

*Isaiah 30.15:  In returning and rest shall ye be saved; in quietness and in confidence shall be your strength.*

It is so hard to remain silent when we are insulted and put down unfairly.  We long to retaliate, or to just defend ourselves. But experience shows that such defenses only escalate into greater disputes and arguments.  Anger begets anger!

These Bible verses are a great lesson to me.  Silence is often golden in difficult circumstances like the one above.  Our best defense is probably no defense.  Calmness, quietness and perhaps removing oneself from the scene can often do more good than anything else.

If we picture the shadow of a great rock, we can feel strength, refreshing coolness, restraint, and wisdom.  Isaiah paints a picture of people who fear God, who will be leaders in justice, honor and truth.

In these tense days there seem to be so many wars around the world, tempers are heated and people are so sure they are right.  The world is divided into those who are anti-war or pro-war.  We know that in similar circumstances, when Lincoln was President, he was frequently on his knees praying. He relied on God's wisdom, not his own, respectfully disagreeing with those who differed in opinion from him.

*Dear Father:  When we are faced with difficult and tumultuous times, we pray for your holy presence with us, guiding us and strengthening us and our leaders for whatever lies ahead.  In Christ's name, Amen.*

# March 7

*I Corinthians 12.6: There are diversities of operations, but it is the same God which worketh all in all.*

*Isaiah 45.7: I form the light and create darkness: I make peace, and create evil: I, the Lord, do all these things.*

When we see a friend suffering pain and illness, it is hard to accept that God is allowing this misery. It is often true that the suffering itself causes us to develop greater closeness to God and to deepen our faith and dependency on Him — all worthy goals.

But we know God is good and God is love. The mystery of good and evil is beyond our understanding. One day when we stand before God, the questions of pain and suffering may be answered. For now, we must be content with studying the scriptures for wisdom and understanding to accept all that God has in store for us. In the Bible we see every circumstance in life, and we can put our own lives in perspective. We can use our short span of years to worship God and do His will so that when we stand under judgment before Him, we may hear Him say, "Well done, my good and faithful servant."

*Dear Father: We know our days are numbered. Help us to apply our heart with wisdom. In Christ's name, Amen.*

# March 8

*II Timothy 2.15: Study to show thyself approved unto God, a workman that needeth not to be ashamed.*

*Galatians 6.9: And let us not be weary in well-doing; for in due season we shall reap if we faint not.*

We cannot always know exactly what God wills for us to do, or perhaps, not to do. But what we usually do know is where our duty lies. We know we should complete some clearly unfinished task, call on an elderly friend who is no longer able to get out, or stop nagging a friend or spouse to do something they don't want to do. These kinds of duties are not easy, but I think in our hearts we know doing them will be pleasing to God.

A few of my students start memorizing a piece well, but somehow "grow weary" towards the end and cannot seem to just finish the memorization. Of course it means they will not be able to perform that piece at all, and usually they then want to move on to another piece. I feel badly for them, for it is a habit that prevents them from achieving their very best.

The ability to finish tasks we begin is very important in living happy and fulfilling lives. Sometimes we fail because we are spreading ourselves too thin, trying to do too many tasks at the same time. That is a juggling act, and can lead to failure in completing any of them well. If I prioritize and set limits on the amount of work or music to learn or duties before me, then I may be able to do everything well and "not be ashamed" of my work. Whatever we do, we can do it as unto the Lord, "excellence in all things, and all things to God's glory."

*Dear Father: Help us today to finish some of those tasks that are dear to your heart. In Jesus' name, Amen.*

# March 9

*Deuteronomy 12.18: Thou shalt rejoice before the Lord thy God in all that thou puttest thine hands into.*

*Colossians 3.15: Be ye thankful.*

The old popular song lyrics that say "laughing in the rain, be happy again," have it right. Our rejoicing in all that God sends us will be a recipe for happiness unparalleled.

If we are thankful for the work God has provided, we will do it with joy. I think I am enjoying my dear students more than ever before; we laugh together and work hard together in such a warm and cooperative spirit. I am very thankful for them.

William Law wrote that a thankful spirit "turns all it touches into happiness."

What a transformation it can make in our lives if we wake each morning thanking God for the gift of a new day! Whatever our circumstances, there is always so much for which we can be grateful.

When we face various trials or disappointments, then, most of all, we should ask God what lessons He is teaching us. It is a blessing if we can learn patience, goodness and hope in the face of adversity. These are character traits that will sustain us throughout our entire lives and prepare us for future adversities, which every one of us will surely experience.

But, if we focus on what may be hurtful or painful in our lives, we can become bitter and make ourselves miserable. This is not how God wants us to live.

*Dear Father: Teach us to give thanks in all things. In Christ's name, Amen.*

# March 10

*Isaiah 43.2: When thou passest through the waters, I will be with thee; and through the rivers, they shall not overflow thee: when thou walkest through the fire, thou shalt not be burned; neither shall the flame kindle upon thee.*

*Jeremiah 1.8: I am with thee to deliver thee.*

Our lives can be turned upside down in a moment. Disaster can strike in a sudden automobile accident or with the diagnosis of a terrible malignancy or by the unexpected death of our closest friend or loved one. I have just heard of the death of the daughter of a close friend and my heart aches for her pain.

When we walk through these depths and our human strength and courage fail us, God has promised to be with us and to deliver us. He does not promise to spare us from suffering and sorrow but to be with us in it all and strengthen us by his strong hand. He is faithful and completely trustworthy.

But we must do our part. We must not worry or "stew" or fret. We must face our adversity with courage, showing our trust in God and relying on Him totally. We are to remain cheerful and show a smiling face to the world. We are told to forget ourselves and our own pain and strive to help others who are hurting, too.

*Dear Father: Thank you for being with us, through fire and flood. Help us to help others as they, too, pass through great times of sorrow. In Christ's name, Amen.*

# March 11

*Psalms 55.22: Cast thy burden upon the Lord, and He shall sustain thee; He shall never suffer the righteous to be moved.*

The New International Version (NIV) translates this verse, "He will never let the righteous fall." While no one can claim to be without fault, "All have sinned…" we can be forgiven, and we can take all of our burdens and cares and lay them down at the feet of Jesus. He promises to carry them for us and transform our character along the way.

After the fire, I found my thoughts were mostly very sad and depressed for several months. I could not seem to picture the future at all. I kept reliving those horrible images of the night the house burned.

We cannot change many of the sad or unhappy circumstances of our lives. But we can try to bear them bravely, putting our own problems away, entrusting them to God --- and then get on with trying to help others and be a comfort to others. As we put aside our selfish cares and self-centeredness and focus on others, we will be filled with peace and joy. Surely a life of service to others is a life well lived. This is not to say that we should go around as a "do-gooder", but just with a mindset of helpfulness, courtesy and kindness to all whom we meet. Then we will often find our own cares and problems greatly diminished in importance.

*Dear Father: Thank you for carrying today's burden. In Jesus' name, Amen.*

# March 12

*Numbers 6.24-26: The Lord bless thee and keep thee; the Lord make His face to shine upon thee and be gracious unto thee. The Lord lift up His countenance upon thee and give thee peace.*

This beautiful benediction closes many, many Christian church services. It is so familiar that we perhaps are putting on our scarves and gloves during it---preparing to leave.

But these are precious words and promises. The Lord God, creator of the universe, has promised to bless us and to be gracious to us, to look with favor upon us and to grant us His peace!

As a professor of music, I often beam at my students because I am so happy for them when they have played well or mastered a difficult passage or given an exceptionally moving performance.

I imagine our beloved Lord, smiling on us as we "bumble" our way through life, but nevertheless are leaning on Him. His favor and His blessing are all we long for, and all we should ever need. Whatever our circumstances, if God is blessing us, we are blessed indeed and can live in peace and harmony.

*Dear Father God: Every day we seek your face and every day you are there. So great is Thy faithfulness. Thank you. In Jesus' name, Amen.*

# March 13

*John 15.5: He that abideth in me, and I in him, bringeth forth fruit.*

*Psalms 90.17: Let the beauty of the Lord our God be upon us.*

If we are indwelt by the Holy Spirit, our outer appearance should reflect it. Not that we will suddenly become beauty queens, but there can be real differences in our expressions, our smiling face, and the light in our eyes.

Although we will still sin and make mistakes, if our hearts belong to Christ, and the Holy Spirit is guiding and directing us, we will be changed people.

*Galatians 5.22 says, "The fruit of the spirit is love, joy, peace, patience, kindness, goodness, faithfulness, gentleness, and self-control".*

These traits should be very obvious to those around us or with whom we associate. If we do not exemplify these traits, we need to search our heart deeply and ask ourselves why? If we provoke others and envy others, we are living selfishly and this is incompatible with a life committed to Christ.

We must be yielded completely, giving up our selfish desires and self-centered behaviors. We need to abide in Him and allow His Holy Spirit to transform us into his likeness. This is a mysterious process, but only then will the true "beauty of the Lord be upon us."

*Dear Father: May we show forth the fruit of Your Holy Spirit today and every day. In Jesus' name, Amen.*

# March 14

*Psalms 17.6: I have called upon Thee, for Thou wilt hear me, O God! Incline Thine ear unto me, and hear my speech.*

*Psalms 62.8: Ye people, pour out your heart before Him! God is a refuge for us.*

Recently I taught advanced make-up lessons so that I could fly down to Florida for nine nights of spring vacation. So I was more than usually tired from the teaching. It seemed like the students were desperate to perform in the Wednesday master class, which lasted for over two hours. Then I went home to pack, close up the house, pay the last bills, and have a miserable trip to the airport. The driver was 30 minutes late, the cab reeked of cigarette smoke, and because of a mix-up with my electronic ticket, my seat was given away and I was put on standby! I was told to rush to the gate, but then had to stand for 15 minutes in a security line certain I would miss the standby selection. It was all totally exhausting. The flight, which I did make, was oversold, very crowded and there was turbulence most of the way. Thankful to be on terra firma, I then had another cab trip to Naples where I unpacked and fell into bed.

This morning, though, as warm Florida sunshine pours through the windows, I am tired, but thankful to have this precious vacation time. It truly feels like a reward for the weeks of hard teaching. I feel God has known my fatigue and He has given me this wonderful refuge!

*Dear Father: Thank you giving us times of work and times of relaxation. All our days are in your hands. Grant us to use every day wisely, In Christ's name, Amen*

# MARCH

## March 15

*Psalms 69.16: Hear me, O Lord, for Thy loving-kindness is good: turn unto me according to the multitude of Thy tender mercies.*

*Psalms 119.76: Let, I pray Thee, Thy merciful kindness be for my comfort, according to Thy word unto Thy servant.*

When we face harshness, criticism and unjust cruelty, conditions that exist frequently together in our fallen and sin-filled world, how comforting it is to rest in the tender mercies and loving kindness of the Holy God.

We cannot depend on our fellow man to do the kind and good thing. We cannot count on receiving justice and love from another human being.

Only God is never-failing in His goodness, comfort and compassion. And what is truly wonderful is that He wants us to depend upon Him alone, to totally rely on Him.

He can lift us out of our individual pits of depression and trials as we turn each of them over to Him. He can use them for good, teaching us precious lessons of tolerance, patience and forgiveness. We cannot change others, but we can be transformed ourselves through His divine power.

*Dear Father: Forgive us if we seek any other source but you for our deepest needs of mercy and kindness. Thank you for your faithfulness. In Christ's name, Amen.*

# March 16

*I Corinthians 10.31: Whether therefore ye eat, drink, or whatsoever ye do, do all to the glory of God.*

*Ephesians 6.7: . . . With good will doing service, as to the Lord and not unto men.*

There is peace and joy in doing the most menial task when we commit it to the Lord. He can transform our least pleasurable work into holy work. It could change our attitude toward our obligations and duties if we pictured doing them for Jesus! If we picture our superior or our boss to be God, wouldn't we work with greater zeal and enthusiasm? I also don't think we would cut any corners!

There used to be so many laws about what one should or should not eat or drink. And still today, many people disapprove of alcoholic beverages of any kind. The Bible tells us that if it will offend or weaken the faith of a brother by what we eat or drink, we should abstain for that reason, not that it is a sin to drink wine. The same would apply to refraining from eating rich food with a loved one who cannot because of health or diet, just so as not to tempt them. In other words, we are to think of others first, and do all we can to encourage them. This is truly doing service, with good will.

*Dear Father: We so often fail to do service with good will. Forgive us our self-centeredness and help us this day to do all we do as unto the Lord. In Christ's name, Amen.*

# March 17

*Ruth 2.19: Where hast thou gleaned today?*

This verse refers to picking up left-over wheat in the fields, a practice in ancient times that helped widows and the poor survive. But it can also mean to us, "What have we done with the gift of time, or what duty have we left undone?"

These precious vacation days are going by so fast, just visiting with friends, setting up the kitchen and shopping, playing golf, swimming, all so enjoyable, but it seems the time is slipping through my fingers.

I at least "do my fingers" at the harp each day, that is, a limited amount of practice necessary to maintain my calluses. I am so fortunate that one of my best harps escaped the fire by being here in Florida.

There have been lunches and dinners planned for every day except today, so I hope to really relax and perhaps spend the afternoon on the beach.

Yesterday was Sunday, and I was so happy to go to my church home here, the First Baptist Church of Naples. That church always has an uplifting and inspiring service.

I hope that I will return to Bloomington rested and refreshed and ready to go back to the last intensive six weeks at the university. I think my "duty" while here is to rest and relax!

*Dear Father: Thank you for giving us times to rest and times to do meaningful work. We commit all our days to Thee. In Christ's name, Amen.*

# March 18

*I Peter 3.8: Finally, be ye all of one mind, having compassion one of another; love as brethren, be pitiful, be courteous.*

Simple courtesy, in the small matters of life seems to be lacking in our world today. Because families so rarely sit down and enjoy meals together, often it means that children are not taught good table manners, not to mention courtesy in other areas.

Even in Japan where courtesy is an ingrained part of the culture, people push and shove to get onto a train or subway.

But, Peter is writing on a deeper level, that all we do should emanate from a compassionate heart full of love and pity for reach other. That is the one mind we should share. If we truly are compassionate, even if we disagree about different matters, we will be patient and courteous to each other.

We have the strongest role model in Jesus, who when falsely accused and vilified by men, remained silent. But, as we strive to remain silent, we must not give bitterness or resentment a root in our hearts. Daily, we must erase hurts and trust God for our well-being. In Him alone will we every find true love and self-affirmation, not from others.

*Dear Father: Thank you for this new day, and for giving us a clean slate and compassionate hearts. In Christ's name, Amen.*

# March 19

*Titus 2.10: Showing all good faith, so that in everything they may adorn the doctrine of God our Savior.*

This chapter in Titus gives guidelines for behavior to all, old and young, men and women, free or slave. Verse 11 says, "For the grace of God has appeared bringing salvation to all people...training us to live self-controlled, upright and godly lives in this present age."

We must never give up; God calls us to be faithful. Whether we are called to great and important tasks (in the world's eyes) or to small and humble deeds, we are called to be faithful.

We are also called to teach what is good. I think as a music professor part of my job is to prepare my students to live good, thoughtful and upright lives; to show integrity in their musical lives, be dependable and well-prepared. As they join the profession hopefully these lessons will remain and they will be good colleagues, helpful to one another.

I love to see the friendships develop in my classes. I know, looking back over 50 years of teaching, that these friendships among my students will always be meaningful. And when my students travel to Europe or Asia or South America, almost in every country, they will have harpist friends.

Surely faithful friendship is one of God's great gifts to us.

*Dear Father: Help us to be faithful to You in all we do today. In Jesus' name, who was faithful even unto death, Amen.*

# March 20

*Matthew 4.10: Thou shalt worship the Lord thy God, and Him only shalt thou serve.*

*Psalms 119.2 Blessed are they that keep His testimonies and that seek Him with the whole heart.*

The striving for success or fame or wealth in this world is really futile, unless blessed by the Lord. We are told in the Bible to "seek first the kingdom of God and His righteousness, and all these things will be added to you."

We are to worship and serve only God, and not any material thing. He wants our whole heart; we are to wholeheartedly serve Him, not just by going to church once a week but by a constant commitment to seek His will in every aspect of our lives.

Nowhere does God promise us wealth or success in terms of material things if we put Him first in our lives, but He promises us peace and His presence, both greater blessings than anything else we can hope for..

His peace surpasses our human understanding. If He is with us throughout our lives and we are resting in the sure knowledge of our salvation through the blood and resurrection of Jesus Christ, we can have that peace. And even as we face terrorism threats and the anxieties of war, we can know that whatever befalls us, we are ready to face our Creator and are assured of eternity with Him.

*Dear Father: You have given us a clear roadmap how we are to live. Thank you for your Word, which is our guide each day through our trials and our triumphs. In Christ's name, Amen.*

# March 21

*Matthew 6.32: Your heavenly Father knoweth that ye have need of all these things.*

I have always loved Matthew 7.9, "which one of you, if his son asks him for bread, will give him a stone…if you then, who are evil know how to give good gifts to your children, how much more will your Father who is in Heaven, give good things to those who ask him!" These verses follow Jesus' words, "Ask and it will be given to you; seek and you will find; knock and it will be opened to you."

God knows what we need and what is best for us. We often pray for things we think we want and need, when we really are not ready for them or we might even be hurt by them. That is why we can rest completely in God's will, knowing He alone knows what is right for us, and His timing is always perfect.

Sometimes He withholds from us in one area of our lives, while blessing us deeply in another area. In the popular television show now only seen on re-runs, "Father Knows Best," the father is often seen making mistakes, even though well-intended. But our Heavenly Father never makes mistakes. We can be at peace about that.

*Dear Father: Every good and perfect gift comes from you. Thank you Lord. In Jesus' name, Amen.*

# March 22

*Ecclesiastes 3.1:To everything there is a season, a time for every purpose under heaven.*

After this verse, there follows the famous verse, "A time to be born, and a time to die," and verse 8, "a time of war and a time of peace."

As our troops are attacking Iraq, we as a country are anxious for their safety, and we wish war were not necessary. Before the hostilities had barely begun, the grandson of one of my neighbors was killed in a helicopter crash.

Our country has been blessed with many years of peace. Then 9-11 happened, and we were attacked. Our leaders believe it is a time to eliminate the threat that Iraq's leadership poses, to give their weapons of mass destruction to terrorists who would hold the world hostage. So, I believe this may be a right time for war, even while praying it will be over quickly with a minimum loss of civilian lives.

As we realize our days are numbered, we should always look at how we spend them. God has a purpose for every life. At every age and in each season, He wants to use us.

*Dear Father: We pray for your provision for our brave troops, keep them safe and protect them. In Jesus' name, Amen*

# March 23

*3 John 5: Beloved, thou doest faithfully, whatsoever thou doest.*

*2 Corinthians 13:9: And this also we wish, even your perfection.*

I have often been asked what traits I most value in a student. While there are many that will serve their work well, I believe flexibility and the ability to adapt are among the most important. It is vital to be flexible, to be able to change easily from one fingering to another, or position, or tempo, or dynamic. On a different level, it is also important to have the ability to be able to learn quickly a new piece required for an orchestra concert, or to be able to follow a conductor's direction on the spot, changing interpretation or tempo.

I think as Christians, God desires us to be flexible too, and pliable under His direction. He wants us to be totally yielded to His will, in the smallest things as well as in the weightiest. With humility and obedience He wants us to do our duties daily, without complaining.

His goal is to make us conform to the perfect image of Christ. Our goal is to be the best musicians we can be and trust Him to perfect us as we are yielded to His will.

*Dear Father: Mold us and make us after Thy Will while we are waiting, yielded, and still. In Christ's name, Amen.*

# March 24

*Psalm 4:8L I will lay down in peace to sleep; for Thou, Lord, only makest me dwell in safety.*

*Psalm 127:2: He giveth His beloved sleep.*

Peaceful sleep is surely one of God's greatest gifts. When we are yielded to His will and are aware of his merciful watchfulness over us, we should be able to sleep and to rest from the day's labors.

However, there are times s when we toss and turn and are unable to find that blessed release of sleep. Sometimes it is because God wants to talk to us or teach us something. It is a good idea to turn on the light and read the Bible or a devotional book. It also is a wonderful uninterrupted time for prayer.

When I cannot sleep, I often sing favorite hymns or praise songs (quietly!) and think of those people I wanted to pray for: friends who are ill, or traveling, or going through some crisis or bereavement. I think these times when sleep eludes me can be used to good purpose.

*Dear Father: Thank you for the gift of sleep. We pray for our brave soldiers who are unable to sleep. In Jesus' name, Amen.*

# March 25

*Psalm 85:8: I will hear what God the Lord will speak, for He will speak peace unto His people.*

How can God speak to us when we fill every moment with work or busyness? It is not that He doesn't want us to work or to do those tasks set before us. But God wants us to put Him first. He longs for us to stop and to simply abide in Him. Only then can he speak to our hearts; only then can we whisper to Him our deepest concerns.

We need to turn off the television, get by ourselves and converse with our Creator.

My college students, many of whom have their own harps in their apartments, still prefer to come to school to do their four hours of practice. It is because they are free of interruptions in the practice rooms, away from the phone and roommates and disturbances. Only in that quiet place can they do the serious work of memorizing and intense concentration.

In the same way, we need to get away by ourselves, alone with God, for true communion with Him to take place. We need to schedule such time and it will bring us great peace.

*Dear Father: Forgive us for rushing here and there, and for devoting such a small proportion of our lives to time alone with you, our highest priority. In Christ's name, Amen.*

# March 26

*Hebrews 1:14: Are they not all ministering spirits?*

Yesterday in class, I heard performances by mature musicians, winners of prizes in competitions. There was much to admire in their playing.

But then two younger underclassmen played also, and they were electrifying, playing perhaps far less perfectly, but with such zest, enthusiasm, and musical intensity that we were all riveted!

This is always a humbling experience for me as a teacher. It is the vital personal spark in an artist that is the most important ingredient, and one which cannot be taught! It is a God-given gift, and I can only hope to nurture it in each of my students.

In each of our lives, from the humblest to the greatest, God has given us unique, special gifts, and He knows the plans and uses He has for them. He nurtures them in us, and encourages us throughout our lives, as we depend upon Him and trust Him. What a blessed collaboration we have when we are yielded completely to God, allowing Him to guide and direct us.

*Dear Father: Each day help us to grow into the ministering spirit you would have us be. In Christ's name, Amen.*

# March 27

*1 John 4:12: If we love one another God dwells in us, and His love is perfected in us.*

*1 John 3:24: And he that keeps His commandments dwells in Him, and He in him. And hereby we know that He abides in us, by the Spirit which He has given us.*

If we are governed by love, it should be apparent to all around us. Love is the opposite of selfishness; it puts others first and forgets self. Love exudes kindness and sympathy. Goodness flows naturally from a loving heart like a rippling brook.

The opposite is also true. An angry and bitter heart spreads ill-will, disappointment, hurt feelings, and selfishness. Envy and covetousness are the same. They poison the actual air we breathe.

The only cure for the latter is the cleansing blood of Jesus Christ. He alone can lift the burden of unforgiveness and pull out the roots of bitterness. He alone can wash us inside and out and make us "whiter than snow." He alone can replace an angry heart with a loving heart.

*Dear Father: We come to you with our public and private sins of selfishness and brokenness. Forgive us and make us new creatures, abide in us we pray. In Christ's name, Amen.*

# March 28

*Ephesians 5:20: Giving thanks always for all things unto God.*

A thankful heart rarely has room in it for unforgiveness or bitterness. As we learn to be thankful for everything, both the hard and the easy, we move into a posture of total acceptance of God's will.

As we trust Him to bring good out of every difficult trial and hidden sorrow, we are able to thank Him for these hard events, knowing that everything He allows is for our ultimate good.

Even as I grieved and mourned my lost home and harps, God was preparing a new house for me with love and compassion.

When a relationship turned to pain and unhappiness, He brought relief and lifted me up by the smiling warmth of my dear students.

Out of every tragic situation, underneath we see the loving arms of our Savior. He will not give us more pain than we can bear, and He will safely carry us through the dark valleys, inevitable in any life.

As we experience this, we learn to trust Him even more, unto death.

*Dear Father God: Thank you for all you give us, gifts of love meant for our good. In Jesus' name, Amen.*

# March 29

*Psalm 91:10: There shall no evil befall thee.*

*Proverbs 1:33: Whoever listens to me will live in safety and be at ease, without fear of harm.*

The beautiful hymn Blessed Assurance sums up our faith in Jesus Christ. We are heirs, inheriting salvation because of His sacrifice on the cross. We know that we will suffer in this human life, but no matter what sorrows and trials we may be asked to bear, we have the promise of a future with Christ in heaven. So, we do not live in fear, but in the blessed assurance of His promises and protection!

As we follow the tragedies of war in the world, we pray for the safety of those in harms' way. We pray that God's mighty, all-powerful hand will hover over the world, and end the cruel suffering taking place. We pray for wisdom for leaders throughout the world.

We must not be crushed by the present nor fear for the future. God calls us to endure whatever he sends us, nobly and courageously. He will bring good out of everything He allows to befall us.

*Dear Father God: Even though we cannot begin to understand why tragedies happen, we trust you to use every circumstance for good. Thank you for giving us courage to bear all in your strength. In Christ's name, Amen.*

# March 30

*Psalm 73:24: Thou shalt guide me with Thy counsel, and afterward receive me to glory.*

*Hebrews 4:9: There remaineth therefore a rest to the people of God.*

The old saying, "Advice is cheap" is too true. Friends will often want to help us out of dilemmas by offering their advice. God can use friends to help us hear His wise counsel, if they, in turn, are relying on Him themselves.

It is also important for us to test advice given us to see if it bears up and agrees with the Bible. God will never contradict Himself.

We should also always pray, committing our problems and decisions, being very specific about them. I remember how deeply I prayed before making the decision to rebuild a house on my old lot. I was given much advice, and I truly relied on the Lord for wisdom. I expected and trusted that my prayers would be answered., and they were!

God's timing is perfect. He will direct our path if we commit it to Him.

*Dear Father: Thank you for your Word, for answered prayer and for the Godly advice of friends. May you direct our path today. In Christ's name, Amen.*

# March 31

*Job 5:23, 24: Thou shalt be in league with the stones of the field, and the beasts of the field shall be at peace with thee. And thou shalt know that thy tabernacle shall be in peace.*

It was a joy to return to Bloomington last week and to find that spring had arrived. After a bitter winter with constant snow and ice, I was so happy to see the first brave crocus and daffodils blooming. The brilliant pure white of the star magnolias and yellow forsythia brightened every street. After being covered with snow, the green grass also seemed especially vivid this year.

Although the final weeks at the university are crowned with recitals, I finally managed to go on an hour-long walk in my old yard, now bare and empty with no house. But it meant so much to me to pick some daffodils and forsythia and to just feel a part of that yard again.

I believe one of God's greatest gifts is a love of nature. Each flower and tree makes me aware of His unfathomable love. Truly, as the old Bible School song says so well, "only God can make a flower . . . only God can make a tree."

We draw near to God when we are in touch with the wonders of His creation.

*Dear Father: Thank you for the beauty of the world you have created for us. In Christ's name, Amen.*

# About the Author

Susann McDonald is recognized as one of the world's leading harpists and pedagogues. She holds the title of Distinguished Professor of Music at Indiana Unviersity's renowned Jacobs School of Music where she chairs the largest harp department in the world. Her many students hold prestigious positions with major orchestras such as the Philadelphia Orchestra, the Chicago Symphony, New York Philharmonic, Los Angeles Philharmonic, the Metropolitan Opera, the Pittsburgh Symphony, the Detroit Symphony, the Munich Philharmonic, the Orchestra Nationale de France, and numerous others.

In October of 2003, her home in Bloomington, Indiana was destroyed by an electrical fire. Before the fire, she was writing a series of devotionals as part of her morning prayer and Bible study time. This book is the result of her reflections and enduring faith in the following years as she struggled with the loss and built a new home.

These daily devotions are a journal of her experiences before and after the fire, as she also shares her life as an artist and teacher. It has been said that she is truly raising a whole generation of harpists who come to her to experience the inspiration that she exemplifies and the love of the harp which she shares so generously.

Printed in the United States
76057LV00001B/1-33